SUCCESSFUL GARDENING

A-Z of ALPINES &
WATER PLANTS

Published by The Reader's Digest Association Limited.

First Edition Copyright © 1995
The Reader's Digest Association Limited,
Berkeley Square House, Berkeley Square, London W1X 6AB

Copyright © 1995
The Reader's Digest Association Far East Limited
Philippines Copyright 1995
The Reader's Digest Association Far East Limited

Consultant editor: Lizzie Boyd

Typeset in Century Schoolbook

PRINTED IN SPAIN

ISBN 0 276 42097 7

Opposite: Rock and water are basic features in nature's landscape,
and miniature versions create ideal habitats for a host of plants.

Overleaf: Water irises and hostas grow into masive clumps in
the boggy ground at the edges of streams and ponds.

Pages 6-7: White-flowered candytufts and purple aubrietas
spread a colourful carpet over rocks and walls.

Reader's
Digest

PUBLISHED BY THE READER'S DIGEST ASSOCIATION LIMITED
LONDON NEW YORK MONTREAL SYDNEY CAPE TOWN

Originally published in partwork form
by Eaglemoss Publications Limited

SUCCESSFUL GARDENING

A-Z of ALPINES &
WATER PLANTS

CONTENTS

SPECIAL FEATURES

A-Z OF ALPINES

A-Z OF WATER PLANTS

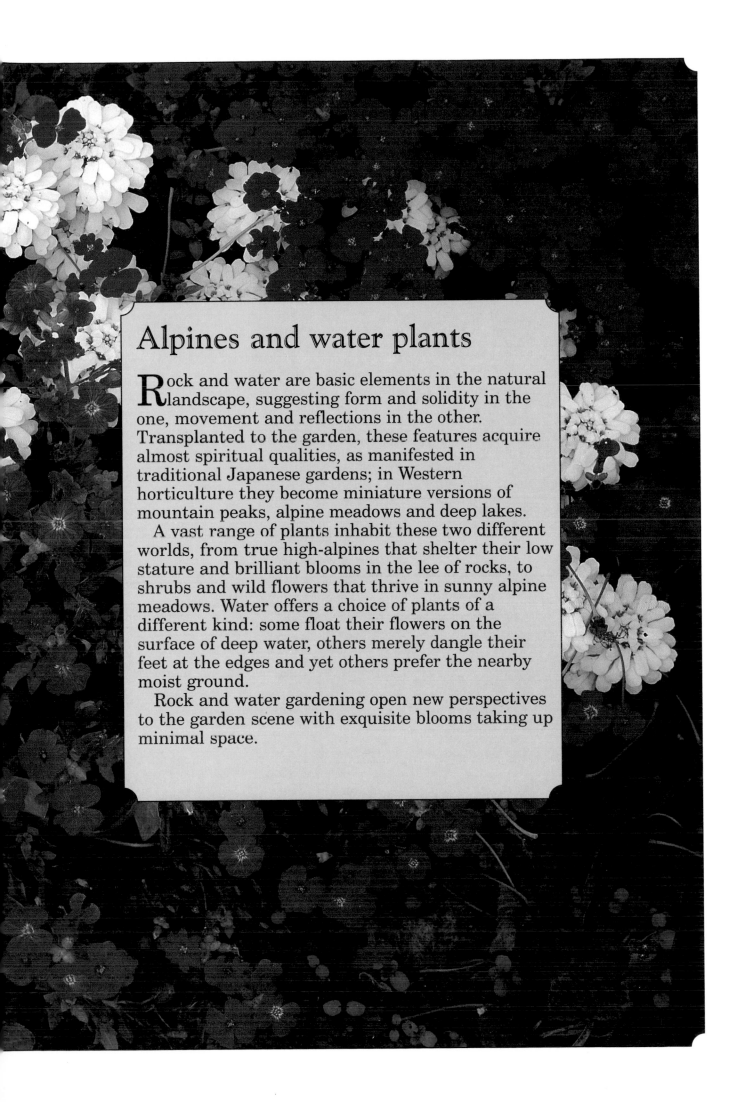

Alpines and water plants

Rock and water are basic elements in the natural landscape, suggesting form and solidity in the one, movement and reflections in the other. Transplanted to the garden, these features acquire almost spiritual qualities, as manifested in traditional Japanese gardens; in Western horticulture they become miniature versions of mountain peaks, alpine meadows and deep lakes.

A vast range of plants inhabit these two different worlds, from true high-alpines that shelter their low stature and brilliant blooms in the lee of rocks, to shrubs and wild flowers that thrive in sunny alpine meadows. Water offers a choice of plants of a different kind: some float their flowers on the surface of deep water, others merely dangle their feet at the edges and yet others prefer the nearby moist ground.

Rock and water gardening open new perspectives to the garden scene with exquisite blooms taking up minimal space.

Alpine habitats Common thyme rapidly spreads to a wide mat while *Saxifraga paniculata* remains a tight, lime-encrusted rosette.

A-Z of alpines

True alpine plants come from high mountainous regions, surviving in the minimum of soil among barren rocks and exposed to biting winds and sharp winter frosts. They survive and flourish above the tree line because they have adapted to the harsh conditions and grow close to the ground in the shelter of rocks, which reflect summer heat, and are protected in winter by heavy snow blankets. Their blooms are comparatively large and brilliantly coloured, their leaves small, often leathery, and their roots penetrate deep into the gravelly subsoil from which they obtain essential moisture and nourishment.

These high-altitude plants – Mount Atlas daisies and lewisias, for example – are the most difficult to grow as garden plants. They need fast-draining soil and usually bright light, and while they are fully hardy, they cannot tolerate our heavy rainfall in autumn and winter. Excessive wetness round their leaf rosettes and roots leads to total collapse and death. For this reason, such alpines are often grown surrounded by deep collars of grit or fine stone chippings to aid drainage and should be protected in winter with overhead panes of glass raised on bricks. Often they perform better grown in pans in an alpine house.

Happily there are numerous other rock garden plants which, though not true alpines, are of dwarf, creeping or trailing habit. They include shrubs and conifers, small bulbs, perennials, annuals, ferns and succulents. Their requirements are less exacting than those of high-alpine plants, and they will thrive without fuss in well-drained soil and in open sites.

ALPINE GARDENS

**Dwarf perennials, bulbs, shrubs and conifers
for year-round interest can be grown in rockeries,
raised beds, sink gardens and tufa blocks.**

The miniature mountain landscapes that rock gardens represent can take many forms. In large gardens, a properly constructed rockery can be an impressive feature with stone outcrops and rocky ledges interspersed with scree beds and alpine meadows and perhaps a pool.

The perfect rockery should be in proportion with the rest of the garden, sited in an open position and preferably built on a gentle slope so that it appears to be a natural outcrop. Whenever possible, local stone should be used, with the rocks embedded vertically and horizontally to expose the different strata and to provide ledges for trailing plants and sheltered pockets for rosette-type alpines. Sharp drainage is essential, and this can be helped by mixing gravel or stone chippings into the planting mixture.

However, a rockery is not essential for the enjoyment and cultivation of rock plants. Raised beds are popular alternatives and have the advantage of bringing the flowers closer to eye level. Dry-stone walls constructed without mortar can host any number of trailing and compact plants, and soil pockets between paving stones can be filled with carpeting alpines.

Troughs and sinks are ideal for miniature landscapes complete with dwarf willows or conifers, and tufa blocks, though expensive, make charming alpine containers. Tufa is a highly porous lava rock, easily drilled to make planting holes for small lime-loving alpines such as the Kabschia saxifrages.

An alpine house is basically a cold greenhouse with extra ventilators. Here, particularly rare alpines can be grown in pots plunged into moist beds of sand or chippings; they flourish through the year, undeterred by the weather.

▼ **Summer rockery** The blue-flowered *Campanula portenschlagiana* is one of the easiest rock plants, blooming throughout summer and spreading to large clumps. It associates well with the clear pink *Dianthus* 'Daphne'.

▲ **Chequerboard paving** A sunny sitting area is paved with stone slabs and gravel, the crevices planted with creeping alpines. Sweet thyme scents the air, and sempervivums and saxifrages mound their rosettes.

▶ **Alpine pans** Shallow pots of colourful sempervivums are sunk in a bed of gravel to ensure perfect drainage. Lumps of tufa rock heighten the illusion of an alpine scree.

▼ **Sink gardens** Well-weathered stone sinks are ideal for miniature alpine landscapes. They are planted with compact plants and dwarf conifers, with pieces of rock and a gravel topping as realistic touches.

◀ **Small and colourful** Late spring is the high season in the rock garden when aubrietas, phlox and alyssum smother themselves with bright blooms. Dwarf rhododendrons on the upper ledges add deeper colours, and miniature and carpeting conifers strike notes of calm.

▼ **Wall carpets** The top of dry-stone walls and pockets between the stones support a multitude of creeping and trailing rock plants. Their roots gain a foothold in bits of soil while the stems cling or cascade in ripples of brilliant colours.

▲ **Alpine container** A hollowed-out tree stump has become home for a collection of alpine succulents. The evergreen, fleshy-leaved sempervivums form perfect rosettes in shades of green often flushed or tipped with red. A top covering of small pebbles keeps the rosette bases dry.

▶ **Alpine meadow** A gently sloping scree bed fans out into a little summer meadow, bright with a carpet woven from different types of rock pinks, thyme and miniature irises.

▲ Tufa rockery Tufa, a porous volcanic rock, is ideal for rock gardens. It is able to retain water for roots to absorb in dry weather, and has a high lime content which is enjoyed by many alpine plants. Tufa's weathered appearance blends well with other types of rock gardens, such as sinks. Natural stone sinks are becoming increasingly rare, but modern glazed sinks covered with hypertufa make acceptable alternatives.

▶ Brilliant colour Despite their small size alpines produce comparatively large magnificent blooms in many different colours. Here, spring-flowering alpines are shown to their best advantage against a background of dwarf conifers and carpeting evergreens.

Abies

dwarf fir

Abies nordmanniana 'Golden Spreader'

☐ Height up to 75cm (2½ft)
☐ Spread up to 1.2m (4ft)
☐ Foliage shrub
☐ Moist, acid soil
☐ Full sun or light shade
☐ Hardy conifer

Dwarf conifers deserve a place in every rock garden, providing tall accent points among ground-hugging and trailing alpines. Being evergreen they are also valuable for winter interest. The genus *Abies* (dwarf silver fir) contains several suitable varieties, conical in shape and bearing aromatic, needle-like foliage. They take many years to reach their maximum height and produce cones.

Popular species

Abies balsamea 'Hudsonia' (dwarf balsam fir) is a round-topped spreading shrub, eventually growing up to 75cm (2½ft) high. The dense foliage is glossy mid green with two white bands on the underside of the leaves.

Abies cephalonica 'Meyer's Dwarf' (dwarf Greek fir) has horizontally spreading branches and shining green needles which are white underneath. It grows 30cm (1ft) tall and 90cm (3ft) wide and thrives on chalky soils.

Abies concolor 'Glauca Compacta' (dwarf white fir), syn. 'Compacta', has a compact but irregular growth habit with grey-blue leaves. It takes 10 years to reach 60-90cm (2-3ft) high.

Abies nordmanniana 'Golden Spreader' (dwarf Caucasian fir), syn. 'Aurea Nana', has wide-spreading branches, and leaves which are golden yellow above and pale yellowish white below. It grows up to 30cm (1ft) tall and 90cm (3ft) wide.

Abies balsamea 'Hudsonia'

Abies concolor 'Glauca Compacta'

Abies procera 'Glauca Prostrata' (dwarf noble fir) has blue-grey foliage and low-spreading branches, reaching up to 30cm (1ft) tall and 90cm (3ft) wide.

Cultivation

Plant in late autumn in slightly acid or neutral, moist but well-drained soil. Full sun is best for golden varieties, though light shade is acceptable and will give protection from late spring frost. Avoid exposed positions.

Propagation Home propagation is impractical, and new stock is better bought in.

Pests and diseases Firs may suffer from die-back or rust or be infested by sap-sucking insects which produce tufts of white waxy wool on leaves and branches.

Acaena
New Zealand burr

Acaena novae-zelandiae

☐ Height 2.5-15cm (1-6in)
☐ Spread 45-75cm (1½-2½ft)
☐ Foliage, and burrs in late summer
☐ Any well-drained soil
☐ Sun or partial shade
☐ Hardy perennial

New Zealand burr is a low-growing, carpeting plant grown for its tiny leaves and the burrs which mature in late summer. They are bristly, globular seed heads, which follow the insignificant flowers. The burrs are carried well above the low carpet of leaves, and may be scarlet, reddish, amber or purple.

Acaenas grow vigorously, and should not be planted near choice plants which might be swamped. As well as making good ground cover, they can be planted between paving stones or on walls.

Popular species
Acaena adscendens forms a dense mass of tangled stems covered with blue-grey leaves with toothed edges. It grows taller than most, up to 15cm (6in) high.
Acaena 'Blue Haze', syn. 'Pewter', has blue-green leaves on red stems, and pale brown burrs. It grows up to 10cm (4in) high, with a spread of 60cm (2ft).
Acaena buchananii, only 5cm (2in) high but 60cm (2ft) across, has pea-green leaves and amber burrs.
Acaena 'Copper Carpet' is similar

Acaena 'Blue Haze'

to *A. buchananii*, but with coppery leaves and reddish burrs.
Acaena microphylla, the most commonly grown species, up to 5cm (2in) high and 60cm (2ft) across, has bronzed foliage and scarlet burrs.
Acaena novae-zelandiae has green leaves and purple burrs.

Cultivation
Set out young plants from early autumn to early spring in any well-drained garden soil. New Zealand burrs thrive in full sun, but can also tolerate some shade.
Propagation Sow seeds in a cold frame between early autumn and early spring. Alternatively divide and replant existing stock between early autumn and early spring.
Pests and diseases Trouble free.

Acantholimon
prickly heath

Acantholimon glumaceum

☐ Height 15-20cm (6 8in)
☐ Spread 30cm (1ft)
☐ Flowers early summer to early autumn
☐ Any well-drained soil
☐ Sunny position
☐ Hardy evergreen perennial

Prickly heath is grown for its mats of needle-like leaves, and for its loose spikes of starry flowers produced from early summer to early autumn. It is rather slow-growing, but long-lived. The choice species described come from Armenia and Asia Minor and are those most commonly available.

Popular species
Acantholimon glumaceum has dark green spiky leaves forming compact mats up to 15cm (6in) high. Mauve to rose-pink flowers, 12mm (½in) across, are borne in 10cm (4in) spikes throughout summer. This is the most reliable species.
Acantholimon olivieri, syn. *A. venustum*, grows 15-20cm (6-8in) high. It forms loose tufts of silver-grey foliage; pale rose flowers, 8mm (⅓in) across, are carried well above the leaves. It resents winter wet around the roots and is best grown on a wall.

Cultivation
Prickly heaths thrive on gritty, well-drained soil and in an open, sunny position. Plant in spring and dead-head after flowering.
Propagation Sow seeds under glass in late winter or root cuttings of non-flowering basal shoots in a cold frame in summer.
Pests and diseases Trouble free.

Achillea

dwarf yarrow

Achillea clavenae

Achillea tomentosa

Achillea x kellereri

☐ Height 10-23cm (4-9in)
☐ Spread 20-30cm (8-12in)
☐ Flowers from late spring to early autumn
☐ Any well-drained soil
☐ Full sun
☐ Hardy perennial

Dwarf yarrow is an easy, reliable rockery plant, grown as much for its aromatic, grey-green or silver, usually feathery leaves as for the flowers. These may be the yellow, flat-topped heads typical of yarrow, though some species have daisy-like white flowers. The plant is useful for growing in poor soil, such as crevices in paving or in walls, where it may live longer and flower more freely than if given a rich loam.

Popular species
Achillea ageratifolia grows 20cm (8in) high, with tight rosettes of narrow, deeply toothed silver leaves. The white, daisy-like flowers are borne in mid and late summer.
Achillea clavenae, syn. *A. argentea*, has oval, irregularly toothed bright silver leaves. Heads of white daisy-like flowers are borne profusely on 15cm (6in) high stems in late spring and early summer.
Achillea x *kellereri* is a hybrid derived partly from *A. clavenae*. It grows 15cm (6in) high and 25cm (10in) across and has similar bright silver leaves. The flower clusters are smaller and tighter.
Achillea 'King Edward', syn. *A.* x *lewisii*, grows 10-15cm (4-6in) high and 20cm (8in) across, with grey-green leaves and lemon-yellow flower heads up to 6cm (2½in) wide. They are borne from late spring to early autumn.
Achillea x *kolbiana* has feathery grey leaves and white flower heads, up to 10cm (4in) across, throughout summer. It grows up to 20cm (8in) high and wide.
Achillea tomentosa grows up to 23cm (9in) high, with downy grey leaves forming a dense mat 30cm (1ft) wide. The flat yellow flower heads are borne on 15cm (6in) stems, from mid summer to early autumn.

Cultivation
Plant yarrows from mid autumn to early spring in any well-drained garden soil in a sunny position. Cut faded flower stems back to the ground in autumn.
Propagation In early spring, divide the roots into sections, each with four or five young shoots, and replant immediately in their permanent positions.
Pests and diseases Generally trouble free.

Adenophora
ladybells

Adenophora tashiroi

☐ Height 20-30cm (8-12in)
☐ Spread up to 30cm (1ft)
☐ Flowers in summer
☐ Any well-drained soil
☐ Full sun or light shade
☐ Hardy perennial

Very similar in appearance to campanulas, ladybells are grown for their clusters of blue, lavender or violet-blue bell-shaped, nodding flowers. The two Asiatic species described here are suitable for growing in a rock garden. Though tall, they are slender, delicate-looking plants.

Popular species
Adenophora sinensis, which comes from China, has 30cm (1ft) high stems and slender spikes of blue flowers in mid summer.
Adenophora tashiroi is smaller, only 20-25cm (8-10in) high. The flowers are violet-blue and appear singly, or with just a few blooms to a spike.

Cultivation
Plant in autumn or spring, in well-drained soil, in full sun or in a lightly shaded spot.
Propagation Sow seed in late spring. Alternatively, divide large clumps into several smaller ones in spring and replant, though ladybells resent disturbance.
Pests and diseases Slugs and snails may eat the leaves.

Adonis
adonis

Adonis amurensis

☐ Height 23-38cm (9-15in)
☐ Spread 30cm (1ft)
☐ Flowers late winter to early spring
☐ Any well-drained soil
☐ Sun or partial shade
☐ Hardy perennial

The bright yellow flowers of adonis appear in late winter and early spring when few flowers are about. They open out flat when the sun shines, into shiny bowl shapes, set against a background of bright green feathery leaves forming neat round clumps. The plants die down completely in summer.

Adonis make admirable plants for the rock garden or as an edging to borders.

Popular species
Adonis amurensis is the earliest to flower, in late winter; it grows 23-38cm (9-15in) high. The single-petalled flowers open out to 5cm (2in) across, displaying a large central boss of stamens. 'Flore-pleno' is a double-flowered form.
Adonis vernalis grows 23-30cm (9-12in) high, with bright yellow flowers 5cm (2in) across. They are borne in early spring.

Cultivation
Adonis will grow in any well-drained but moisture-retentive soil. Plant in a sunny or partly shaded spot from mid summer to mid autumn, with the crowns 2.5cm (1in) below the soil level.
Propagation Divide and replant the roots in autumn.
Pests and diseases Generally trouble free.

Aethionema
stone-cress

Aethionema 'Warley Ruber'

☐ Height 10-23cm (4-9in)
☐ Spread 30-45cm (1-1½ft)
☐ Flowers mid spring to mid summer
☐ Any well-drained soil
☐ Full sun
☐ Hardy evergreen sub-shrubby perennial

Stone-cress is an ideal rock garden plant, forming a thick mat of leaves and bearing abundant clusters of pink or white flowers. It revels in hot dry spots, and is also a lime-lover, suitable for planting in pockets and crevices in rock gardens or dry-stone walls.

Popular species
Aethionema grandiflorum (Persian stone-cress) is a loosely branched species with narrowly oval grey-green leaves; it grows up to 23cm (9in) high. Delicate pink flowers, arranged in 4-5cm (1½-2in) wide domed heads, appear in profusion from late spring to mid summer.
Aethionema iberideum grows 15cm (6in) high, with oval blue-green leaves. The white flowers are freely produced in 5cm (2in) terminal clusters from late spring to mid summer.
Aethionema pulchellum is similar to *A. grandiflorum* but with a more compact habit of growth; it bears smaller leaves and shorter flower stalks. The flowers are a darker pink and appear from late spring to mid summer.
Aethionema 'Warley Rose' is a hybrid only 10-15cm (4-6in) high, with linear grey-green leaves. Deep rose-pink flowers appear in broad spikes 5-7.5cm (2-3in) long in mid and late spring.

Aethionema iberideum

Aethionema pulchellum

Aethionema 'Warley Ruber' is similar to 'Warley Rose' but with deeper coloured flowers.

Cultivation
Plant in any well-drained soil and in full sun between early autumn and early spring. After flowering, remove faded stems.

Propagation Increase 'Warley Rose' and 'Warley Ruber' by soft cuttings of non-flowering shoots taken in early or mid summer. Root them in a cold frame, then pot up individually and grow on in the frame for planting out in the flowering positions in mid spring.

Other aethionemas can be increased from seed sown in a cold frame or greenhouse in early spring.

Pests and diseases Generally trouble free.

Ajuga
bugle

Ajuga reptans 'Multicolor'

☐ Height 10-30cm (4-12in)
☐ Spread 15-45cm (6-18in)
☐ Flowers late spring to mid summer
☐ Any moist soil
☐ Partial shade
☐ Hardy perennial

A useful ground-cover plant, bugle combines attractive foliage with erect spikes of blue, pink or white flowers. It thrives in moist, shady areas.

Popular species
Ajuga pyramidalis grows 23cm (9in) high, with toothed green leaves and erect pyramid-shaped spikes of whorled blue flowers in late spring.

Ajuga reptans (bugle) is too invasive for rock gardens, but excellent for ground cover. Attractive foliage varieties include 'Atropurpurea' ('Purpurea', purple); 'Burgundy Glow' (purple, bronze and cream); 'Multicolor' ('Rainbow', bronze, pink and cream); and 'Variegata' (grey-green, cream).

Cultivation
Plant in ordinary moisture-retentive soil between autumn and

Ajuga reptans 'Atropurpurea'

spring. Avoid deep shade for coloured-leaved bugles; *A. pyramidalis* thrives in shade.

Propagation Divide and replant between autumn and spring.

Pests and diseases Trouble free.

Alchemilla

lady's mantle

Alchemilla erythropoda

☐ Height 15-23cm (6-9in)
☐ Spread 25-30cm (10-12in)
☐ Flowers in summer
☐ Moist but well-drained soil
☐ Sunny or partially shaded site
☐ Hardy perennial

Dwarf lady's mantles are grown mainly for their rounded, deeply divided leaves which have a central depression that catches drops of rainwater and angles them into many-faceted sparkling diamonds. The small round flower clusters are pleasant but unremarkable, unlike those of their relation, *Alchemilla mollis*, a border perennial with lime-green flowers.

Popular species
Alchemilla alpina grows up to 23cm (9in) high, with neat tufts of rounded, silvery green leaves divided into narrow leaflets. The flower clusters are green.
Alchemilla erythropoda grows only 15cm (6in) high and the leaves have a bluish tinge. The small round flower heads are yellow, turning russet-red.

Cultivation
Plant lady's mantle between mid autumn and early spring in a sunny or partly shaded spot, in any moist but well-drained garden soil. The plants are suitable for large rock gardens, for edging and ground cover.
Propagation Sow seeds in early spring, or divide and replant established plants between autumn and spring.
Pests and diseases Trouble free.

ALKANET – see *Anchusa*

Allium

ornamental onion

Allium moly

☐ Height 15-38cm (6-15in)
☐ Spread 15cm (6in)
☐ Flowers spring and summer
☐ Any well-drained soil
☐ Sun or partial shade
☐ Hardy bulb

Ornamental onions (*Allium*) are related to culinary onions, and some produce typically onion-like globular flower clusters, carried singly on stiff upright stems. Most also have the typical onion smell. The leaves are strap-shaped and form low tufted clumps.

Popular species
Allium karataviense grows up to 15cm (6in) high and has broad leaves tinted metallic red. The globular flower heads, 10cm (4in) across, are soft grey-pink and borne in late spring.
Allium moly grows about 30cm (1ft) high. It is an invasive species, with grey-green leaves. The bright yellow, star-shaped flowers are borne in loose clusters in early summer.
Allium oreophilum, syn. *A. ostrowskianum*, grows 15-30cm (6-12in) high, with small tufts of leaves at ground level. The deep cerise-pink flowers are carried in dense heads in early summer.

Allium oreophilum

'Zwanenburg' has exceptionally richly coloured flowers.
Allium roseum grows 30-38cm (12-15in) high with long, broad leaves; pink star-shaped flowers are borne in clusters in early summer.

Cultivation
Plant ornamental onions in early to mid autumn in a sunny spot in any well-drained soil. Cover the bulbs to three or four times their own depth. Dead-head the flowers, leaving the stalks to feed the bulbs. Leave clumps untouched until they are congested.
Propagation Split clumps in autumn or as growth starts in spring and replant.
Pests and diseases Young plants may be eaten by slugs.

Alyssum

alyssum, gold dust

Alyssum saxatile

□ Height 5-30cm (2-12in)
□ Spread 30-45cm (1-1½ft)
□ Flowers late spring to early summer
□ Any well-drained soil
□ Sunny site
□ Hardy evergreen sub-shrub

Alyssum is one of the most popular of all rock garden plants, vigorous and so free-flowering that the leaves are often completely hidden. It is long-lived and thrives in sunny rock gardens or tumbling over dry-stone walls and banks.

Popular species

Alyssum montanum grows about 15cm (6in) high as a dense mat of grey, hairy, oblong-oval leaves. The scented yellow flowers are borne in early and mid summer.

Alyssum saxatile forms bold clumps of grey-green tapering leaves, and reaches 23-30cm (9-12in) high. The dense masses of yellow flower clusters are produced from mid spring to early summer. Numerous varieties include: 'Citrinum' (lemon-yellow flowers); 'Compactum' (15cm/6in, golden yellow flowers); 'Dudley Nevill' (buff-yellow flowers); and 'Plenum' (golden yellow double flowers).

Alyssum serpyllifolium is prostrate, growing no more than 5cm (2in) high, but spreading and trailing to 30cm (12in). It bears grey leaves and clear yellow flowers in early summer.

Alyssum wulfenianum is another prostrate species, with trailing woody stems bearing small grey

Alyssum saxatile 'Dudley Nevill'

leaves. The flowers are tiny but a good strong yellow.

Cultivation

Plant alyssum in full sun and in any well-drained soil between early autumn and early spring. Cut back hard after flowering to produce bushy plants.

Propagation Increase named varieties by cuttings taken in early summer and rooted in a cold frame. Species are easily grown from seed sown in a cold frame in early spring.

Pests and diseases Young plants are vulnerable to slugs and flea beetles. Downy mildew may attack, causing the leaves to curl.

Anacyclus

Mount Atlas daisy

Anacyclus depressus

□ Height 5cm (2in)
□ Spread 30cm (1ft)
□ Flowers early to late summer
□ Any well-drained soil
□ Sunny site
□ Hardy evergreen perennial

Mount Atlas daisy (*Anacyclus depressus*) is a colourful little plant, its red buds contrasting with the open, daisy-like white flowers, and both set off by delicate grey-green ferny foliage. It grows as a low mat, only 5cm (2in) high and up to 30cm (1ft) across. Flowering throughout summer, the blooms have petals that are white above, and red on the reverse side.

Cultivation

Plant Mount Atlas daisy in a sunny spot in well-drained gritty soil between early autumn and mid spring. Dead-head after flowering. During wet winters protect the plants from rain with raised panes of glass.

Propagation Take cuttings of non-flowering shoots in early to mid spring or mid to late summer and root in a cold frame. Plant out spring cuttings in early autumn, summer ones the following spring.

Pests and diseases Blackfly or greenfly may infest the foliage, sucking the sap and making plants sticky and sooty.

Anchusa

alkanet, bugloss

Anchusa caespitosa

□ Height 5cm (2in)
□ Spread 20cm (8in)
□ Flowers in spring
□ Well-drained gritty soil
□ Sunny site
□ Hardy perennial

One species of alkanet, or bugloss, is suitable for growing in the rock garden or the alpine house. Other species are popular tall border plants, but the tufted alkanet (*Anchusa caespitosa*) is almost prostrate.

Tufted alkanet forms compact rosettes of slender, strap-shaped, deep green, slightly reddish and hairy leaves with wavy edges. It grows no more than 5cm (2in) high but spreads to an evergreen carpet 20cm (8in) wide.

A cluster of large, brilliant gentian-blue, star-shaped, almost stemless flowers appears in the centre of each leaf rosette in spring. Each flower has a bright white eye in the centre.

The plant has a strong, vigorous root system which penetrates deep into the ground. With age it becomes less floriferous.

Cultivation

Plant tufted alkanet in a sunny position in well-drained gritty soil any time between mid autumn and early spring.

It can also be grown successfully in a pot in an alpine house. It should be repotted every year after flowering has finished as it soon outgrows its container. Keep it dry in winter.

Propagation Because of its long root system, tufted alkanet is not suitable for regular lifting and division. Instead, take root cuttings in mid or late winter and plant them in a cold frame; they should have rooted and be ready for setting out in a nursery bed by late spring. Transfer them to their final positions from mid autumn onwards.

Pests and diseases Generally trouble free.

Andromeda

bog rosemary

Andromeda polifolia, var. *angustifolia*

□ Height 15-45cm (6-18in)
□ Spread 30cm (1ft) or more
□ Flowers late spring to early summer
□ Acid moist soil
□ Semi-shaded site
□ Hardy evergreen shrub

Bog rosemary (*Andromeda polifolia*) grows in peat bogs and marshy places in the wild and is a good plant for cool shady places in the rock garden. Like other members of the heather family, it will thrive only in acid soils.

Bog rosemary can grow 45cm (18in) high, but several compact-growing forms are available, notably 'Compacta' and the pink-flowered 'Macrophylla', which eventually form dense hummocks. Bog rosemary has wiry stems and leathery, narrow-oval leaves. The pale pink, bell-shaped flowers are freely borne in tight clusters on the tips of the shoots in late spring and early summer.

'Alba' is a white-flowered variety; *angustifolia* has leaves that are grey-felted on the undersides.

Cultivation

Plant bog rosemary in rich, acid and moist soil at any time between autumn and spring, in a cool, partially shaded site.

Propagation Lift and divide mature plants in autumn or early spring. Alternatively, layer long shoots in autumn, or increase by hardwood cuttings.

Pests and diseases Trouble free.

Androsace

rock jasmine

Androsace primuloides

Androsace imbricata

- ☐ Height 2.5-10cm (1-4in)
- ☐ Spread 10-60cm (4in-2ft)
- ☐ Flowers late spring to mid summer
- ☐ Sharply-drained soil
- ☐ Sunny site
- ☐ Hardy evergreen perennial

Rock jasmines are true alpine plants from high mountains, many of which cannot tolerate wet British winters and need the protection of an alpine house. Those described here are suitable for growing in rock, scree or trough gardens, with some protection from winter rain.

Rock jasmines are prized for their dainty tussocks or ground-hugging mats of leaves, and tiny primrose-like flowers, carried singly or in dense clusters.

Popular species

Androsace carnea grows up to 7.5cm (3in) high, forming a clump of dark green, needle-like leaves. The small pink or white flowers are carried in small clusters on erect stalks in early summer. The variety *A. c. laggeri* bears small clusters of deep pink flowers in late spring.

Androsace imbricata, syn. *A. vandellii*, is 5cm (2in) high and forms dense tussocks of silver-felted leaves. In late spring it bears a mass of stemless, white flowers with golden eyes. Somewhat diffi-

cult, it needs a deep collar of grit to ensure perfect drainage.

Androsace lanuginosa is a prostrate, trailing plant, ideal for growing high up in crevices on the shady side of a rockery. The silver-leaved stems spread to 30-45cm (1-1½ft). Clusters of pink flowers are borne in summer.

Androsace primuloides, syn. *A. sarmentosa*, forms a mat of leaf rosettes 10cm (4in) high and up to 60cm (2ft) across, which turn from mid green in summer to a woolly grey-green in winter. The profuse clusters of pink flowers are borne from mid spring to early summer. The species is one of the easier rock jasmines and less prone to winter rot.

Androsace sempervivoides grows in 5cm (2in) high rosettes of overlapping leathery green leaves, with short erect flower stems carrying pink blossoms in early summer.

Androsace villosa produces tufts of small grey-green leaves clustered at the ends of hairy, often red runners, growing into mats about 5cm (2in) high and 23-30cm (9-12in) across. The flowers, in early summer, are white or pale pink with a red eye.

Cultivation

Plant rock jasmines in early to mid spring in gritty, sharply-drained soil and in full sun. It is advisable

to protect them from winter rain with raised panes of glass.

In the alpine house, grow the plants in shallow pots of loamy compost mixed with plenty of limestone grit. Cover the surface with fine chippings to aid drainage.

Propagation Detach rosettes in early summer and root in a cold frame. Overwinter in pots and plant out the following mid spring. Take 5cm (2in) basal shoots of *A. lanuginosa* and treat in the same way as rosettes.

Alternatively, sow seeds in mid or late winter and leave outdoors for about a fortnight; freezing temperatures hasten germination.

Pests and diseases Root aphids and mealy bugs may check the plants' growth.

Antennaria

antennaria, cat's ear

Antennaria dioica 'Rubra'

☐ Height 5-15cm (2-6in)
☐ Spread up to 45cm (1½ft)
☐ Flowers late spring to early summer
☐ Any well-drained soil
☐ Sunny site
☐ Hardy evergreen perennial

Antennaria is an unspectacular but useful evergreen ground-cover plant, suitable for carpeting areas where spring bulbs are planted and for growing in cracks between paving stones.

Popular species
Antennaria dioica, syn. *A. tomentosa*, has narrow silver-grey leaves that form 2.5cm (1in) high woolly mats up to 45cm (1½ft) across. Erect stems, 5-15cm (2-6in) high, bear small heads of white, pink-tipped, tufted flowers in late spring and early summer.

'Minima' grows 5cm (2in) high and 15cm (6in) wide, with bright pink flowers; 'Nyewoods' is 7.5cm (3in) high, with deep pink flowers; 'Rosea' grows 15cm (6in) high, with green and silver foliage and rose-pink flowers; and 'Rubra' grows 10cm (4in) high with deep pink flowers.

Antennaria parvifolia

Antennaria parvifolia, syn. *A. dioica aprica*, has silver-grey foliage and silver-white flowers in early summer.

Cultivation
Plant in any well-drained soil in a sunny spot between early autumn and early spring.
Propagation Divide and replant established plants in early spring.
Pests and diseases Trouble free.

Anthemis

anthemis

Anthemis rudolphiana

☐ Height 7.5-30cm (3-12in)
☐ Spread up to 90cm (3ft)
☐ Flowers spring to late autumn; foliage
☐ Any well-drained soil
☐ Sunny site
☐ Hardy perennial

Low-growing anthemis species are grown as much for their feathery, aromatic foliage as for their daisy-like flowers. *A. nobilis* (common chamomile) is a foliage plant popular for chamomile lawns and can make an attractive feature in a rock garden, its jewel-like green leaves setting off brightly coloured flowers.

Popular species
Anthemis cupaniana is a spreading, cushion-forming species, up to 30cm (1ft) high and 45-90cm (1½-3ft) across. It makes bright accent points with its silvery, feathery foliage and large white daisy flowers borne singly on long stems, from late spring until early autumn.
Anthemis montana, syn. *A. macedonica*, forms 15cm (6in) high mats of small green leaves; it bears a profusion of small white flowers in early summer.
Anthemis nobilis (common chamomile) itself is rather invasive and is most commonly seen as the double-flowered 'Flore-pleno'. This carpets the ground with tiny green leaves and pompon-shaped white flowers on 7.5cm (3in) stems all summer long.

The non-flowering variety 'Treneague' makes a mossy, aromatic emerald-green carpet 23cm (9in) high. This is the variety commonly planted for a

Anthemis cupaniana

chamomile lawn, which needs no mowing, just an occasional clipping over. Chamomile lawns can be walked on a moderate amount, although they are not as hardwearing as grass. As they are bruised underfoot the leaves release a delicate fragrance.

Anthemis rudolphiana, syn. *A. biebersteiniana*, has filigree silver foliage, and yellow daisy flowers borne on 23cm (9in) stems in summer. It grows 15cm (6in) high.

Cultivation

Plant flowering anthemis in any well-drained soil in a sunny site from early autumn to early spring. To grow an alpine lawn, set young plants of *A. nobilis* 'Treneague' 15cm (6in) apart in an open position in early to mid spring.

Propagation Divide and replant established plants. Or take cuttings of basal shoots (lateral shoots of *A. nobilis*) in spring and root in a cold frame. Plant out in early autumn.

Pests and diseases Trouble free.

Anthemis nobilis 'Treneague'

Anthyllis

anthyllis

Anthyllis montana

- ☐ Height 10-45cm (4in-1½)
- ☐ Spread up to 30cm (1ft)
- ☐ Flowers mid to late summer
- ☐ Any well-drained soil
- ☐ Sunny site
- ☐ Hardy shrubby perennial

Although some species can grow rather tall, anthyllis deserves a place in the rock garden as it continues to flower into late summer, when many alpines are past their best. It has attractive feathery foliage and pea-like flowers.

Popular species

Anthyllis hermanniae 'Compacta' grows 30cm (1ft) or more tall, but is of compact habit. Its bright yellow flowers are borne in such profusion that they smother the foliage completely.

Anthyllis montana is rather looser in habit and has clover-like, rose-red flowers, and foliage covered with fluffy silver hairs. It reaches 10-15cm (4-6in) or more in height. 'Rubra' has exceptionally deep pink flowers.

Anthyllis vulneraria (ladies' fingers) can grow up to 45cm (1½ft) tall though it is usually shorter; it bears flowers which range from cream and yellow to orange and red.

Cultivation

Plant anthyllis in full sun in any sharply-drained soil in autumn or early spring. It appreciates chalky soils.

Propagation Take softwood cuttings and root in a cold frame in early to late summer.

Pests and diseases Aphids may infest the foliage.

ANTIRRHINUM – see *Asarina*

Aquilegia
columbine

Aquilegia nivalis

Aquilegia flabellata 'Nana Alba'

☐ Height 10-30cm (4-12in)
☐ Spread 15-30cm (6-12in)
☐ Flowers late spring to mid summer
☐ Well-drained moist soil
☐ Sunny or lightly shaded site
☐ Hardy perennial

Columbines are familiar border plants, with spurred funnel-shaped, often bicoloured flowers and delicate, deeply divided, grey-green leaves. Dwarf types are ideal for rock gardens.

Popular species

Aquilegia alpina grows up to 30cm (1ft) high and across. The flowers, in late spring, are blue or blue-and-white, but the plant hybridizes freely to produce other colours. Varieties include 'Mini Star', a dwarf mixed colour strain with pink and white flowers.

Aquilegia bertolonii has 10cm (4in) stems, each carrying a single large rich blue flower in late spring.

Aquilegia flabellata grows 25cm (10in) or more high, with purple-blue flowers from late spring to mid summer. The dwarf 'Nana' has lilac and cream flowers; 'Nana Alba', even smaller, has white flowers.

Aquilegia nivalis grows 10-20cm (4-8in) high, with large purple and purple-black flowers.

Aquilegia flabellata

Aquilegia scopulorum grows 15cm (6in) high, with mauve-blue flowers in summer, and blue-grey leaves.

Cultivation

Plant between autumn and spring in sun or partial shade, in any fertile, moist but well-drained soil. Dead-head after flowering.

Propagation Sow seed in summer, or divide plants between autumn and spring.

Pests and diseases Leaf miners and aphids may infest the plants.

Aquilegia alpina 'Mini Star'

Arabis

rock cress

Arctostaphylos

bearberry

Arabis caucasica 'Pink Pearl'

Arabis caucasica 'Plena'

Arctostaphylos uva-ursi

☐ Height 10-23cm (4-9in)
☐ Spread 23-60cm (9-24in)
☐ Flowers spring and summer
☐ Any well-drained soil
☐ Partial shade
☐ Hardy evergreen perennial

Rock cress is deservedly one of the most popular of all rock garden plants. It is easy to grow, covers the ground with dense hummocks of grey-green foliage and bears a profusion of attractive flowers over long periods.

Popular species

Arabis blepharophylla grows 10cm (4in) high, with a spread of 23cm (9in). It bears tufts of stiff leaves with hairy margins. The pink, rose-purple or white flowers are borne from early to late spring.
Arabis caucasica, syn. *A. albida*, grows 23cm (9in) high and can spread up to 60cm (2ft). Clusters of white flowers are produced from late winter until early summer. The species can be too invasive for a rock garden, though it can be planted in a wall to restrain it. The variety 'Plena' is more compact; it is less free-flowering, but has double blooms.

Other compact varieties include 'Pink Pearl' and 'Rosabella' (pink flowers). 'Variegata' is a slow-growing form grown mainly for its gold-and-silver marked leaves; the flowers are white, sometimes flushed pink.

Arabis ferdinandi-coburgii 'Variegata'

Arabis ferdinandi-coburgii 'Variegata' grows only 10cm (4in) high, with a spread of 23cm (9in). It bears white flowers in late spring, and green leaves attractively striped with cream all year round.

Cultivation

Set plants out in well-drained soil in partial shade from early to mid autumn or in early spring. Trim *A. caucasica* and its varieties hard back after flowering.
Propagation Root non-flowering leaf rosettes in a cold frame from early to mid summer. Pot up and plant out in early spring. *A. caucasica* can also be divided and replanted in early autumn. *A. blepharophylla* can only be raised from seed.
Pests and diseases Generally trouble free.

☐ Height 10-15cm (4-6in)
☐ Spread up to 1.2m (4ft)
☐ Flowers late spring; edible autumn berries
☐ Lime-free moist soil
☐ Full sun or light shade
☐ Hardy evergreen shrub

Bearberry can be grown in rock gardens but it makes a better ground-cover plant, thriving in light shade or sun. It will not tolerate lime, and needs acid soil and plenty of room to ramble. It is a member of the heather family. The one species in cultivation is *Arctostaphylos uva-ursi*, a near prostrate sub-shrub which spreads rapidly, rooting where it touches the ground to form a dense mat, 10-15 cm (4-6in) high, of shiny, leathery, oval leaves. In spring it bears pendent, urn-shaped white flowers flushed with pink; they are followed by glistening scarlet, edible berries in autumn.

Cultivation

Plant bearberry in early autumn or mid spring. It thrives in cool and moist, acid soil, poor and sandy, and in sun or partial shade.
Propagation Layer long shoots in early spring and separate from the parent plant after one year. Or take heel cuttings in late summer.
Pests and diseases Trouble free.

Arenaria

sandwort

Arenaria montana

☐ Height 2.5-23cm (1-9in)
☐ Spread up to 45cm (1½ft)
☐ Flowers spring and early summer
☐ Any sharply-drained soil
☐ Sunny or partially shaded site
☐ Hardy evergreen perennial

Sandwort is a rather inconspicuous plant, but valuable in the rock garden for its ability to creep over rocks. It is evergreen, with leaves so tiny that the plant has a moss-like appearance. Small, usually white flowers cover the plant in spring and early summer.

Popular species

Arenaria balearica is ideal for a shady rock garden with moist soil. It is prostrate, reaching only 2.5cm (1in) in height, but spreading to 45cm (1½ft). Tiny white flowers are produced abundantly on 2.5cm (1in) high stems from early spring to mid summer.
Arenaria grandiflora has larger, more showy, funnel-shaped white flowers carried on 23cm (9in) stems from late spring to late summer. The dense foliage is bright green. It does best in a sunny position.

Arenaria montana thrives in full sun. It grows about 15cm (6in) high, with clouds of glistening white flowers produced in early summer above dark green leaf mats. Planted in narrow crevices to show it off to best advantage it will eventually cascade down rocks.
Arenaria purpurascens (pink sandwort) bears numerous short-stemmed lilac-purple flowers in mid and late summer. It thrives in full sun.

Cultivation

Plant in sun or shade, according to species, in sharply drained, gritty soil during late spring. While the plants are young protect them from winter wet with straw or panes of glass.
Propagation Divide and replant *A. balearica, A. grandiflora* and *A. purpurascens* in early to mid spring. Root non-flowering basal cuttings of *A. montana* in a cold frame in summer. Plant out in early spring.
Pests and diseases Generally trouble free.

Armeria

thrift

Armeria maritima 'Alba'

☐ Height 7.5-30cm (3-12in)
☐ Spread 15-30cm (6-12in)
☐ Flowers mid spring to mid summer
☐ Any well-drained soil
☐ Sunny site
☐ Hardy evergreen perennial

The delightful little thrifts are almost essential in a rock garden or as low fronting to a border. They grow in small, neat, grassy clumps, with globular flowers on short sturdy stalks. The flowers are usually pink or white, and are borne so profusely that the foliage can hardly be seen. Miniature species are particularly effective planted in stone sinks or troughs.

Popular species

Armeria caespitosa, syn. *A. juniperifolia*, is a compact species, growing only 7.5cm (3in) high, with a maximum spread of 23cm (9in). The pink flower heads are almost stemless and appear from mid to late spring. The leaves are grey-green. 'Bevan's Variety' has deeper pink flowers and dark green foliage.
Armeria maritima is the native British sea pink, a common sight along coasts and in seaside gardens. It is extremely hardy and grows up to 30cm (1ft) high, with globular pink flower heads produced in profusion from late spring to mid summer.
Popular garden varieties

Arnica
mountain tobacco

Arnica montana

☐ Height 30-38cm (12-15in)
☐ Spread 15-30cm (6-12in)
☐ Flowers in summer
☐ Alkaline, neutral or acid soil
☐ Sunny site
☐ Hardy perennial

Mountain tobacco is an uncommon plant, but worth seeking out for its showy flowers. It grows, from rhizomatous roots, in attractive rosettes of slender oval leaves and bears large daisy-like flowers on tall stems in summer. Arnicas are not the easiest of plants, but where they are happy, they can be quite invasive.

Popular species
Arnica alpina grows 30-38cm (12-15in) high, from rosettes of narrow, grey-green and hairy leaves. A profusion of large bright yellow flowers appears in late summer.
Arnica montana resembles *A. alpina* but has broader basal leaves and golden-yellow flowers.

Cultivation
Plant in well-drained soil and full sun during autumn or spring. They succeed in all types of soil though *A. montana* flourishes in acid soil.
Propagation Divide and replant in mid spring.
Pests and diseases Trouble free.

Armeria maritima 'Dusseldorf Pride'

include: 'Alba' (white flowers); 'Birch Pink' (shell pink, grey foliage); 'Bloodstone' (deep red flowers); 'Dusseldorf Pride' (crimson-magenta flowers); 'Laucheana' (rich pink flowers); and 'Vindictive' (rich glowing red flowers).
Armeria montana (mountain thrift), syn. *A. alpina*, forms a small tufted cushion only 7.5cm (3in) high. The flowers, carried on 2.5cm (1in) stems in early and mid summer, are deep pink.

Cultivation
Set young plants in ordinary well-drained soil between early autumn and mid spring. They need full sun. Dead-head after flowering.

Propagation Divide and replant in early to mid spring. Alternatively, sow seed in a cold frame in early to mid spring. Pot the seedlings singly and plunge in an outdoor nursery bed until planting out in permanent positions from early autumn.

Alternatively, take basal cuttings during mid to late summer and root in a cold frame.
Pests and diseases The plants are prone to rust, which shows in spring on the leaves and stems as small white blisters that burst open. Later, purple spots with light brown pustules develop.

Artemisia
artemisia

Artemisia schmidtiana 'Nana'

☐ Height 5-13cm (2-5in)
☐ Spread 23cm (9in)
☐ Foliage plant
☐ Any well-drained soil
☐ Sunny site
☐ Hardy evergreen sub-shrub

Miniature versions of the familiar silver-leaved *Artemisia* grown in borders fulfil the same function in the rock garden, providing a pastel background for other more colourful plants. The evergreen leaves have a sharp but pleasant scent if crushed.

Popular species
Artemisia brachyloba is one of the smallest species, growing slowly into a mat less than 2.5cm (1in) high. The silvery leaves are finely divided. Stems, 7.5-10cm (3-4in) high, bear insignificant yellow flowers in summer.
Artemisia lanata, syn. *A. nitida* and *A. pedemontana*, grows up to 5cm (2in) high in shining silvery cushions up to 23cm (9in) across. Tiny yellow flowers appear from mid summer to early autumn.
Artemisia laxa, syn. *A. mutellina*, forms a mat of silver-grey leaves

only about 5cm (2in) high. The pale yellow flower spikes are tall – up to 20cm (8in) high – but are best removed so that the foliage can be seen to best effect.
Artemisia schmidtiana 'Nana' has very finely cut glistening silver-grey leaves, growing in a neat dome 7.5-13cm (3-5in) high. Dull yellow flowers, enclosed in round, woolly silver bracts, appear in early autumn.
Artemisia stelleriana 'Mori's Form' grows in low rosettes of deeply lobed grey-white felted leaves.

Cultivation
Plant during spring in any well-drained soil in full sun.
Propagation Take semi-hardwood heel cuttings in late summer and root in a cold frame. Pot up rooted cuttings and plunge outdoors in a sheltered bed; move them to their final positions the following spring.
Pests and diseases Colonies of aphids may settle on the leaves. They may also be attacked by rust – pale brown spots on the undersides developing into almost black pustules.

Asarina
asarina, creeping snapdragon

Asarina procumbens

☐ Height up to 5cm (2in)
☐ Trails to 45cm (1½ft) or more
☐ Flowers summer and autumn
☐ Any well-drained soil
☐ Partially shaded site
☐ Hardy evergreen perennial

Asarina procumbens, syn. *Antirrhinum asarina*, is a trailing plant with rounded or broadly heart-shaped, softly hairy, grey-green leaves up to 5cm (2in) long, borne on sticky stems. It grows no more than about 5cm (2in) high but is capable of spreading and trailing to 45cm (1½ft) or more.

Throughout summer and early autumn it produces a succession of charming snapdragon-like creamy yellow flowers which often have a pinkish flush.

Asarina will grow in the minimum of soil and is excellent for crevices in a wall or angles between walls and paving – but make sure to site it on the shady side as it likes a cool root run even though it originates from the South of France.

Cultivation
Plant asarina in autumn or spring in a partially shaded site in any well-drained soil, or in crevices in a wall or between paving stones.
Propagation Root stem cuttings in late summer; the plant self-seeds freely.
Pests and diseases Trouble free.

Asperula
woodruff

Asperula suberosa

Asplenium
spleenwort

Asplenium trichomanes

☐ Height 15-25cm (6-10in)
☐ Spread 15-25cm (6-10in)
☐ Foliage plant
☐ Well-drained, moist rich soil
☐ Shady site
☐ Hardy evergreen fern

The graceful evergreen fronds of spleenwort provide a useful contrast to mat- or clump-forming plants grown in the rock garden. It likes shade, and is often grown in vertical crevices on the north side of walls or rocks.

Popular species
Asplenium adiantum-nigrum (black spleenwort) grows up to 23cm (9in) high. Its glossy, black-stemmed fronds with a triangular outline grow in pairs.
Asplenium ceterach (rusty-back fern), syn. *Ceterach officinarum*, has a height and spread of 15cm (6in) and bears tufted, dark green fronds with brown scaly undersides. It will tolerate a sunny site.
Asplenium trichomanes (maidenhair spleenwort) grows about 25cm (10in) tall, with wiry, arching, black-stalked fronds bearing many pairs of rounded pinnae.

Cultivation
Plant from mid spring to autumn in good, moist but well-drained soil, and in light shade. *A. trichomanes* needs alkaline soil.
Propagation Sow the dust-like spores in early spring; or divide and replant mature plants in spring.
Pests and diseases Slugs and scale insects may infest the fronds.

☐ Height 2.5-7.5cm (1-3in)
☐ Spread 10-20cm (4-8in)
☐ Flowers early to mid summer
☐ Moist, well-drained soil
☐ Sunny site
☐ Hardy perennial

One of the prettiest of ground-cover plants, woodruff forms low cushions of green or grey-green leaves, smothered with delicate pink tubular flowers from early to mid summer. Most species are easy to grow, given a well-lit position in moisture-retentive soil. A few do better in the protection of an alpine house.

Popular species
Asperula lilaciflora caespitosa grows 5-7.5cm (2-3in) high and about 15cm (6in) across. It forms a dense mat of narrow, awl-shaped, bright green leaves. The tubular, deep pink flowers are borne in clusters from early to mid summer. The plant grows well in sink and trough gardens.
Asperula nitida forms a 2.5cm (1in) high carpet of grey-green leaves and bears tiny starry pink flowers. It is ideally grown in an alpine house, but can also be planted in a trough or sink garden placed in a sheltered position.
Asperula suberosa, syn. *A. athoa*, grows 5-7.5cm (2-3in) high, in low carpets, up to 23cm (9in) across, of grey hairy leaves. The flowers are a delicate shell pink. The plant is intolerant of winter wet, and is at its best in a sunny crevice, scree bed or an alpine house.

Cultivation
Plant woodruff from mid autumn to early spring in any well-drained but moist soil in a sunny site. Cut back *A. suberosa* by one-third after flowering in order to keep it tidy. Protect it from winter wet with raised panes of glass or cloches.
Propagation Take soft cuttings of non-flowering basal shoots in mid to late spring. Root in a cold frame, then pot up rooted cuttings singly. Grow on in an outdoor nursery bed. Plant them in their final positions in spring of the following year.
Pests and diseases Generally trouble free.

Aster

aster

Aster alpinus

☐ Height 15-23cm (6-9in)
☐ Spread 30-45cm (1-1½ft)
☐ Flowers early to mid summer
☐ Any good well-drained soil
☐ Sunny, open site
☐ Hardy perennial

Alpine or dwarf asters are as popular in the rock garden as are their larger cousins in borders and summer bedding. They are easy to grow, hardy and extremely free flowering. The flowering period is generally earlier than that of the taller varieties – most come into flower from early summer onwards.

Their soft grey-green leaves provide a perfect colour contrast to the daisy-like flowers that appear in many shades in the pink to red and blue to purple range, each with a prominent golden centre.

Popular species

Aster alpinus grows 15cm (6in) high in clumps which can reach 45cm (1½ft) across. The grey-green leaves are narrow and lance-shaped. The flowers, up to 4cm (1½in) across, come in varying shades of mauve, blue-purple and white, with bright orange-yellow centres. They are at their height in mid summer.

Numerous named varieties include 'Albus' (pure white); 'Beechwood' (outstanding lavender-blue flowers); 'Glory' (blue flowers), and 'Wargrave Variety' (pale purple flowers tinged with pink).
Aster natalensis grows to 10-15cm (4-6in) high, forming a creeping mat of grey-green hairy leaves; it bears clear blue flowers with orange-yellow centres in early summer. It needs sharply-drained soil if it is to do well.
Aster tibeticus grows 15cm (6in) high, with slender, lance-shaped mid green leaves. The purple-blue flowers, 2.5-5cm (1-2in) across, appear in early summer.

Cultivation

Plant asters in fertile well-drained soil in a sunny site between mid autumn and early spring. Cut faded flower stems back to soil level after flowering.
Propagation Divide and replant the roots at any time between mid autumn and early spring.
Pests and diseases Powdery mildew appears on the leaves. Aster wilt may be troublesome.

Aubrieta

aubrieta

Aubrieta deltoidea 'Argenteo-variegata'

☐ Height 7.5-10cm (3-4in)
☐ Spread 45-60cm (1½-2ft) or more
☐ Flowers early spring to early summer
☐ Well-drained, alkaline soil
☐ Sunny site
☐ Hardy evergreen perennial

The sight of clumps of purple and pink aubrieta tumbling over garden walls and rockeries is one of the great joys of early spring. Because it is such a common plant, and so easily grown, aubrieta is sometimes undervalued, but it is a plant no rock garden should be without. However, it does need to be cut hard back once its glorious flowering display is over, otherwise it will romp away all summer, smothering other more choice and delicate plants before they can put on their own show.

Only one species is in general cultivation – *Aubrieta deltoidea* – but there are a great many named varieties. The plants grow in loose mounds or mats, trailing slightly, up to 10cm (4in) high, with a spread of 60cm (2ft) or more. The leaves are slightly downy and mid to deep green, or sometimes variegated. The species itself bears purple, cross-shaped flowers, but the named varieties offer a range of shades: lavender, purple, mauve, crimson and pink. The individual four-petalled flowers are no more than 2cm (¾in) across, but are produced in dazzling profusion.

31

Bolax
bolax

Bolax glebaria

Aubrieta deltoidea

☐ Height 13mm-5cm (½-2in)
☐ Spread 15-23cm (6-9in) or more
☐ Foliage plant
☐ Well-drained soil
☐ Sunny site
☐ Hardy evergreen perennial

Bolax glebaria, syn. *Azorella tri-furcata*, is an uncommon plant, more of a curiosity than a beauty, though when seen flowering in full sun it gives an impression of molten gold.

The plant grows up to 5cm (2in) high, forming hard ever-green hummocks or rosettes of leathery, glossy, light apple-green leaves divided into three oval lobes. The tiny golden yellow flowers are stemless and are borne in clusters of four. 'Nana', an even smaller form, growing only 13mm (½in) high, is good for troughs and paving cracks.

Cultivation
Plant bolax between autumn and spring in any sharply-drained soil in full sun. It is also suitable for growing in an alpine house.
Propagation Take basal cut-tings in summer and root in a cold frame. Pot up in early spring and plant in the final sites in autumn. Or divide plants in spring.
Pests and diseases Trouble free.

BONNET BELLFLOWER – see *Codonopsis*
BROOM – see *Cytisus, Genista*
BROOM, HEDGEHOG – see *Erinacea*

Popular varieties
'Argenteo-variegata' has leaves edged with creamy white, and lavender-purple flowers.
'Carnival' and **'Cobalt Violet'** have blue-violet flowers.
'Church Knowle' and **'Joy'** have pale mauve to lavender-blue flowers.
'Dr. Mules' has double, violet-mauve flowers.
'Gurgedyke' and **'J.S. Barker'** have deep purple flowers.
'Royal Cascade' bears flowers in shades of red.

Cultivation
Plant aubrieta between early autumn and early spring in well-drained, preferably alkaline soil and in a sunny site. Cut rock gar-den plants hard back after flower-ing to prevent the plants from becoming straggly; aubrietas trailing over walls can be allowed to grow unchecked.
Propagation Sow seeds under glass in late winter or early spring. Pot up the seedlings when well rooted and plunge outside. Transfer to final positions in autumn.

Alternatively, root basal cut-tings from established plants in a cold frame.
Pests and diseases Downy mildew may affect the leaves.

AURICULA – see *Primula*
AVENS – see *Geum*
AVENS, MOUNTAIN – see *Dryas*
BABY'S BREATH – see *Gypsophila*
BEARBERRY – see *Arctostaphylos*
BELLFLOWER – see *Campanula*
BELLFLOWER, BONNET – see *Codonopsis*
BELLFLOWER, TRAILING – see *Cyananthus*
BINDWEED – see *Convolvulus*
BLOODROOT – see *Sanguinaria*
BLUEBERRY – see *Vaccinium*
BLUETS – see *Houstonia*
BOG ROSEMARY – see *Andromeda*

Bruckenthalia

spike heath

Bruckenthalia spiculifolia

- ☐ Height 15-20cm (6-8in)
- ☐ Spread 30cm (1ft)
- ☐ Flowers early summer
- ☐ Well-drained lime-free soil
- ☐ Sunny site
- ☐ Hardy evergreen shrub

There is only one species of spike heath: *Bruckenthalia spiculifolia*. It is easy to grow, but being a member of the heather family, it needs lime-free soil. The plant is grown for its 2.5cm (1in) long spikes of bell-shaped flowers which are borne between late spring and early summer. They are white in bud, opening to very pale pink. The leaves are typically heather-like: vivid green, small, narrow and bristle-tipped. The plant forms thick ground-covering mats up to 20cm (8in) high and 30cm (1ft) across.

Cultivation
Plant spike heath in mid to late spring or mid to late autumn in well-drained but moisture-retentive, lime-free soil, in a sunny position.
Propagation Divide established plants in spring when they become straggly. Replant rooted portions at 30cm (1ft) spacings. Or take semi-ripe cuttings in late summer and root in a cold frame.
Pests and diseases Trouble free.

BUGLE – see *Ajuga*
BUGLOSS – see *Anchusa*

Bulbocodium

spring meadow saffron

Bulbocodium vernum

- ☐ Height 10-15cm (4-6in)
- ☐ Spread 5-10cm (2-4in)
- ☐ Flowers early spring
- ☐ Well-drained soil
- ☐ Sunny site
- ☐ Hardy bulbous perennial

Spring meadow saffron (*Bulbocodium vernum*, syn. *Colchicum bulbocodium*) is a striking sight when in flower. The almost stemless blooms appear before the leaves, giving them the appearance of being temporarily settled on the ground rather than growing from it. It is closely related to *Colchicum*, the autumn crocus, which has the same curious characteristic of bearing flowers well before leaves.

Each corm produces a cluster of up to three pinkish or violet-coloured, funnel-shaped flowers in early spring. The leaves are narrow and strap-like, and the plants die back by early summer. They look charming in sunny pockets in the rock garden.

Cultivation
Plant the corms 7.5cm (3in) deep during early autumn, in any well-drained soil and in an sunny site.
Propagation Lift the clusters of corms every three to four years in early autumn. Split them up and replant in new positions immediately. Unless the corms are lifted and split up regularly, flowering will be impaired.
Pests and diseases Trouble free.

BUTTERCUP – see *Ranunculus*

Calamintha

calamint

Calamintha grandiflora

- ☐ Height 10-23cm (4-9in)
- ☐ Spread 15-30cm (6-12in)
- ☐ Flowers spring and summer
- ☐ Any well-drained soil
- ☐ Sunny site
- ☐ Hardy perennial

Calamint forms neat hummocks of mint-like aromatic leaves, covered for long periods in small, tubular, pink to purple flowers.

Popular species
Calamintha alpina grows 10-15cm (4-6in) high in freely branching tufts, and bears whorls of purple, hooded flowers during late spring and summer.
Calamintha grandiflora grows up to 23cm (9in) high, with bright lavender-pink tubular flowers produced throughout summer.

Cultivation
Plant calamint in any well-drained soil in a sunny site during autumn or spring.
Propagation Divide and replant in autumn, or take cuttings in late spring and root in a cold frame.
Pests and diseases Mint rust may affect young shoots.

Calceolaria

slipper flower

Calceolaria darwinii

☐ Height 5-30cm (2-12in)
☐ Spread 30-45cm (1-1½ft)
☐ Flowers late spring to early autumn
☐ Any well-drained moist soil
☐ Full sun or partial shade
☐ Hardy and half-hardy perennials

Miniature forms of slipper flower, some no more than 5cm (2in) high, are just as delightful as their larger relations grown as pot plants or in bedding schemes. The strange pouch-shaped flowers, beautifully marked and mottled, are borne from late spring right through to early autumn.

Dwarf slipper flowers can be grown on sheltered ledges in the rock garden, in troughs and sinks and in the alpine house.

Popular species

Calceolaria biflora is moderately hardy, and grows 15-30cm (6-12in) high from a basal rosette of oval leaves. The 2.5cm (1in) long flowers are yellow and are borne on 30cm (1ft) high stems in mid to late summer.

Calceolaria darwinii, moderately hardy, grows only 5-10cm (2-4in) high, with narrow oval leaves. The bright yellow flowers, 2.5-4cm (1-1½in) long, are spotted chestnut-brown and have a white horizontal band across the lower lip. They appear in early summer. The plant needs a sheltered position and is often grown in an alpine house.

Calceolaria fothergillii is similar to *C. darwinii* but has soft hairy leaves, and smaller flowers, sulphur-yellow with crimson spots.

Calceolaria 'John Innes'

Calceolaria 'John Innes' is a hardy hybrid, growing 10-15cm (4-6in) high, with lance-shaped pale to mid green leaves. In late spring erect stems carry one or two 4cm (1½in) long bright yellow flowers, spotted with brown.

Calceolaria polyrrhiza is a creeping, moderately hardy species. It grows 7.5-10cm (3-4in) high, with lance-shaped mid green leaves. The 2.5cm (1in) long yellow flowers appear in early and mid summer.

Calceolaria tenella is a mat-forming species, with trailing stems which root as they grow. It is 7.5-10cm (3-4in) high, with oval, bright green leaves. In light sandy soil it will spread freely, and is hardy if given a sheltered site. Bright yellow flowers, 4cm (1½in) long, appear from late spring to early autumn.

Cultivation

Slipper flowers require a fertile, well-drained but moisture-retentive soil; plant in mid to late spring. A sunny site is best, but the plants will tolerate partial shade. *C. darwinii* and *C. tenella* do best in rich, lime-free soil.

Remove faded flower stems after flowering. Protect from excessive winter wet with raised panes of glass.

Propagation Sow seeds in mid summer and place in a cold frame or greenhouse. Pot the seedlings up singly and grow on in a frost-free frame. They should be ready for planting out in their permanent positions in mid spring of the following year.

Alternatively, divide and re-plant hardy species in spring.

Pests and diseases Aphids and slugs may cause problems. *C. darwinii* can be decimated by red spider mites.

CALIFORNIAN FUCHSIA – see *Zauscheria*

Campanula

bellflower

Campanula carpatica 'Chewton Joy'

Campanula garganica 'Hirsuta'

- ☐ Height 5-30cm (2-12in)
- ☐ Spread 15-60cm (6-24in)
- ☐ Flowers late spring to early autumn
- ☐ Any well-drained soil
- ☐ Sun or partial shade
- ☐ Hardy herbaceous and semi-evergreen perennials

Bellflowers form a vast genus and include many border plants growing up to 1.2m (4ft) high. Dwarf species and varieties are ideal for planting in rock gardens, in walls, paving, trough gardens and as edgings to beds and borders. Like their taller relations, dwarf bellflowers are extremely easy-going, flourishing in sun or partial shade, and producing flowers in shades of blue for long periods.

The typical flower is bell-shaped, usually pendent but sometimes erect; some species have open cup-shaped blooms and others star-like ones. The leaves are generally heart-shaped with toothed edges.

Popular species

Campanula allionii, syn. *C. alpestris*, spreads by underground stems, from which grow rosettes of narrow, slightly hairy leaves. It grows 5-7.5cm (2-3in) high, with a spread of 15cm (6in), and bears large purple-blue flowers.

Campanula arvatica forms creeping mats of small leaf rosettes. Each rosette produces a stem carrying star-shaped, upturned, deep violet-blue flowers. The plant grows only 5cm (2in) high, but spreads to 30cm (12in). 'Alba' has white flowers.

Campanula carpatica grows 15-30cm (6-12in) high in clumps up to 38cm (15in) across. It is invasive and most suitable for edging. The large, cup-shaped flowers are blue, purple or white and appear

Campanula cochleariifolia

Campanula arvatica 'Alba'

Campanula raineri

from early summer to early autumn. Numerous varieties include 'Bressingham White' (pure white); 'Chewton Joy' (china-blue); and 'Jewel' (deep violet-blue flowers).

Campanula cochleariifolia (fairy's thimble), syn. *C. pusilla*, grows only 7.5-15cm (3-6in) high, but spreads to 30cm (12in). The small pendent bell-shaped flowers in blue or white appear from early summer to early autumn.

Campanula garganica grows up to 15cm (6in) high and twice that across, bearing profuse sprays of star-shaped blue flowers from late spring to early autumn. 'W.H. Paine' has lavender-blue flowers with white centres. 'Hirsuta' has grey hairy leaves and lavender-blue starry flowers.

Campanula portenschlagiana, syn. *C. muralis*, is invasive, growing 15cm (6in) high, but spreading to 60cm (2ft). Deep blue-purple, bell-shaped flowers are borne between mid summer and late autumn. This species does best in shade, in crevices in paving or walls.

Campanula poscharskyana grows up to 25cm (10in) tall and 60cm (2ft) across, with starry lavender flowers appearing between early summer and early autumn.

Campanula pulla is only 7.5-10cm (3-4in) high and wide, and is best grown in partial shade. The leaves form broad tufts of shiny mid green rosettes. The pendent, purple, bell-shaped flowers appear in early summer.

Campanula raineri grows in 7.5-10cm (3-4in) high tufts of grey-green leaves. Erect, bell-shaped, china blue flowers are borne in mid summer.

Campanula rotundifolia (harebell) grows 15-30cm (6-12in) high and up to 45cm (1½ft) across. Bell-shaped slate-blue to purple-blue flowers appear from early to late summer.

Campanula zoysii is a choice species, best grown in an alpine house. It grows only 7.5cm (3in) high, with numerous leaf rosettes rising from creeping stolons. The distinctive light blue flowers are oval in outline, pinched at the mouth and expand to a puckered ruff. They are borne in mid summer.

Cultivation
Plant bellflowers between early autumn and mid spring, in any fertile well-drained soil (*C. allionii* does better in lime-free soil). Most plants do well in sun or light shade.

Propagation Divide and replant clump-forming species in early spring. Alternatively, raise from seed sown in mid autumn or spring in a cold frame.

Pests and diseases Slugs and snails are the chief enemies.

CAMPION – see *Lychnis, Silene*
CANDYTUFT – see *Iberis*

Cardamine
cardamine

Cardamine pratensis 'Flore Pleno'

- ☐ Height 10-25cm (4-10in)
- ☐ Spread 30cm (12in)
- ☐ Flowers early to mid spring
- ☐ Any moist soil
- ☐ Sun or partial shade
- ☐ Hardy perennial

Cardamines belong to the cress family, and are moisture-loving plants, some with watercress-like leaves. The most commonly grown species is *Cardamine pratensis*, the cuckoo flower or lady's smock, which grows wild in damp meadows. It is suitable for cool, shady rockeries, and wild and woodland gardens.

Popular species
Cardamine pratensis (cuckoo flower, lady's smock) grows 25cm (10in) or more high, and spreads to 30cm (12in) across. The mid green leaves are divided into rounded leaflets; the white or pale lilac flowers are borne in loose sprays in early spring. 'Flore Pleno' is a taller, improved form with larger, double flowers.
Cardamine trifolia grows only 10-15cm (4-6in) high but spreads to 30cm (12in) with mats of round toothed evergreen foliage and small clusters of white flowers.

Cultivation
Plant cardamines in any moist soil in partial shade or sun during spring or autumn.
Propagation Divide and replant established plants after flowering.
Pests and diseases Trouble free.

Carlina
stemless thistle

Carlina acaulis

- ☐ Height 2.5-10cm (1-4in)
- ☐ Spread 15-23cm (6-9in)
- ☐ Flowers in summer
- ☐ Any well-drained soil
- ☐ Sunny site
- ☐ Hardy perennial

Thistles are generally troublesome weeds, but several members of the thistle family are grown as ornamental garden plants, such as the cornflower (*Centaurea*), whose clear blue flower heads are a familiar sight in herbaceous borders and cottage gardens.

One thistle is suitable for rock gardens – *Carlina acaulis* (stemless or alpine thistle). It comes from the European Alps and more southerly mountain regions, such as the Pyrenees, and has been cultivated in Britain since the early 17th century. It has successfully escaped from gardens and self-seeded and now flourishes in the wild on the downlands of southern Britain, favouring the chalky soil found there.

The plant grows 2.5-10cm (1-4in) high, occasionally more, with spreading rosettes of long, deeply divided, spiny greyish leaves up to 15cm (6in) long. The off-white or pale brown thistle-like flowers, 5-10cm (2-4in) across, are almost stemless and stud the leaf rosettes throughout summer.

Cultivation
Plant stemless thistle in any sharply-drained poor soil in a sunny site in spring or autumn.
Propagation Increase by seeds sown in autumn.
Pests and diseases Generally trouble free.

Cassiope
cassiope

Cassiope mertensiana

- ☐ Height 5-30cm (2-12in)
- ☐ Spread 23-45cm (9-18in)
- ☐ Flowers mid to late spring
- ☐ Moist acid soil
- ☐ Shady and cool site
- ☐ Hardy evergreen shrub

Cassiope is a member of the heath family and will only grow in acid, peaty soil. Native to arctic mountainous regions, it does best in cool climates and thrives in shady, sheltered rock gardens and walls. Prostrate varieties make good ground cover.

Popular species
Cassiope x 'Edinburgh' forms a compact shrub up to 20cm (8in) high and wide, with erect stems. The tiny overlapping leaves are dark green. White, urn-shaped flowers are carried in dense spikes at the tips of the branches during late spring.

Cassiope lycopodioides is a prostrate, mat-forming species spreading to 30cm (1ft). The nodding white, bell-shaped flowers have red stalks and calyxes and are borne in profusion.

Cassiope mertensiana grows 30cm (1ft) high and wide, with dark green, scale-like leaves. The flowers are creamy white and carried in early spring on short stalks at the tips of the branches.

Cassiope x 'Muirhead' forms a bushy shrub, 20cm (8in) or more high and wide, with grey-green branching shoots. The white flowers are almost stemless.

Cassiope tetragona grows 10-23cm (4-9in) high and bears dense, dark green, scale-like leaves. The ivory-white flower bells, in late spring, are borne on short stalks.

Cassiope wardii grows to 30cm (1ft) high, and spreads by underground stems. The white bell flowers are tinged with red.

Cultivation
Plant cassiopes in acid, cool and moist soil, in a lightly shaded site, during autumn or spring.

Propagation Take heel cuttings, about 5cm (2in) long, in early autumn and root in a cold frame. Carpeting species can be increased by division or runners in autumn, and upright types by layering at the same time.

Pests and diseases Trouble free.

CAT'S FOOT – see *Antennaria*
CELANDINE, LESSER – see *Ranunculus*

Celmisia
celmisia

Celmisia coriacea

- ☐ Height 2.5-23cm (1-9in)
- ☐ Spread 30-60cm (1-2ft)
- ☐ Flowers late spring and early summer
- ☐ Rich moist, acid soil
- ☐ Sunny or lightly shaded, sheltered site
- ☐ Hardy evergreen perennial

Celmisias are grown for their white daisy flowers with golden centres, and handsome foliage. Many have thickly felted and silvery leaves. The majority come from New Zealand and are sometimes called New Zealand daisies. They do best in cool and moist areas.

Popular species
Celmisia argentea grows in tight tufts 5-7.5cm (2-3in) high and 15cm (6in) across, with tiny, narrow, silver-haired leaves. The white flowers are stemless and appear on the tips of the shoots in late spring.

Celmisia bellidioides forms creeping mats 2.5-7.5cm (1-3in) high and 30cm (1ft) wide. One of the easiest species to grow, it bears glossy dark green, round and leathery leaves. The flowers appear in early summer.

Celmisia coriacea grows 23-30cm (9-12in) high and wide. The sword-shaped leaves are silver above and thickly felted underneath. The flowers appear in early summer.

Celmisia sessiliflora is tiny, forming 2.5cm (1in) high mats of needle-like grey-green leaves

Centaurea

knapweed, alpine cornflower

Centaurea simplicaulis

☐ Height 25cm (10in)
☐ Spread up to 25cm (10in)
☐ Flowers late spring to mid summer
☐ Well-drained soil
☐ Sunny site
☐ Hardy perennial

Most knapweeds or cornflowers are too tall for the rock garden, but a couple of near-hardy species make dainty additions, with their cornflower-like flowers in summer.

Popular species

Centaurea argentea, syn. *C. ragusina*, has deeply divided felted leaves with white hairs, and yellow flowers carried on short, sturdy stems in summer. This species is not reliably hardy and is often pot-grown in an alpine house. *Centaurea simplicaulis* grows 25cm (10in) high and wide and makes fine ground cover for small bulbs. The leaves, dark green above, have silvery undersides. The pink-mauve flowers are carried on 15cm (6in) high stems during late spring and early summer; they are followed by attractive fluffy seed heads, and should not be dead-headed.

Cultivation

Plant knapweed in any well-drained soil in full sun during autumn or spring.
Propagation Increase by sowing seeds or by division.
Pests and diseases Trouble free.

Celmisia walkeri

which throw up short-stemmed flowers in early summer. It is best grown in an alpine house.
Celmisia walkeri, syn. *C. webbii*, grows about 23cm (9in) high and forms mounds, up to 60cm (2ft) across, of narrow, leathery grey-green leaves that are white and hairy on the undersides. The finely rayed, large daisy flowers are carried on thin wiry stems, 30-38cm (12-15in) high, in early summer.

Cultivation

Plant New Zealand daisies during autumn or spring in rich, preferably acid, moist but well-drained soil in a sheltered site which receives plenty of light but does not dry out during hot weather. Protect from winter wet with raised panes of glass or cloches.

Propagation Sow seeds in spring and germinate in a cold frame. Seeds seldom ripen in Britain and germination of imported seed is often unreliable. Division and cuttings in summer are more reliable methods. Once plants are established, take cuttings from side rosettes and root in a cold frame.
Pests and diseases Generally trouble free.

Centaurium

centaurium

Centaurium scilloides

☐ Height 7.5cm (3in)
☐ Spread up to 15cm (6in)
☐ Flowers late spring and summer
☐ Well-drained soil
☐ Sun
☐ Hardy perennial

Centaurium scilloides, syn. *Erythraea diffusa*, is a delightful little plant, growing in 7.5cm (3in) high tufts of small, round, shiny green leaves. It produces a mass of clear lilac-pink flowers, carried on short stems, from late spring and throughout summer. When fully open to the sun the flat-faced flowers resemble those of the spring gentian (*Gentiana verna*) in appearance, although they are pink rather than blue.

Centaurium is a native British species which grows wild on southern downlands. It thrives in paving cracks and crevices and is ideal for trough and sink gardens.

Cultivation

Plant centaurium during autumn or spring in any well-drained soil in a sunny position.

Propagation Increase by division in spring or autumn. The plant is often short-lived and propagation by seed is a more reliable method.

Pests and diseases Generally trouble free.

Cerastium

cerastium, mouse-ear chickweed

Cerastium alpinum

☐ Height 5-15cm (2-6in)
☐ Spread 23-60cm (9-24in) or more
☐ Flowers late spring to late summer
☐ Any well-drained soil
☐ Sunny site
☐ Hardy evergreen perennial

Cerastium is a popular rock garden plant, but species should be chosen and sited with care, as some are extremely vigorous and invasive, rapidly smothering their neighbours. Such rampant species are more suitable for ground cover.

Cerastiums are grown for their soft silvery grey leaves and small delicate white flowers. In some species these are borne so profusely that the plants appear to turn white, giving them the common name snow-in-summer.

Popular species

Cerastium alpinum grows 5-10cm (2-4in) high with a spread of 23cm (9in). It forms mats of grey to pale green lance-shaped leaves. It bears clusters of white star-shaped flowers, 2cm (¾in) across, from late spring and through summer.

Cerastium biebersteinii (snow-in-summer) grows 10-15cm (4-6in) high and spreads to 60cm (2ft) or more. The slender, lance-shaped leaves are a woolly silver-grey. The white cup-shaped flowers, in early summer, are 2-2.5cm (¾-1in) across.

Cerastium lanatum is so similar to *C. alpinum* that it is usually classified as a sub-species. It forms attractive woolly silver

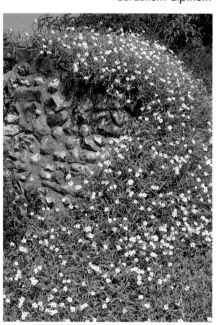

Cerastium tomentosum

tufts, with insignificant flowers.

Cerastium tomentosum (snow-in-summer) grows 10-15cm (4-6in) high and rapidly spreads to 60cm (2ft) or more. It closely resembles *C. biebersteinii*, but the leaves are less woolly and silvery. The flowers are slightly smaller and star-like.

Cultivation

Plant cerastiums in early to mid spring or in early autumn, in any well-drained soil in a sunny site. Protect *C. lanatum* from winter rain with raised sheets of glass, or grow it in an alpine house.

Propagation Divide and replant in early to mid spring.

Pests and diseases Generally trouble free.

Chamaecyparis

dwarf false cypress

Chamaecyparis pisifera 'Filifera Aurea'

Chamaecyparis lawsoniana 'Gnome'

☐ Height 15-90cm (6in-3ft)
☐ Spread up to 60cm (2ft)
☐ Foliage shrub
☐ Any well-drained soil
☐ Sun or light shade
☐ Dwarf evergreen conifer

False cypresses are hardy evergreen conifers native to North America, Japan and Taiwan. They differ from true cypresses in having foliage in sprays flattened into one plane.

The species can reach 12m (40ft) or more high, but numerous dwarf forms, many with golden foliage, are suitable for the rock garden. Some of these eventually become too tall, but as they are very slow-growing this takes many years to happen.

Dwarf cypresses are particularly useful in a rock garden, giving year-round interest and colour with their conical, globular or prostrate shapes and foliage that contrasts well with colourful flowering rock plants. The heights given are those a plant can be expected to reach after ten years.

Popular species

Chamaecyparis lawsoniana (Lawson's cypress) varieties are generally narrowly conical, with a pointed top and drooping leading shoots. 'Minima' grows about 30cm (1ft) high; it forms a globular or round-topped plant. 'Nana' is taller – about 60cm (2ft) and broadly conical. Both are reliable dwarf forms, usually seen as the blue-green varieties 'Minima Glauca' and 'Nana Argentea'. 'Minima Aurea' and 'Aurea Densa' are attractive golden forms. 'Gnome', of rounded, slow growth, has dark green foliage; 'Pygmaea' is exceptionally slow-growing with a rounded top.

Chamaecyparis obtusa (Hinoki cypress) is a Japanese species often used for bonsai culture. It has produced numerous dwarf forms, including some of the smallest conifers known. 'Nana' grows 15-20cm (6-8in) high, with dark green foliage carried in tight rounded sprays. 'Nana Gracilis' is faster growing, with larger, shell-like sprays of darker green. 'Nana Aurea' is a golden form of similar size. 'Pygmaea' bears flat, fan-shaped branchlets, forming a 15-20cm (6-8in) high semi-prostrate shrub spreading to 60cm (2ft) across. The foliage is bronze-green, tinged reddish-brown in winter.

Chamaecyparis lawsoniana 'Pygmaea'

Chiastophyllum
lamb's tail

Chiastophyllum oppositifolium

☐ Height 10-15cm (4-6in)
☐ Spread up to 30cm (1ft)
☐ Flowers late spring to early summer
☐ Well-drained, moist soil
☐ Sunny or partially shaded site
☐ Hardy evergreen perennial

Chamaecyparis pisifera 'Plumosa Flavescens'

Chamaecyparis pisifera (Sawara cypress) includes a number of dwarf forms of widely differing appearance. 'Boulevard' is fairly large at about 90cm (3ft) high, but worth growing for its pyramid of silvery blue foliage, at its brightest in light shade. 'Nana' is extremely slow-growing and forms a dense, flat-topped dome of dark green foliage sprays. Both 'Aureovariegata' and 'Nana Aureovariegata' have bright golden new growths, which fade in winter.

The Filifera types of the species have thin thread-like foliage. 'Filifera' is the tallest, at 75cm (2½ft). 'Filifera Aurea' is smaller, and makes a bright golden domed shrub, which keeps its colour all year round if planted in an open position. 'Filifera Nana' is slow-growing and forms a compact rounded and flat-topped shrub. 'Plumosa Flavescens' forms a dense, compact shrub with soft dark green foliage sprays, pale golden when young.

Cultivation
Dwarf cypresses flourish in any well-drained soil, in an open sunny position or in moderate shade. Golden varieties are best grown in full sun to preserve their colour through the seasons.

Plant container-grown specimens in mid autumn on light soils, mid spring on heavy soils. This ensures that the roots remain moist during their settling-in period.

When dwarf conifers eventually grow too large for the rock garden they can sometimes be transplanted to another site as they do not grow deep roots. Afterwards, water them plentifully during dry spells.

Some conifers may fork – produce two leading shoots. Some forms of *C. lawsoniana* are especially prone to this. If forking occurs, prune away the weaker shoot as soon as possible.

Propagation Dwarf conifers are grown from cuttings grafted on to a proven rootstock. Home propagation is difficult.

Pests and diseases Honey fungus may cause the death of plants.

CHAMOIS CRESS – see *Hutchinsia*
CHECKERBERRY – see *Gaultheria*
CHEIRANTHUS – see *Erysimum*

Lamb's tail (*Chiastophyllum oppositifolium*, syn. *Cotyledon oppositifolia*), is evergreen, and grown as much for its flowers as for its fleshy, rounded, coarsely toothed leaves. It belongs to the *Crassula* family. The succulent leaves form low, compact rosettes that spread to mats 30cm (1ft) or more wide. The yellow flowers are carried in arching sprays in late spring and early summer.

Lamb's tail – the name comes from the appearance of the flower sprays – is suitable for growing in walls and crevices where the flower spikes can arch over freely without touching the ground. It thrives in sun, but with some shade over the roots.

Cultivation
Plant lamb's tail during autumn in a sunny spot in free-draining, gritty soil and surround with mineral chippings. Alternatively, plant it in partial shade in rock crevices or walls.

Propagation Take tip cuttings in early summer. Allow the cut surfaces to heal before rooting them in compost. Alternatively, separate and replant offsets.

Pests and diseases Mealy bugs may show as unsightly tufts of white waxy wool on new growth.

Chionodoxa

glory-of-the-snow

Chionodoxa luciliae

☐ Height 10-20cm (4-8in)
☐ Spread 5-10cm (2-4in)
☐ Flowers late winter to late spring
☐ Ordinary well-drained soil
☐ Sunny or partially shaded site
☐ Hardy bulb

The blue star-like flowers of these hardy bulbous plants bring colour to the rockery from late winter to late spring.

Popular species

Chionodoxa gigantea reaches some 20cm (8in) high. Its white-eyed, violet-blue flowers appear from late winter to early spring. The variety 'Blue Giant', 15cm (6in) high, is bright blue.

Chionodoxa luciliae has light blue flowers with white centres. They appear in late winter to early spring and are carried 15cm (6in) above the ground. A white-flowered form – 'Alba' – and two pink-flowered forms – 'Rosea' and 'Pink Giant' – are also available.

Chionodoxa sardensis has slender stems carrying nodding sky-blue flowers with tiny white centres from early to late spring. It grows 10-15cm (4-6in) high.

Cultivation

Plant the bulbs in autumn, setting them 5-7.5cm (2-3in) deep and 10cm (4in) apart in any well-drained soil in sun or partial shade.

Propagation Glory-of-the-snow self-seeds freely. Plants can also be divided when the leaves die down after flowering.

Pests and diseases The plants may be damaged by slugs.

Chrysanthemum

alpine chrysanthemum

Chrysanthemum hosmariense

☐ Height 15-25cm (6-10in)
☐ Spread 30-38cm (12-15in)
☐ Flowers late spring to early autumn
☐ Well-drained soil
☐ Sunny site
☐ Hardy evergreen sub-shrubs

Dwarf chrysanthemums add bright splashes to a rock garden, with their attractive, often silvery mounds of foliage and handsome daisy-like flowers.

Popular species

Chrysanthemum alpinum is a short-lived evergreen perennial, only 15cm (6in) high but spreading to form tufts 30cm (12in) wide. The finely dissected leaves are deep green; large white daisy flowers are borne on short stalks in mid and late summer.

Chrysanthemum haradjanii, syn. *Tanacetum densum* 'Amani' or *T. haradjanii*, bears silvery, deeply cut, fern-like foliage. It grows about 25cm (10in) high and 38cm (15in) across, with clusters of bright yellow, groundsel-like flowers in late summer.

Chrysanthemum hosmariense, syn. *Leucanthemum hosmariense*, is a sub-shrubby species, 15-20cm (6-8in) high and 30cm (12in) or more across. It bears deeply cut, bright silver-green foliage, and

Chrysanthemum haradjanii

white, yellow-centred flowers from late spring until early autumn.

Cultivation

Plant from early autumn to mid spring in any well-drained soil in full sun.

Propagation Take 5-7.5cm (2-3in) long cuttings in early to mid summer and root in a cold frame. Alternatively, divide and replant in autumn or spring.

Pests and diseases Trouble free.

CINQUEFOIL – see *Potentilla*
CLOVER – see *Trifolium*

Codonopsis

bonnet bellflower

Codonopsis ovata

☐ Height 23-60cm (9-24in)
☐ Spread 30cm (12in)
☐ Flowers in summer
☐ Well-drained fertile soil
☐ Sunny or lightly shaded position
☐ Hardy perennial

Bonnet bellflowers, from the Himalayas and Japan, are lax climbing plants, seen to best effect sprawling over a rocky ledge or scrambling through other plants.

Popular species

Codonopsis clematidea has white, blue-tinged, bell-shaped flowers with browny gold and black markings inside. They appear in early to mid summer; the small oval leaves are mid green. The plant grows 30-60cm (1-2ft) high – tall for a rock garden plant if given support, but it is most effective where it can droop its stems over a wall or ledge.

Codonopsis ovata has oval, hairy, light green leaves. In mid to late summer it bears pale blue flowers with orange-purple markings. The plant grows 23cm (9in) high and 30cm (12in) across.

Cultivation

Plant between mid autumn and mid spring in a sunny or lightly shaded position and in fertile, well-drained soil.

Propagation Take cuttings of basal shoots in spring and root in a cold frame. Alternatively, sow seed in early spring in a cold frame and plant out in mid autumn.

Pests and diseases Trouble free.

COLCHICUM – see *Bulbocodium*
COLUMBINE – see *Aquilegia*

Convolvulus

bindweed

Convolvulus sabatius

☐ Height 15-20cm (6-8in)
☐ Spread 30-60cm (1-2ft)
☐ Flowers late summer and early autumn
☐ Any well-drained soil
☐ Sheltered sunny site
☐ Near-hardy perennial

Because of their invasive habit, most *Convolvulus* species, including the pernicious weed, spread rampantly and at great speed over as much ground as is made available to them. One species is suitable for growing in a rock garden; this is *Convolvulus sabatius* (syn. *C. mauritanicus*), a delightful little plant from North Africa.

It is not fully hardy and needs a warm, sunny and sheltered rock crevice where its trailing stems form a mat, about 15cm (6in) high and up to 60cm (2ft) wide. It bears a succession of blue, trumpet-shaped flowers with white throats from late summer to early autumn. It has round, soft grey-green, hairy leaves.

Cultivation

Plant in mid to late spring in any well-drained soil in a warm, sunny and sheltered spot. In winter, protect from the cold and wet with panes of glass or cloches. Alternatively, grow in an alpine house.

Propagation Take 3-5cm (1½-2in) heel cuttings of basal or side-shoots in summer and root in a well-ventilated cold frame. Pot up the rooted cuttings, overwinter in a frost-free frame and plant out in late spring.

Pests and diseases Generally trouble free.

CORNFLOWER – see *Centaurea*

Corydalis

corydalis

Corydalis cheilanthifolia

☐ Height 10-30cm (4-12in)
☐ Spread 10-30cm (4-12in)
☐ Flowers late spring to mid autumn
☐ Well-drained soil
☐ Sunny site
☐ Hardy perennial

The dainty little corydalis species are enchanting plants for rock gardens, dry-stone walls and cracks in paving. All have delicate fern-like foliage and a long display of tubular spurred flowers.

Popular species

Corydalis ambigua reaches 10-15cm (4-6in) high and across. In late spring and early summer it bears blue, purple or white flowers with upturned spurs. The leaves, composed of rounded leaflets, appear in pairs. The plant dies down by mid summer.

Corydalis cashmeriana is one of the most beautiful species with glacier-blue flowers appearing from late spring to late summer, and with handsome blue-green fern-like leaves. It forms a tuft 15cm (6in) high and 23cm (9in) across. It requires cool conditions and in the south of England succeeds best in an alpine house; in northern gardens it does well out of doors. Even under the right conditions, however, it is a capricious plant and can suddenly die for no obvious reason.

Corydalis cheilanthifolia is one of the most popular rock garden plants. It grows about 25cm (10in) high and bears bold tufts of ferny leaves; bright yellow flowers appear throughout late spring and early summer. It is excellent for ground cover and edging and self-seeds freely.

Corydalis lutea (common yellow

Corydalis wilsonii

corydalis) grows wild in Britain, often colonizing in old walls and paving crevices. It bears dainty light blue-green ferny leaves, and its yellow flowers, borne on arching stems some 30cm (1ft) high, appear from mid spring to mid autumn. It self-seeds freely.

Corydalis wilsonii has blue-green prostrate rosettes of ferny leaves, and upright spikes of bright canary yellow flowers in summer. It grows up to 25cm (10in) high and wide.

Cultivation

Plant corydalis (with the exception of *C. cashmeriana*) in early spring in any fertile, well-drained soil, in a sunny site; *C. lutea* also tolerates shade.

Grow *C. cashmeriana* in an alpine house, in 15-20cm (6-8in) pans of potting compost; repot annually in spring. The species will survive outdoors in Scotland if planted in cool, rich lime-free soil.

Propagation *C. cheilanthifolia* and *C. lutea* self-seed freely. Sow seeds of other species in a cold frame in late winter to early spring or early to mid autumn. Prick out the seedlings, overwinter in a cold frame and plant out in early to mid spring.

Pests and diseases Generally trouble free.

Cotula

cotula

Cotula atrata var. *luteola*

☐ Height 2.5-5cm (1-2in)
☐ Spread 30-50cm (12-20in)
☐ Foliage plant
☐ Well-drained gritty soil
☐ Sunny site
☐ Moderately hardy evergreen perennial

With their invasive habit, cotulas, from New Zealand, are excellent for carpeting and for filling gaps between paving slabs. They are mainly grown for their evergreen foliage although they also flower during summer and early autumn.

Popular species

Cotula atrata var. *luteola* forms a mat of fleshy green fern-like foliage about 30cm (1ft) across and 5cm (2in) high. It bears tiny pincushion-like flowers of cream and rosy-pink with a prominent dark red and black centre.

Cotula potentillina has creeping stems covered in green fern-like leaves. It spreads up to 50cm (20in) across but reaches only 2.5cm (1in) high.

Cotula squalida grows as a lush mat of deeply cut bright green foliage. It is 2.5cm (1in) high and up to 45cm (1½ft) across.

Cultivation

Plant in mid to late autumn in cracks between paving slabs, or a rockery with gritty, well-drained soil, in full sun.

Propagation Divide and replant in autumn.

Pests and diseases Trouble free.

CRANE'S-BILL – see *Geranium*

Crassula

crassula

Crassula sarcocaulis

☐ Height 2.5-15cm (1-6in) or more
☐ Spread 15-38cm (6-15in)
☐ Flowers in summer; attractive foliage
☐ Sharply-drained soil
☐ Sunny sheltered position
☐ Near-hardy evergreen perennials and sub-shrubs

The *Crassula* genus is best known for its house plants, but a few species are suitable for rock gardens in sheltered, mild areas. They have succulent leaves and small starry flowers.

Popular species

Crassula milfordae, a perennial, forms dense cushions of tiny grey-green rosettes 2.5cm (1in) high and 30-38cm (12-15in) across. In winter the leaves are tinted bronze. Crimson buds open into small white flowers in summer.

Crassula sarcocaulis, a sub-shrub, is best grown in an alpine house. Reaching 15cm (6in) high and wide, its woody stems bear small pointed green leaves flushed red in summer. Abundant clusters of minute pink flowers open from crimson buds in late summer.

Cultivation

Plant *C. milfordae* in late spring in sharply-drained soil, in full sun. Grow *C. sarcocaulis* in an alpine house.

Propagation Take leaf cuttings in spring or summer. Or raise new plants from seed in spring.

Pests and diseases Poor drainage can cause grey mould.

CREEPING JENNY – see *Lysimachia*
CREEPING SNAPDRAGON – see *Asarina*

Crepis

hawkweed

Crepis aurea

- ☐ Height 10-23cm (4-9in)
- ☐ Spread 23-30cm (9-12in)
- ☐ Flowers in summer
- ☐ Any well-drained soil
- ☐ Sunny site
- ☐ Hardy perennial

Hawkweeds are ultra-hardy plants which will grow in the poorest soil. Many species are persistent weeds, but those listed here are decorative perennials for the rock garden or front of a border. They bear dandelion-like flowers in summer.

Popular species

Crepis aurea has basal tufts of oblong, light green leaves and orange-bronze flowers borne on short stems from mid summer onwards. The plant reaches 10-20cm (4-8in) high.
Crepis incana has rosettes of narrow grey-green leaves covered in soft hairs. The numerous soft pink flowers are carried on 23cm (9in) high stems from mid to late summer.

Cultivation

Plant in well-drained soil, including poor types, from late summer to early autumn in a sunny site.

Crepis incana

Propagation In mid spring sow seeds in pans or boxes of seed compost in a cold frame. Prick out the seedlings into boxes or pots and transplant to the permanent position in late summer or early autumn. Alternatively, lift, divide and replant clumps in mid to late spring.
Pests and diseases Trouble free.

CRETAN DITTANY – see *Origanum*

Crocus

crocus

Crocus vernus

- ☐ Height 5-10cm (2-4in)
- ☐ Spread 7.5-10cm (3-4in)
- ☐ Flowers spring, autumn or winter
- ☐ Well-drained soil
- ☐ Sunny site or dappled shade
- ☐ Hardy corm

These hardy dwarf bulbs or corms are a welcome source of spring and autumn colour in rockeries and sink and trough gardens. As well as a large number of true species in cultivation, hundreds of named varieties are available in a wide choice of colours.

Unless otherwise stated, the species and varieties listed grow 7.5-10cm (3-4in) high.

Popular species and varieties
Crocus biflorus (Scotch crocus) produces white flowers flushed purple-blue in late winter and early spring.
Crocus byzantinus flowers in mid autumn before the foliage develops. It has two sets of petals – the inner ones are pale purple and the outer, larger ones are deep purple. The plant is best grown in shade.
Crocus chrysanthus has golden yellow flowers. It blooms in the open in late winter, or slightly earlier if grown in pots in a cold greenhouse.

Numerous hybrids have been developed and include: 'Advance' (yellow and violet); 'Blue Bird' (violet and white); 'Cream Beauty' (cream); 'E.A. Bowles' (yellow and bronze); 'Gipsy Girl' (gold and brown); 'Goldilocks' (yellow with a bronze-purple base); 'Herald' (primrose-yellow and brown); 'Ladykiller' (purple and pale lilac); 'Princess Beatrice' (blue with a

Crocus chrysanthus 'Goldilocks'

Crocus speciosus 'Oxonian'

yellow base); 'Snow Bunting' (white); and 'Zwanenburg Bronze' (bronze and golden yellow).

Crocus imperati flowers from mid to late winter. The outer petals are buff streaked with purple and the inner ones are satin-purple.

Crocus kotschyanus, syn. *C. zonatus*, has lilac-blue flowers spotted with bright orange at the base. It flowers in early to mid autumn before the leaves form.

Crocus sieberi has pale mauve flowers with a yellow base in late winter and early spring. Varieties include: 'Bowles' White' (pure white); 'Tricolor' (deep lilac-blue, white bands and yellow base); and 'Violet Queen' (violet-blue).

Crocus speciosus flowers in mid autumn, bearing lilac blooms with yellow anthers and scarlet stigmas. It is one of the easiest crocuses to grow and several popular varieties have been developed, including 'Aitchisonii' (pale lavender-blue); 'Conqueror' (deep sky-blue); 'Globosus' (violet-blue); and 'Oxonian' (lilac-purple).

Crocus susianus, syn. *C. angustifolius*, is one of the oldest crocus species still grown. Its flowers, only 6-7.5cm (2½-3in) tall, are bronze outside and golden yellow inside. They appear in winter. This species does well in an alpine house or outdoors.

Crocus tomasinianus has lilac flowers in late winter. 'Ruby Giant' and 'Whitewell Purple' are in shades of purple.

Crocus vernus, syn. *C. neapolitanus*, has variable flowers which may be white, lilac or purple and sometimes striped. The variety 'Vanguard' is light blue. The early-spring flowering species is one of the parents of the larger-flowered Dutch crocuses.

Cultivation

Plant as soon as the corms are available: the spring-flowering species in autumn, and autumn-flowering species in early summer. Crocuses grow in any well-drained soil in sun or dappled shade. Set the corms in groups 5-7.5cm (2-3in) deep and 7.5-10cm (3-4in) apart.

Winter and early-spring flowering species are ideal for growing in pots in a cold greenhouse or the home. Plant them in pans of potting compost. Allow six to eight corms to each 15cm (6in) pan.

Crocus chrysanthus

Do not remove dead flowers when they fade and allow the leaves to turn brown and die down naturally.

Propagation After the leaves die down, lift the corms, remove any cormlets and replant. *C. tomasinianus* and *vernus* increase naturally.

Pests and diseases Birds peck at flower buds, and mice and leatherjackets eat corms in the ground.

CUCKOO FLOWER – see *Cardamine*

Cyananthus

trailing bellflower

Cyananthus lobatus

- ☐ Height 5-10cm (2-4in)
- ☐ Spread 30-45cm (1-1½ft)
- ☐ Flowers late summer and autumn
- ☐ Well-drained but moist lime-free soil
- ☐ Sunny site
- ☐ Hardy trailing perennial

The bright blue funnel-shaped flowers of this trailing alpine plant are reminiscent of gentians. They are worthy of a place in the rock garden and prized for their autumn display.

Popular species

Cyananthus lobatus bears bright blue flowers at the tips of its creeping stems in late summer and early autumn. It is 10cm (4in) high and has a spread of 30-38cm (12-15in). 'Albus' has ivory-white flowers and 'Dark Seedling' bears deep violet flowers.

Cyananthus microphyllus, syn. *C. integer*, the easiest to grow, has small-leaved trailing stems spreading to 30cm (1ft) and carries blue-purple flowers in early autumn. It grows 7.5cm (3in) high.

Cyananthus sheriffii bears powder-blue flowers in early autumn. It is 5cm (2in) high and creeps to 45cm (1½ft) across.

Cultivation

Plant in early to mid spring in a sunny position in rich lime-free soil. The fleshy roots need good drainage and constant moisture. Protect *C. sheriffii* from winter rain.

Propagation Take 3-5cm (1½-2in) cuttings of basal shoots between mid spring and early summer and root in a cold frame.

Pests and diseases Trouble free.

Cyclamen

cyclamen

Cyclamen coum

- ☐ Height 10-15cm (4-6in)
- ☐ Spread 10-15cm (4-6in)
- ☐ Flowers late summer to mid spring
- ☐ Well-drained, rich soil
- ☐ Sheltered, shaded site
- ☐ Hardy and near-hardy bulbous plants

The tiny, delicate-looking but tough cyclamens are ideal for providing colour when little else is in flower. The hardy species flourish in shady rockeries and beneath trees; half-hardy types do best in an alpine house.

Popular species

Cyclamen x *atkinsii*, a 10cm (4in) high hybrid, has crimson-purple flowers from early winter to early spring. 'Album' is white with a pink base and 'Roseum' is pink. All have rounded green leaves marbled with silver.

Cyclamen balearicum is a semi-hardy species best grown in an alpine house. The white flowers, flushed pink at the base, appear in spring after the leaves. It grows 10-15cm (4-6in) high.

Cyclamen coum, 10cm (4in) tall, flowers from early winter to early spring. Its mid green leaves are marbled silver. 'Album' is white; and the 'Pewter' selection bears flowers in shades of pink.

Cyclamen europaeum, syn. *C. purpurascens*, is one of the hardiest species and bears fragrant, carmine flowers from mid summer to early winter. The mid green leaves have silver markings. The plants reach 10cm (4in) high.

Cyclamen hederifolium (ivy-leaved cyclamen), syn. *C. neapolitanum*, has profuse rose-pink flowers in autumn, followed by deep green leaves with silver markings which persist until late spring. 'Album' is white-flowered.

Cyclamen libanoticum is semi-hardy and best grown in a cool, shaded greenhouse. It has green, ivy-shaped leaves with a white zone, and pale pink flowers in late winter and early spring. It grows 15cm (6in) high.

Cyclamen repandum, syn. *C. vernale*, has rich pink scented flowers in mid spring. The mid green leaves are marbled silver. It grows 10cm (4in) high.

Cultivation

Plant hardy species in late summer to early autumn, setting them in groups 15cm (6in) apart and 2.5-5cm (1-2in) deep. They need well-drained, humus-rich soil in a shady, sheltered site.

Plant half-hardy species in pans of potting compost and keep cool, moist and shaded in a greenhouse.

Propagation Seed propagation is the only means of increase.

Pests and diseases Mites may infest greenhouse species.

Cytisus
broom

Cytisus x beanii

Cytisus x kewensis

- ☐ Height 5-60cm (2-24in)
- ☐ Spread 30cm-1.2m (1-4ft)
- ☐ Flowers mid to late spring
- ☐ Any well-drained soil
- ☐ Sunny site
- ☐ Hardy deciduous shrub

Broom (*Cytisus*) is a deservedly popular shrub in the mixed border or shrubbery, grown for its profusion of sweet pea-shaped, typically golden yellow flowers. Most brooms are full-sized shrubs, too large for the rock garden, but a few are suitable, especially slow-growing mat-forming types. Small species are at home in large rock gardens, where they can cascade their flowering stems over rocky ledges.

Popular species
Cytisus ardoini is the smallest species, growing only 5-10cm (2-4in) high, and spreading slowly to 30cm (1ft) or more across. The tiny three-lobed, grey-green leaves are hairy. Bright yellow flowers, 12mm (½in) long, are borne in mid to late spring in clusters of two and three, sometimes up to six, almost smothering the lax, mat-forming stems.

Cytisus x *beanii* grows 45-60cm (1½-2ft) high and spreads to 90cm (3ft). The linear leaves are mid green and downy. Golden yellow, 12mm (½in) long flowers are borne singly or in clusters of up to three on the previous year's growth in late spring. 'Cottage' is a compact, upright variety, with a profusion of pale creamy yellow flowers.

Cytisus decumbens is prostrate, growing about 15cm (6in) high and 30cm (12in) wide. The solitary flowers are rich yellow and appear in profusion during late spring and early summer.

Cytisus demissus spreads slowly to form a low carpet, 7.5cm (3in) high and up to 30cm (12in) across. The tiny leaves are bright green, covered with silky, silvery hairs. The large bicoloured flowers, golden yellow and russet brown, are borne in early summer.

Cytisus x *kewensis* grows 30-60cm (1-2ft) high. It is of lax, drooping habit and can spread up to 1.2m (4ft). The three-lobed leaves are mid green. Cream-white or soft yellow, 12mm (½in) long flowers appear during late spring in great profusion, singly or in twos or threes in the axils of the previous year's shoots.

Cultivation
Plant brooms in any well-drained soil during autumn or early spring in a warm sunny site. They will tolerate chalky soil, though they may be short-lived in such situations. Buy pot-grown plants as brooms are particularly sensitive to root disturbance.

Prune straggly growths immediately after flowering to encourage new shoots to sprout. Do not cut back into old wood as die-back often occurs.

Propagation Take 7.5cm (3in)

Cytisus demissus

long heel cuttings of young side-shoots in late summer and root in a cold frame. Alternatively, sow seeds in pots in spring and germinate in a cold frame.

Pests and diseases Generally trouble free, but gall mites can cause disfiguring growths.

Daphne

daphne

Daphne cneorum 'Eximia'

- ☐ Height 7.5-90cm (3-36in)
- ☐ Spread up to 1.8m (6ft)
- ☐ Flowers mid spring to early summer
- ☐ Good well-drained soil
- ☐ Sunny site
- ☐ Hardy deciduous and evergreen shrubs

The great charm of the daphnes is the wonderfully fragrant, colourful flowers that chiefly appear in late spring and early summer. They are tubular at the base, expanding into four lobes, and are usually borne in clusters. Several species are dwarf or mat-forming and suitable for the rock garden or the front of a border.

Popular species

Daphne alpina, a deciduous species, grows up to 45cm (1½ft) high and 40cm (16in) across, with grey-green leaves and white flowers in late spring, followed by red berries.

Daphne arbuscula, an evergreen, grows up to 15cm (6in) high and 30cm (12in) across, with shiny, leathery and dark green leaves crowded together at the ends of the branches. The rose-purple flowers are borne in clusters in late spring and early summer.

Daphne blagayana is a mat-form-

Daphne arbuscula

Daphne blagayana

ing, evergreen species, growing 15cm (6in) high and spreading up to 1.8m (6ft). The leathery, mid green leaves are crowded towards the tips of the branches, giving the plant a sparse appearance. The creamy white flowers are borne in clusters in late spring.

Daphne cneorum (garland flower) grows 15cm (6in) high and spreads to 60-90cm (2-3ft). It is evergreen and the most widely grown daphne, although sometimes difficult to establish. The slender stems bear small, oval, deep green leaves and dense terminal clusters of rose-pink flowers. 'Alba' has white flowers and is less vigorous. 'Eximia' is a particularly fine form, larger than the species. *D. cneorum* var. *pygmaea* is fully prostrate and free flowering.

Daphne genkwa is rather tall – up to 90cm (3ft), and more difficult to establish than the other species. It is deciduous and outstanding with its lavender-blue, slightly scented flowers borne in mid to late spring.

Daphne petraea is a slow-growing evergreen 7.5-15cm (3-6in) high, with a spread of 30cm (12in). The glossy dark green, leathery leaves are crowded on the twiggy stems. Rose-pink flowers appear in terminal clusters of two or three in late spring. The species is not fully hardy and is best grown in an alpine house or a sunny, sheltered sink garden. 'Grandiflora' has larger flowers.

Daphne retusa

Daphne retusa is an evergreen bushy shrub of rounded habit, slowly reaching 90cm (3ft) in height and 45-60cm (1½-2ft) across. It has leathery, lustrous dark green leaves, and pale pink to purple flowers in late spring and early summer; they are followed by bright red berries in autumn.

Cultivation

Plant daphnes in early autumn or mid spring in fertile, well-drained soil, including chalky soil, in sun or partial shade.

Propagation Take heel cuttings from mid summer to early autumn and root in a cold frame; grow on and transplant to permanent positions one or two years later.

Pests and diseases Aphids may check young growth. Cucumber mosaic virus and leaf spot may mark and distort the leaves.

Dianthus
rock pink

Dianthus deltoides 'Brighteyes'

Dianthus sylvestris

- Height 10-45cm (4-18in)
- Spread 15-60cm (6-24in)
- Flowers late spring to early autumn
- Well-drained neutral or alkaline soil
- Sunny site
- Hardy evergreen perennial

No alpine garden should be without rock pinks. They are truly delightful plants with neat clumps of grassy evergreen foliage and dainty flowers, almost always scented. Numerous species and named varieties are available.

Popular species and varieties

Dianthus x *allwoodii* (modern rock pinks) are hybrids of complex parentage. They flower profusely, usually in early summer and again in autumn, and have grey-green leaves. Dwarf varieties, up to 15cm (6in) high, include 'Annabel' (double, sugar pink); 'Little Jock' (semi-double, rich pink); 'Pike's Pink' (double, pink); 'Waithman Jubilee' (crimson flecked white); and 'Whatfield White' (pure white).

Dianthus alpinus forms mid to deep green mats of foliage up to 10cm (4in) high and 15cm (6in) across. The large flowers vary in colour from pale pink to purple with a pale eye ringed with purple spots. 'Albus' is cream white.

Dianthus arenarius, 20-30cm (8-12in) high, forms a dense mat,

Dianthus x *allwoodii* 'Waithman Jubilee'

30cm (12in) across, of green or grey-green leaves. The flowers are white with fringed petals and a green eye; they appear in summer.

Dianthus x *arvernensis* (Auvergne pink) has a height and spread of only 15cm (6in), with grey leaves and, from late spring to mid summer, numerous rose-pink flowers.

Dianthus deltoides (maiden pink) grows up to 23cm (9in) high, with deep to mid green leaves, sometimes purple tinged. The flowers are borne from early summer to autumn. Popular varieties include 'Brighteyes' (white with pink eye); 'Samos' (deep red flowers, purple leaves); and 'Wisley Variety' (deep red flowers).

Dianthus gratianopolitanus, syn. *D. caesius* (Cheddar pink), is a variable native, summer-flowering species 10-30cm (4-12in) high and 23-30cm (9-12in) or more wide. The leaves are grey-green,

Dianthus alpinus

Dianthus gratianopolitanus

Dianthus x allwoodii 'Whatfield White'

Dicentra

Dutchman's breeches

Dicentra cucullaria

- ☐ Height 7.5-15cm (3-6in)
- ☐ Spread 7.5-15cm (3-6in)
- ☐ Flowers mid spring to early summer
- ☐ Rich, well-drained soil
- ☐ Sheltered and shady site
- ☐ Hardy perennial

Dutchman's breeches is the rather unromantic name given to *Dicentra cucullaria*, a small species related to the bleeding heart (*D. spectabilis*), a popular border plant. The common name refers to the flowers, which are divided into two and vaguely resemble pairs of baggy breeches hanging up to dry.

The plant has a height and spread of 7.5-15cm (3-6in), with fleshy, pale to mid green, deeply dissected leaves. The flowers are up to 2.5cm (1in) long, white or pale pink, with yellow tips. They droop gracefully along the flower stalks from mid or late spring to early summer.

and the flowers soft pink with fringed petals. Varieties include 'La Bourboulle' (syn. 'La Bour-bille', only 15cm/6in across, blue-grey foliage and strongly scented pink flowers).

Dianthus neglectus, syn. *D. pavonius* (glacier pink), forms dense grey-green tufts of foliage 7.5cm (3in) high and up to 23cm (9in) wide, with pale pink to deep crimson flowers in summer.

Dianthus superbus (fringed pink) grows 23-45cm (9-18in) high, with white or lavender-pink, fringed flowers in summer.

Dianthus sylvestris (wood pink) forms clumps of silvery grey foliage. The single, luminous pink, fringed flowers are borne in early and mid summer on wiry stems 10-25cm (4-10in) high.

Cultivation
Plant rock pinks in full sun in any well-drained soil in spring or autumn. Sinks, troughs, retaining walls and gaps between paving stones are good sites.

Propagation Only the species come true from seed, easily germinated in late spring or early summer. Alternatively, take cuttings of side-shoots in summer and root in a cold frame.

Pests and diseases Powdery mildew, aphids and root aphids may be troublesome.

Cultivation
Plant Dutchman's breeches between mid autumn and early spring in well-drained but moist, humus-rich soil. Choose a shady site sheltered from late spring frosts and strong winds. Once planted, leave the plants undisturbed as the roots are brittle.

Propagation If crowded, divide and replant between autumn and spring; or take root cuttings in spring and root in a cold frame.

Pests and diseases Generally trouble free.

Dionysia
dionysia

Dionysia aretioides

- ☐ Height up to 5-10cm (2-4in)
- ☐ Spread 15-30cm (6-12in)
- ☐ Flowers spring and early summer
- ☐ Sharply-drained, gritty soil
- ☐ Alpine house
- ☐ Evergreen perennial

Although most species of *Dionysia* are fully hardy and can be grown in tufa rock outdoors, they dislike winter wet so much that they are best grown in the protection of an alpine house. Their native habitat is the dry limestone mountains of the Middle East.

Dionysia is relatively new in cultivation, and growing it successfully represents a challenge in determining the optimum conditions for each species.

Popular species
Dionysia aretioides is one of the least difficult of the species. It forms dense cushions, 5-10cm (2-4in) high and 15-30cm (6-12in) across, of packed rosettes of softly hairy, grey-green leaves, lightly toothed at the upper edges. Each rosette produces an almost stemless, scented, yellow, primrose-like flower in such profusion that the entire plant is covered with flowers during spring and early summer. It is a variable species; selected forms include 'Gravetye' and 'Paul Furse'.
Dionysia bryoides is similar to *D.*
aretioides, forming a dense green cushion, but bears long-tubed pink flowers.
Dionysia caespitosa has tiny, lightly hairy leaves which overlap on the short stems. The rich yellow flowers are carried in clusters on stems up to 5cm (2in) high.
Dionysia michauxii forms dense round pads of stems covered in scale-like overlapping leaves. The yellow, long-tubed flowers appear singly and are almost stemless.
Dionysia teucrioides has a more loose habit of growth than other species. The leaves are oblong, toothed and softly hairy. Yellow flowers are carried in clusters of one to three.

Cultivation
Grow dionysia in pots in an alpine house in very gritty compost containing some humus, in a sunny position. Sprinkle a deep collar of limestone grit beneath the plant cushions and do not overwater. If attempting to grow the plants out of doors, protect them from winter rain with raised panes of glass.
Propagation Divide mature plants or grow from seed.
Pests and diseases Generally trouble free, allowing for the difficulty of cultivation.

Dodecatheon
shooting star

Dodecatheon hendersonii

- ☐ Height 10-60cm (4-24in)
- ☐ Spread 15-30cm (6-12in)
- ☐ Flowers late spring and early summer
- ☐ Rich moist soil
- ☐ Partial shade
- ☐ Hardy perennial

Dodecatheon has cyclamen-like flowers with upward-curving petals, which accounts for the common name of shooting star. The flowers range in colour from pale pink through crimson to reddish purple. They are carried in loose clusters on tall straight stems rising from low rosettes of large oval leaves, much like primulas, to which the plant is related.

A second common name is American cowslip all the species are native to North America. The species described here are suitable for growing in large rock gardens.

Popular species
Dodecatheon alpinum grows 10cm (4in) or more high, spreading to 15cm (6in). The flowers, which are reddish purple with a yellow tube and purple ring in the throat, appear in early summer.
Dodecatheon dentatum grows 15cm (6in) high and across. It has heart-shaped leaves with serrated edges. White flowers with prominent dark anthers are carried in drooping clusters in late spring and early summer.
Dodecatheon hendersonii grows about 30cm (1ft) high from

Douglasia
douglasia

Douglasia montana

Douglasia vitaliana

Dodecatheon pauciflorum

clumps of kidney-shaped leaves. The flowers are deep pink to pale violet and carried on stout stalks in late spring.

Dodecatheon jeffreyi is one of the taller species, growing up to 60cm (2ft) high and 30cm (1ft) across, with unusually large leaves – up to 30cm (1ft) long. The flowers, borne in late spring and early summer, are reddish purple with purple stamens.

Dodecatheon meadia is the best-known species. It grows 30cm (1ft) high and across, with pale green leaf rosettes. Each flower cluster consists of numerous rose-pink blooms with white bases and bright yellow anthers. They are borne in late spring and early summer.

Dodecatheon pauciflorum grows about 23-30cm (9-12in) high and up to 15cm (6in) across. The bright lilac-pink flowers are produced in loose clusters and have a wavy purple ring in the throat; they appear in mid and late spring. 'Red Wings' has magenta-crimson flowers. The plants die down by early summer.

Cultivation
Plant shooting stars in rich moisture-retentive soil between mid autumn and early spring. They flourish in partial shade but will tolerate sun provided the soil remains moist.

Propagation Divide mature plants in spring or autumn. Alternatively, sow seeds in spring and germinate in a cold frame.

Pests and diseases Trouble free.

☐ Height 2.5-7.5cm (1-3in)
☐ Spread up to 30cm (1ft)
☐ Flowers late spring and early summer
☐ Any well-drained soil
☐ Sunny site
☐ Hardy perennial

A small, cushion-forming or creeping plant, *Douglasia* is closely related to *Androsace* and often confused with it. The species are sometimes listed under *Vitaliana*. The plants are best grown in a stone sink or trough, on a scree bed or in crevices between rocks, so that water drains away freely. Alternatively, grow the plants in pans in an alpine house, where they will be protected from winter wet.

Popular species
Douglasia dentata grows in loose tufts of pale grey rosettes of small spoon-shaped leaves, irregularly toothed at the tips. The violet, primrose-like flowers are carried on 2.5cm (1in) high stems in late spring and early summer.

Douglasia laevigata forms dense clumps, up to 7.5cm (3in) high and 30cm (1ft) across, of small glossy green leaf rosettes. Dense clusters of bright crimson blooms are carried on 2.5cm (1in) stems during late spring and early summer. The species dislikes lime and hot sun.

Douglasia montana is similar to *D. laevigata*, but with larger bright pink flowers, carried singly or in pairs above the foliage in late spring and early summer.

Douglasia nivalis forms loose 2.5cm (1in) high tufts of downy, slender, spoon-shaped leaves. The three- to six-flowered heads of pale pink blooms are almost stemless and appear in mid to late spring.

Douglasia vitaliana, syn. *Androsace vitaliana* and *Vitaliana primuliflora*, is a mat-forming species, 5cm (2in) high and 23cm (9in) across, with bright yellow flowers produced in early summer above tufts of grey-green foliage.

Cultivation
Plant douglasia in good well-drained gritty soil, in a sunny site between mid autumn and early spring. Protect from excessive sun during summer.

Propagation Increase by cuttings in early summer; by dividing established plants in spring or by seed sown in spring.

Pests and diseases Generally trouble free, but aphids may infest leaves in summer.

Draba

whitlow grass

Draba rigida

☐ Height 2.5-10cm (1-4in)
☐ Spread 7.5-23cm (3-9in)
☐ Flowers early spring to early summer
☐ Any well-drained soil
☐ Sunny site
☐ Hardy evergreen perennial

There are 300 species of whitlow grass (*Draba*), of which a handful are suitable for a rock or trough garden or alpine house. Those described form neat hummocks or small tufts of closely packed leaves which are evergreen and decorative all year round. In spring and summer they are smothered in yellow cross-shaped flowers borne on short stems.

Popular species

Draba aizoides grows about 10cm (4in) high, forming tightly packed rosettes of bristly dark green leaves. The flowers appear in large clusters carried on stout stems in early and mid spring.
Draba bruniifolia grows only 5cm (2in) high with loose tufts of hairy leaves. The flower clusters are borne on 10cm (4in) high stems in mid spring.
Draba bryoides forms a green cushion, only 5cm (2in) high and 7.5cm (3in) across, of small rigid leaves; in mid spring a few flowers are carried on thin wiry stems. *D. bryoides* var. *imbricata* has more showy flowers.
Draba mollissima grows only 2.5cm (1in) high and 15cm (6in) across, with hairy, pale grey-green leaves packed into numerous tiny, tightly crowded rosettes. Bright

Draba bruniifolia

yellow flower sprays are borne in early summer.
Draba polytricha grows 5cm (2in) high and forms hard cushions of grey-green leaves covered with small white hairs. The flowers, in mid spring, are pale yellow.
Draba rigida grows 7.5-10cm (3-4in) high in compact mid green cushions formed by minute rosettes of leaves. The yellow flowers appear in mid spring.

Cultivation

Plant drabas in early to mid spring in a sunny site in gritty, sharply-drained soil. Avoid pouring water over the foliage cushions. Cover with raised panes of glass to keep off winter rains.
Propagation Detach non-flowering rosettes in summer and root in a cold frame like cuttings.
Pests and diseases Generally trouble free.

Dryas

mountain avens

Dryas x suendermannii

☐ Height 7.5-10cm (3-4in)
☐ Spread 60-90cm (2-3ft)
☐ Flowers in summer
☐ Sunny site
☐ Hardy evergreen sub-shrub

Mountain avens is a carpeting plant, useful for evergreen ground cover in association with bulbs. White, anemone-like flowers are followed by fluffy seed heads.

Popular species

Dryas octopetala has prostrate woody stems bearing shiny, oak-like leaves, dark green above and silvery beneath. The white, saucer-shaped flowers are borne in late spring.
Dryas x *suendermannii* grows 10cm (4in) high and 60cm (2ft) or more across. It bears small, dark green leathery leaves, and cream-white flowers in early summer.

Cultivation

Plant mountain avens in well-drained soil in a sunny site between early autumn and early spring. Leave undisturbed as the plants resent root disturbance.
Propagation Take heel cuttings in summer and root in a cold frame.
Pests and diseases Trouble free.

DUTCHMAN'S BREECHES – see *Dicentra*
EDELWEISS – see *Leontopodium*

Edraianthus

edraianthus

Edraianthus pumilio

☐ Height 2.5-7.5cm (1-3in)
☐ Spread 15-23cm (6-9in)
☐ Flowers late spring to mid summer
☐ Any well-drained soil
☐ Sunny site
☐ Hardy perennial

Edraianthus is related to campanula, and grown for its profusion of rich purple or purple-blue, upturned, bell-shaped flowers. They are easy if short-lived plants for rock and trough gardens.

Popular species
Edraianthus dalmaticus grows 7.5cm (3in) high, with a spread of 15cm (6in). It forms tufted rosettes of lance-shaped, grey-green leaves. Purple flowers are borne on semi-prostrate stems during mid summer.
Edraianthus graminifolius grows 7.5cm (3in) high and 23cm (9in) across, with rosettes of bristly, needle-shaped, grey-green leaves. Purple flowers are borne from late spring to mid summer.
Edraianthus pumilio grows 5-7.5cm (2-3in) high in compact clumps with strap-shaped, grey-green leaves. Purple-blue flowers cover the plant from late spring to mid summer.
Edraianthus serpyllifolius grows only 2.5cm (1in) high and 7.5cm (3in) wide; it is suitable for a trough. It forms neat cushions with spear-shaped, deep green leaves. Glowing purple flowers, red in bud, are carried on the tips of the stems in early summer. The most commonly grown variety is 'Major' with larger flowers in a deeper shade of purple.

Cultivation
Plant edraianthus between early autumn and early spring in a sunny site, in deep well-drained soil. Protect *E. pumilio* from winter rain with raised panes of glass.
Propagation Take cuttings of non-flowering basal shoots in mid to late summer and root in a cold frame. Alternatively, sow seeds in early spring.
Pests and diseases Generally trouble free, but slugs may feed on young leaves and flowers.

Edraianthus dalmaticus

Epilobium

alpine willow herb

Epilobium glabellum

☐ Height 10-23cm (4-9in)
☐ Spread 30-38cm (12-15in)
☐ Flowers early summer to early autumn
☐ Any well-drained soil
☐ Sunny site
☐ Hardy perennial

Epilobium is a large genus which includes the invasive common willow herb as well as low-growing carpeting plants suitable for the rock garden. The flowers are shallowly funnel-shaped.

Popular species
Epilobium 'Broadwell Hybrid' grows 15cm (6in) high and 23cm (9in) across, with bronzed leaves and, in summer, cream flowers flushed with pink.
Epilobium glabellum grows 23cm (9in) high. It bears a profusion of cream-white flowers throughout summer and early autumn.
Epilobium kai-koense grows 10cm (4in) high, forming a neat mat of purple-green leaves studded with rose-pink flowers.
Epilobium obcordatum grows 15cm (6in) high. It bears a profusion of bright rose-purple flowers in summer.

Cultivation
Plant epilobiums between autumn and spring in any well-drained soil in full sun.
Propagation Take basal cuttings in spring and root in a cold frame.
Pests and diseases Trouble free.

Eranthis
winter aconite

Eranthis x tubergenii 'Guinea Gold'

- ☐ Height 5-10cm (2-4in)
- ☐ Spread 7.5-10cm (3-4in)
- ☐ Flowers mid winter to mid spring
- ☐ Well-drained moist soil
- ☐ Sun or partial shade
- ☐ Tuberous perennial

The hardy little winter aconite is prized for its yellow buttercup-like flowers, which appear early in the year on naked stems above a ruff of deep green leaves.

Popular species
Eranthis cilicia grows 5-7.5cm (2-3in) high with bronze-green foliage. The deep yellow flowers are carried on pink stems in early spring.

Eranthis hyemalis grows 10cm (4in) high, with lemon-yellow flowers in late winter. Good for naturalizing.

Eranthis x tubergenii grows 10cm (4in) high, with rich yellow flowers in early spring. 'Guinea Gold' has deep yellow, fragrant flowers and bronze leaves.

Cultivation
Plant the small tubers as soon as they become available in late summer, setting them 2.5cm (1in) deep and 7.5cm (3in) apart in groups. Sun or partial shade suits them; the soil should be well drained but moisture-retentive.

Propagation Lift the tubers as the plants begin to die down in late spring, break them into sections and replant straight away.

Pests and diseases Birds may peck the flowers.

Erigeron
fleabane

Erigeron x hybridus

- ☐ Height 7.5-60cm (3-24in)
- ☐ Spread 15-38cm (6-15in)
- ☐ Flowers late spring to late summer
- ☐ Moist, well-drained soil
- ☐ Sunny site
- ☐ Hardy perennial

The large genus of fleabane (*Erigeron*) includes a number of low-growing species that enliven the rock garden for long periods with their colourful daisy-like flowers. All have large yellow centres which contrast vividly with the outer ring of orange, pink, mauve, blue or white ray petals. There are also semi-double and double-flowered varieties.

Popular species
Erigeron alpinus grows up to 15cm (6in) high with tufts of hairy lance-shaped leaves, and rose-purple to lavender-coloured flowers.

Erigeron aurantiacus grows 23-25cm (9-10in) high and wide, forming a mat of velvety, grey-green leaves. Solitary, bright orange-yellow flowers are borne on stout leafy stems from early to late summer. The variety 'Sulphureus' has pale yellow flowers.

Erigeron aureus is a clump-forming species growing 7.5-10cm (3-4in) high, with spoon-shaped, mid green leaves. The orange-yellow flowers are borne on violet, hairy stems in mid to late summer.

Erigeron 'Birch Hybrid' is a natural hybrid. It grows 10cm (4in) high and bears creamy yellow flowers between late spring and early summer.

Erigeron compositus grows about 7.5cm (3in) high, forming tiny tufts of deeply cut grey-green woolly leaves. The purple flowers are borne in summer.

Erigeron mucronatus

Erigeron delicatus grows 10cm (4in) high in neat clumps and bears lavender flowers throughout summer.

Erigeron x *hybridus* can grow up to 60cm (2ft) high, but several varieties reach only 25-38cm (10-15in) and make good rock garden plants. Suitable small varieties include 'Dignity' (violet-blue) and 'Dimity' (pink).

Erigeron leiomerus grows 10cm (4in) high and wide, with tufts of grey-green leaves and a profusion of violet-blue flowers throughout summer.

Erigeron mucronatus, syn. *E. karvinskianus*, grows 23-25cm (9-10in) high, with numerous tiny flowers which vary in colour from white to rich pink. It is a creeping species, ideal for walls and crevices in paving, but can become invasive as it self-seeds readily.

Erigeron simplex grows 20cm (8in) high and spreads to 30cm (12in). It bears grey, hairy leaves, and pure white flowers in early and mid summer.

Cultivation

Plant fleabanes between mid autumn and early spring in moist but well-drained soil in a sunny site. Dead-head regularly to prevent self-sown seedlings and to encourage further flowering later in the season. Cut the stems down to ground level in autumn.

Propagation Divide and replant the roots between mid autumn and early spring. Alternatively, sow seeds during mid to late spring in pots or boxes placed in a cold frame. Prick out the seedlings into boxes, then into a nursery bed. Transfer to the final positions in autumn.

Pests and diseases Generally trouble free.

Erigeron alpinus

Erinacea
hedgehog broom

Erinacea anthyllis

☐ Height 25cm (10in) or more
☐ Spread 25cm (10in)
☐ Flowers late spring
☐ Deep well-drained soil
☐ Sunny and sheltered site
☐ Evergreen sub-shrub

Hedgehog broom (*Erinacea anthyllis*, syn. *Erinacea pungens*) bears profuse clusters of violet-blue pea flowers in late spring and early summer. It forms a dome-shaped mound of hard, many-branched, smooth, grey-green stems, tipped with sharp spines. The slender, lance-shaped, grey-green leaves are covered in silky hairs. They are sparse and quickly fall.

In its natural habitats in Spain, France and North Africa it can grow up to 90cm (3ft) high, but it is extremely slow-growing. A cultivated specimen will take several years to reach 23cm (9in) high.

Cultivation

Plant hedgehog broom in alkaline soil in a sunny scree bed – unless it has bright light and sharp drainage it will rot. Alternatively, grow it in an alpine house. Repot only when necessary, after flowering, as the plant dislikes having its roots disturbed.

Propagation Take softwood cuttings in late spring or early summer and root in a propagator unit.

Pests and diseases Aphids may infest young growth.

Erinus

fairy foxglove

Erinus alpinus

- ☐ Height 7.5-10cm (3-4in)
- ☐ Spread 15cm (6in)
- ☐ Flowers early spring to late summer
- ☐ Any well-drained soil
- ☐ Sunny site
- ☐ Hardy evergreen perennial

Fairy foxglove (*Erinus alpinus*) produces a mass of tiny starry flowers which appear from early spring right through to late summer. They almost smother the mid green, spoon-shaped, deeply toothed leaves.

Although not a long-lived plant, fairy foxglove seeds itself freely. It is a good plant to grow in a dry-stone wall, between cracks in paving or in sinks or troughs. As it is evergreen, as well as having a long flowering period, it provides interest all year round.

Popular varieties include 'Albus' (white flowers); 'Dr. Hanelle' (carmine-red flowers); and 'Mrs. Charles Boyle' (clear pink flowers).

Cultivation

Plant fairy foxglove between early autumn and early spring in well-drained soil in a sunny site, in a scree bed or a paved area.

Propagation Collect ripe seed from mature plants and scatter it where the plants are to grow, or in pots of seed compost placed in a cold frame. Named varieties do not come true from seed; instead divide and replant clumps of established plants in early spring.

Pests and diseases Generally trouble free.

Erodium

stork's-bill

Erodium macradenum 'Roseum'

- ☐ Height 2.5-23cm (1-9in)
- ☐ Spread 23-38cm (9-15in)
- ☐ Flowers mid spring to early autumn
- ☐ Well-drained, preferably lime-rich soil
- ☐ Sunny site
- ☐ Hardy perennial

Stork's-bill or heron's-bill belongs to a large genus closely related to the true geranium or crane's-bill, and similar in many respects, though more wiry and elegant in its habit of growth. Several species are small and compact with attractive five-petalled, saucer-shaped flowers, ideal for planting in the rock garden.

Popular species

Erodium absinthioides grows about 15cm (6in) high, with deeply cut, grey-green foliage. Loose heads of rosy-lilac flowers are carried on upright stems in summer.

Erodium chrysanthum grows 10-15cm (4-6in) high and 30cm (12in) across; it forms tufts of deeply divided fern-like silvery foliage. Small sprays of sulphur-yellow flowers are borne from late spring through summer.

Erodium corsicum grows 20cm (8in) high, with downy, soft grey, oval leaves with rounded teeth. The almost stemless flowers are clear pink veined with red and have conspicuous pale centres. The plant is susceptible to winter wet and should be protected with raised panes of glass or grown in an alpine house. 'Rubrum' has rich red flowers.

Erodium macradenum, syn. *E. petraeum* var. *glandulosum*, grows up to 23cm (9in) high, with deeply divided, mid green, fern-like foliage. The lilac flowers have dark violet blotches on the two upper petals. They are borne throughout summer. 'Roseum' has rose-coloured flowers with darker veining.

Erodium reichardii, syn. *E. chamaedryoides*, is exceptionally low-growing – 2.5-5cm (1-2in) high – forming a spreading mat of mid green round-toothed foliage. The flowers, from early to late

Erysimum
alpine wallflower

Erysimum rupestre

Erodium corsicum

summer, are white with pink veins. 'Roseum' has pink flowers with crimson veins, and 'Album' is white-flowered.

Cultivation
Plant stork's-bills during mid spring in well-drained soil in full sun. They do better in an alkaline soil than in an acid one, and grow particularly well in tufa. The half-hardy *E. corsicum* needs a sheltered, sunny site or can be grown in an alpine house.

Propagation Take root cuttings of *E. reichardii* in early spring, from the thickest parts of the root. Leave them in a cold frame and pot up when three or four leaves have formed. Take basal cuttings from other species in mid spring and root in a cold frame.

Pests and diseases Plants may be infested by aphids, particularly when grown in an alpine house.

Erodium reichardii 'Roseum'

☐ Height 15-30cm (6-12in)
☐ Spread 10-30cm (4-12in)
☐ Flowers mid spring to early summer
☐ Any well-drained soil
☐ Sunny site
☐ Hardy perennial

Alpine wallflowers (*Erysimum*) are dainty versions of their large border cousins *Cheiranthus*, with the added advantage that they thrive on poor and chalky soils. The species described here are all perennials, suitable for a rock garden. They are fairly short-lived but self-seed freely.

Popular species
Erysimum alpinum, syn. *Cheiranthus alpinus*, grows about 15cm (6in) high, with lance-shaped dark green leaves. The sulphur-yellow flowers are borne in loose clusters in late spring.

Erysimum capitatum, syn. *Cheiranthus capitatus*, is a sub-shrubby species growing 20-25cm (8-10in) high, with dark green lance-shaped leaves. Large heads of scented cream-white flowers are borne in mid and late spring, and occasionally at other times of the year.

Erysimum helveticum, syn. *E. pumilum*, grows in neat tufts with 7.5cm (3in) high stems carrying fragrant yellow flowers in flat heads in late spring and early summer.

Erysimum linifolium grows 23-30cm (9-12in) high. It is sub-shrubby and semi-evergreen, with narrow blue-grey leaves. Tight clusters of pale lilac flowers are borne in early summer.

Erysimum rupestre, syn. *E. pulchellum*, grows up to 30cm (1ft) high. It has mid green leaves that are spoon-shaped to oblong-oval. Cross-shaped, sulphur-yellow flowers are borne in oval heads from mid spring to early summer.

Cultivation
Plant alpine wallflowers between mid autumn and early spring in full sun. They thrive in any soil, even a poor or chalky one.

Propagation Take heel cuttings in mid or late summer and root in a cold frame. Pot up singly and overwinter in the cold frame; transfer to permanent positions in mid spring.

Pests and diseases Generally trouble free.

ERYTHRAEA – see *Centaurium*

Euryops

euryops

Euryops acraeus

- ☐ Height up to 30cm (12in)
- ☐ Spread 30cm (12in) or more
- ☐ Flowers late spring and early summer
- ☐ Well-drained, but moist soil
- ☐ Sunny site
- ☐ Hardy evergreen shrub

Euryops acraeus, syn. *E. evansii*, is the only species of this genus of evergreen shrubs hardy enough to be grown in Britain. It is a dwarf shrub, suitable for a sunny rock garden. It forms a compact, low-growing mound of woody stems carrying narrow silver-grey leaves. In late spring and early summer it is covered in a profusion of bright yellow daisy-like flowers up to 2.5cm (1in) across.

Euryops comes from the Drakensberg Mountains in South Africa, but is hardy in all but the most severe winters provided it is given a position in full sun.

Cultivation
Plant euryops in well-drained but moist, gritty, even poor soil in a sunny site in mid spring. Set out container-grown plants to minimize root disturbance. Dead-head regularly to encourage a succession of flowers. Prune off straggly or badly placed shoots in spring in order to maintain shape.
Propagation Take semi-ripe cuttings in summer and root in a cold frame.
Pests and diseases Trouble free.

EVENING PRIMROSE – see *Oenothera*
FAIRY FOXGLOVE – see *Erinus*
FALSE CYPRESS (DWARF) – see *Chamaecyparis*
FESCUE GRASS – see *Festuca*

Festuca

fescue grass

Festuca glauca

- ☐ Height 7.5-23cm (3-9in)
- ☐ Spread 10-15cm (4-6in)
- ☐ Ornamental grass
- ☐ Any well-drained soil
- ☐ Sunny site
- ☐ Hardy evergreen grass

Fescue grasses form dense domes of slender leaves topped in summer by blue-grey flower spikes. They provide year-round colour to rock gardens and edgings.

Popular species
Festuca alpina grows 10-15cm (4-6in) high and has bright green thread-like leaves in dense tufts. The pale green flower spikes are borne in late summer.
Festuca glauca grows 15-23cm (6-9in) high as dense clumps of tough blue-grey leaves.

Cultivation
Plant fescue grasses between early autumn and mid spring in a sunny site and in well-drained soil. Cut off the flower spikes before they develop or the clumps lose their neat shape.
Propagation Sow seeds in mid spring in an outdoor nursery bed. Or, divide clumps in autumn.
Pests and diseases Trouble free.

FIR (DWARF) – see *Abies*
FLAX – see *Linum*
FLEABANE – see *Erigeron*
FORGET-ME-NOT – see *Myosotis*

Frankenia

sea heath

Frankenia thymifolia

- ☐ Height 5-7.5cm (2-3in)
- ☐ Spread 60cm (2ft)
- ☐ Flowers mid to late summer
- ☐ Any well-drained soil
- ☐ Sunny site
- ☐ Hardy evergreen perennial

Sea heath belongs to a small genus of evergreen plants which grow wild along sea coasts in temperate and sub-tropical regions, including Britain. The species described are creeping, carpeting plants, useful for year-round ground cover which is not too rampant. Sea heaths are ideal plants for covering the gaps left by spring bulbs.

Popular species

Frankenia laevis is native to Britain and forms a neat carpet, 5-7.5cm (2-3in) high and up to 60cm (2ft) across, of tiny mid green leaves. These gradually turn from orange to crimson in late summer. A profusion of small flesh pink flowers appears in mid summer.

Frankenia thymifolia has creeping 7.5cm (3in) high stems clothed with grey-green downy leaves tinted crimson-red by early autumn. Rose-pink flowers appear during mid summer in numerous tiny, stemless clusters.

Cultivation

Plant sea heath in any well-drained, ideally sandy soil in a sunny site from autumn to spring.
Propagation Divide plants in mid spring and root in a cold frame until re-established.
Pests and diseases Generally trouble free.

Fritillaria

fritillary

Fritillaria verticillata

- ☐ Height 15-60cm (6-24in)
- ☐ Spread up to 20cm (8in)
- ☐ Flowers mid to late spring
- ☐ Rich well-drained soil
- ☐ Sunny or partially shaded site
- ☐ Hardy bulbous perennial

Fritillaries are members of the lily family, with quiet, subtle colours and great charm. They produce linear or slender lance-shaped leaves singly or in pairs, scattered along the upright slender stems which bear pendent bell-shaped flowers. Fritillaries have a reputation for being difficult, and some species are only suitable for an alpine house. Those described here are suitable for growing in groups in sunny rock gardens; the plants die down and disappear below ground by mid summer.

Popular species

Fritillaria acmopetala grows 38-45cm (15-18in) high, and is one of the easiest to grow. It bears mid green, strap-shaped leaves and two or three bell-shaped flowers in mid spring. They have three pale green outer petals surrounding three smaller inner petals, purple-brown outside and yellow-green veined with brown inside.

Fritillaria pallidiflora grows 30-38cm (12-15in) high, and has stout stems which carry lance-shaped, grey-green leaves. Clusters of greenish-yellow bell-shaped flowers appear at the tips of the stems in mid spring.

Fritillaria pudica grows about 20cm (8in) high, with strap-shaped leaves scattered along the stems. The pendent, deep yellow, orange-tinged flowers are bell-shaped and usually borne singly in mid spring.

Fritillaria pyrenaica grows 15cm (6in) or more high, with slender stems set with narrowly lance-shaped grey-green leaves. The bell shaped, drooping flowers are borne singly at the tips of the stems in mid spring; they are deep brown or purple-black and checkered.

Fritillaria verticillata grows up to 60cm (2ft) high, with slender lance-shaped leaves, in opposite pairs or in whorls along the stems. The white, pendent, bell-shaped flowers, with green markings, are borne in loose spikes in mid and late spring.

Fuchsia

trailing, dwarf fuchsia

Fuchsia 'Tom Thumb'

- ☐ Height 5-23cm (2-9in)
- ☐ Spread 60cm (2ft)
- ☐ Flowers summer and autumn
- ☐ Fertile well-drained soil
- ☐ Full sun or light shade
- ☐ Deciduous shrub

The popular, generally hardy fuchsias include a few dwarf types suitable for a rock garden.

Popular species and varieties
Fuchsia hybrids grow about 15-23cm (6-9in) high. They bear typical pendent, tubular flowers that expand into wide bells with prominent stamens; sometimes self-coloured, the flowers are more often bicoloured and borne throughout summer. Popular types include 'Alice Hoffman' (red and white); 'Pumila' (scarlet and violet); and 'Tom Thumb' (carmine-pink and purple).
Fuchsia procumbens is prostrate, only 5cm (2in) high, but spreading and trailing for 60cm (2ft). Each tiny flower consists of a yellow tube with backward-curving green and purple sepals.

Cultivation
Plant fuchsias in any humus-rich well-drained soil once any danger of spring frosts is past, in sun or light shade. In cold districts, cut the plants right down in late autumn and cover with a mulch.
Propagation Take non-flowering tip cuttings in spring and root in a propagator unit.
Pests and diseases Trouble free.

FUCHSIA (CALIFORNIAN) – see *Zauschneria*
GARLAND FLOWER – see *Daphne*

Gaultheria

wintergreen

Gaultheria miqueliana

- ☐ Height 7.5-30cm (3-12in)
- ☐ Spread up to 90cm (3ft)
- ☐ Flowers late spring to late summer
- ☐ Moist acid soil
- ☐ Partial shade
- ☐ Hardy evergreen shrub

Wintergreens are useful ground-cover plants, some species growing only a few inches high, others rather taller. They are decorative all year round, bearing urn-shaped white or pink flowers, followed by attractive globular berries in the autumn. All wintergreens spread through underground runners; they are suitable for large rock gardens, peat beds and as ground cover on banks.

Popular species
Gaultheria adenothrix grows 15-30cm (6-12in) high with hairy, red-brown zig-zag branches bearing pointed dark green, oval leaves. The flowers, from late spring to mid summer, are pink to white, and the berries are crimson.
Gaultheria humifusa is of dense, compact habit but grows only 5cm (2in) high, with rounded, wavy-edged leaves. The bell-shaped flowers are pinkish white and borne in summer, followed by small scarlet berries.
Gaultheria miqueliana grows 30cm (1ft) high and spreads to 90cm (3ft). The leaves are dark green, toothed and oval-shaped. Small white flower clusters appear in early summer and are followed by globular white berries often flushed with pink.

Fritillaria pallidiflora

Cultivation
Plant fritillaries from early to late autumn in a sunny site, as soon as the fleshy bulbs are available. The soil should be well drained and fertile. Handle the bulbs carefully – they are easily bruised and damaged by prolonged exposure to air. Plant 10-15cm (4-6in) deep with the bulbs on their sides so that the hollow crowns do not retain water. Alternatively, surround the bulbs with coarse sand.

Leave the plants undisturbed for at least four years. Cut the stems out at ground level as they die down in summer.
Propagation Seed can be bought, or collected when ripe from plants and sown at once in a cold frame. As it takes six years for the young plants to reach flowering size, it is better to buy new bulbs. Alternatively, take offsets from parent bulbs and grow them on in pots or frames until they reach flowering size.
Pests and diseases Generally trouble free.

Genista

broom

Genista procumbens photo caption area — Gaultheria procumbens

Gaultheria nummularioides is a densely hairy, prostrate shrub up to 15cm (6in) high and 20cm (8in) across. The branches are clothed with rows of leathery, oval leaves. White, pink-flushed flowers are borne in late spring and early summer; the berries are blue-black.

Gaultheria procumbens (partridge-berry, checkerberry) is a creeping species, growing 7.5-15cm (3-6in) high and spreading to 90cm (3ft) or more. The oval, toothed leaves are shiny dark green and clustered at the tips of reddish hairy stems. Tiny white or pink flowers are carried in short terminal sprays during mid to late summer. They are followed by bright red globular berries.

Gaultheria pyrolifolia, syn. *G. pyroloides*, is a prostrate creeping plant of tufted habit, forming dense mats of slender stems barely 10cm (4in) high. The leaves are glossy bright green above, hairy beneath, with toothed edges. The flowers are white flushed with pink and are borne from late spring to mid summer; the berries are black.

Cultivation

Gaultherias require a moist, acid soil with added peat or lime-free organic matter. Plant in early autumn, or in mid to late spring, in partial shade but away from drips from overhanging trees, which damage the leaves.

Propagation Take heel cuttings of lateral shoots in mid to late summer and root in a cold frame. Pot up the following spring and plunge outdoors. Plant out in autumn.

Pests and diseases Generally trouble free.

☐ Height 2.5-90cm (1-36in)
☐ Spread up to 90cm (3ft)
☐ Flowers late spring to late summer
☐ Any well-drained soil
☐ Sunny site
☐ Hardy deciduous shrub

The brooms are valued for their golden-yellow pea flowers and make handsome shrubs for borders or specimen planting. Several species are small enough to be planted in a rock garden.

Popular species

Genista lydia is commonly grown in borders, where it reaches 60-90cm (2-3ft) high and spreads for up to 1.8m (6ft). It can also be used for covering banks or for trailing over rock ledges in large rock gardens. It has arching branches with narrow grey-green leaves. The bright yellow flowers are freely borne in 7.5cm (3in) long sprays on spine-tipped shoots in late spring.

Genista sagittalis forms prostrate mats of winged stems bearing a few dark green leaves. It spreads to 30cm (12in). Closely packed golden flowers appear in terminal clusters in early summer.

Genista sylvestris (Dalmatian broom), syn. *G. dalmatica*, grows 15cm (6in) high and spreads 60-90cm (2-3ft). It forms compact hummocks with narrow dark green leaves. Bright yellow flowers appear in early to mid summer in densely set terminal sprays. It makes excellent ground cover.

Genista sylvestris

Genista tinctoria (dyer's greenweed) is a variable species ranging from a prostrate plant only 15cm (6in) high to an upright shrub with slender grooved stems, 90cm (3ft) high and 1.8m (6ft) across. The slender lance-shaped leaves are dark green. It blooms from early to late summer. Popular varieties include 'Golden Plate', up to 30cm (12in) high and of spreading habit; and 'Plena', growing about 20cm (8in) high, with golden double flowers exceptionally freely produced.

Cultivation

Plant container-grown young specimens in any well-drained soil in full sun, from mid autumn to mid spring. Do not feed or mulch as they grow best on poor, sharply-drained soil.

Propagation Take heel cuttings of lateral shoots in late summer and root in a cold frame.

Pests and diseases Trouble free.

Genista lydia

Gentiana

gentian

Gentiana x macaulayi 'Praecox'

Gentiana x macaulayi 'Kingfisher'

☐ Height 7.5-25cm (3-10in)
☐ Spread up to 45cm (18in)
☐ Flowers spring and summer or autumn
☐ Rich, moist, well-drained soil
☐ Sun or partial shade
☐ Hardy evergreen perennial

Gentians probably have the most stunning blue flowers of any garden plant, and no rock garden would be complete without them. There are two basic types – the European species, which start to flower in spring, and the Asiatic species, which are generally autumn-flowering. The typical gentian bloom is trumpet-shaped, but bell or star shapes also occur. The exquisite gentians are exacting in their demands – the European species usually tolerate lime, while the Asiatic species, which are the easiest to grow, flourish in acid soil.

Most gentians have narrow lance-shaped leaves. Those described here are invaluable in rock gardens, raised beds, sinks and troughs; Asiatic species do well in peat beds.

Popular species and varieties
Gentiana acaulis (trumpet gentian), syn. *G. clusii*, *G. excisa*, from Europe, grows 7.5cm (3in) high, forming a 45cm (18in) wide mat of glossy deep green leaves. The brilliant deep blue flower trumpets, speckled green inside,

Gentiana saxosa

appear in late spring and early summer, but the flowering habit is often unpredictable.

Gentiana farreri grows up to 10cm (4in) high and spreads to 23cm (9in) with tufts of pale green leaves. The upturned, mid blue, white-throated flowers appear from late summer to mid autumn. This Asiatic species tolerates lime.

Gentiana gracilipes, an Asiatic species, grows up to 23cm (9in) high and 30cm (12in) or more wide, with rosettes of slender mid green leaves. The narrow bell-

shaped, purple-blue and green-striped flowers appear on arching stems in mid to late summer. 'Alba' has white flowers.

Gentiana x *macaulayi* grows up to 15cm (6in) high and 45cm (18in) wide, with pale to mid green leaves. The deep blue trumpet-shaped flowers appear in early and mid autumn. It thrives in moist acid soil and partial shade. Popular varieties include 'Kingfisher' (large bright blue flowers with white-striped throats) and 'Praecox' (rich blue flowers).

Gentiana saxosa, from New

Gentiana verna

Gentiana septemfida

Zealand, is half-hardy; it forms 10cm (4in) high tufts of shiny green, spoon-shaped leaves. Small cup-shaped white flowers appear in late summer. Best grown in an alpine house.

Gentiana septemfida forms compact domes of mid green leaves. Clusters of bell-shaped violet-blue flowers appear in summer. This species, which grows about 20cm (8in) high and 30cm (12in) across, is extremely hardy, free-flowering and easy to grow in any soil.

Gentiana sino-ornata is an Asiatic, autumn-flowering species, easy to grow and free-flowering in acid soil. It grows 15cm (6in) high and 30cm (12in) across, with rosettes of slender mid green leaves. The trumpet-shaped, rich blue flowers, 5cm (2in) long, appear in autumn. 'Mary Lyle' has creamy white flowers.

Gentiana verna (spring gentian) is a European species, usually represented by the variety 'Angulosa'. This is a dainty plant, only 7.5cm (3in) high and 15cm (6in) across, with tufts of mid green ovate leaves. The intense blue starry flowers appear from late spring to mid summer. It is short-lived.

Cultivation

Plant gentians between early autumn and early spring, in fertile soil enriched with organic matter, in a sunny or partially shaded site. All gentians need

Gentiana acaulis

moisture-retentive but well-drained soil which should be lime-free for Asiatic species. Water in summer.

Divide *G. sino-ornata* every two to three years in spring.

Propagation Most gentians can be increased by dividing and replanting mature plants in early spring, except for *G. acaulis*, which is best lifted in early summer. Alternatively, take cuttings from basal shoots in late spring and root in a cold frame. *G. verna*

'Angulosa' is best raised from seed sown as soon as it is ripe, and stem cuttings can also be taken immediately after flowering.

Pests and diseases Gentians are usually free of pests, but fungal infection may cause root rot, particularly on poorly drained soil.

Geranium

geranium, crane's-bill

Geranium dalmaticum

G. sanguineum 'Lancastriense Splendens'

Geranium renardii

- ☐ Height 7.5-30cm (3-12in)
- ☐ Spread 15-60cm (6-24in)
- ☐ Flowers late spring to mid autumn
- ☐ Any well-drained soil
- ☐ Sun or partial shade
- ☐ Hardy herbaceous or semi-evergreen perennial

Dwarf forms of the true geranium, or crane's-bill, play as important a role in the rock garden as do their larger cousins in the border. As well as having a long flowering period they are compact or carpeting plants, often with semi-evergreen leaves; some have attractive autumn colouring. The flowers range in colour from white through pale lilac to magenta-pink and crimson-purple. Their common name comes from the shape of the seed heads.

Popular species and varieties

Geranium argenteum grows 15-30cm (6-12in) high and 30cm (12in) wide, with silvery, silky-haired, deeply divided leaves. The flowers are pale pink, with darker veins and borne throughout summer. This species does well in a scree bed.

Geranium cinereum grows 10-15cm (4-6in) high and 30cm (12in) across, with round to kidney-shaped grey-green leaves divided into five or seven wedge-shaped lobes. Crimson-magenta flowers with almost black centres appear from late spring to mid autumn. Popular varieties include: 'Apple Blossom' (pale pink); 'Ballerina' (lilac-pink with dark centre and red veins); and 'Laurence Flatman' (pink flowers marked with crimson).

Geranium dalmaticum grows 15cm (6in) high and forms dense, low cushions of deeply cut rounded leaves. They are glossy mid green, becoming red-tinted in autumn. Delicate clusters of pale pink flowers appear from early to late summer. 'Album' is white.

Geranium farreri, syn. *G. napuligerum*, grows slowly to 15cm (6in) high; it is a good species for a scree. The kidney-shaped, lobed, grey-green leaves form a close mat. Mauve-pink flowers on red stalks are borne in early summer; they have prominent black anthers.

Geranium argenteum

Geranium cinereum 'Ballerina'

Geranium subcaulescens

Geranium pylzowianum grows only 7.5cm (3in) high and spreads to 23cm (9in); it is suitable as ground cover in a rock garden. The mid green leaves are rounded and deeply lobed. Clear pink flowers are borne rather sparsely during early and mid summer.

Geranium renardii grows 23cm (9in) high and up to 60cm (2ft) across, with soft grey-green, deeply lobed, round leaves. Pale lavender, purple-veined flowers are borne from late spring to mid summer. It thrives in poor soil.

Geranium sanguineum (bloody crane's-bill) grows 15-25cm (6-10in) high, spreading about 45cm (1½ft) and makes good ground cover. The leaves are dark green and deeply lobed. The crimson-magenta flowers open from early summer to early autumn. 'Album'

is a slightly smaller, white-flowered variety; 'Lancastriense Splendens' has rose-pink flowers. *G. sanguineum* var. *prostratum* is a dwarf form, only 7.5-10cm (3-4in) high, with pale pink flowers. *Geranium subcaulescens*, syn. *G. cinereum subcaulescens*, grows 10-15cm (4-6in) high with round, lobed, grey-green leaves. Masses of bright crimson-magenta black-centred flowers appear from late spring to mid autumn. Varieties include 'Giuseppii' (crimson-purple) and 'Splendens' (salmon-pink).

Cultivation

Plant geraniums between early autumn and early spring in any well-drained soil, in sun or partial shade. *G. cinereum* is best planted in early spring unless the site is

sheltered and sunny. After flowering, cut the stems back to ground level, to encourage new growth and a second flush of flowers.

Propagation Divide and replant at any time between early autumn and early spring. Alternatively, sow seed in early autumn and overwinter in a cold frame. Set out in nursery rows for the summer and transplant in autumn.

Pests and diseases Slugs may eat young plants. Mildew and rust cause stunting and discoloration.

GERMANDER – see *Teucrium*

Geum

avens

☐ Height 15-30cm (6-12in)
☐ Spread 23-38cm (9-15in)
☐ Flowers late spring to mid summer
☐ Rich neutral to acid soil
☐ Sunny or partially shaded site
☐ Hardy perennial

Avens is a plant with long-lasting appeal. Its neat rosettes of bright green leaves are attractive in themselves. From late spring to mid summer, large saucer-shaped and rose-like, golden-yellow or bright orange flowers rise above the foliage on slender stems. The flowers are followed by attractive fluffy silver-pink seed heads.

Popular species
Geum montanum grows 15-30cm (6-12in) high with a spread of up to 30cm (1ft). The mid green leaves are deeply lobed and borne in pairs along the stems with a larger terminal lobe at the tip. The golden-yellow flowers are 2.5cm (1in) across. 'Maximum' has larger flowers and crinkled dark green leaves.
Geum reptans is very similar to *G. montanum* but slightly larger, growing 23-30cm (9-12in) high and spreading to 38cm (15in). It develops conspicuous red runners, but can be difficult to establish; it is best grown in a sunny scree bed with acid soil.

Cultivation
Plant geums from early autumn to early spring in sun or partial shade in soil enriched with organ-

Geum reptans

Geum montanum (seed heads)

ic matter. *G. reptans* needs lime-free soil.
Propagation Divide plants during early to mid spring and replant at once. *G. reptans* produces small plantlets on its runners which can be detached during summer and treated like seedlings. Or sow seeds in 7.5cm (3in) pots of compost and place in a cold frame. Transfer the seedlings to an outdoor plunge bed in spring and plant out in autumn.
Pests and diseases Generally trouble free.

GLOBE DAISY – see *Globularia*

Globularia

globe daisy

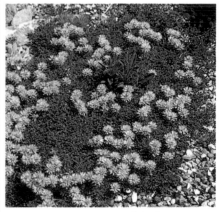

Globularia repens

☐ Height 2.5-23cm (1-9in)
☐ Spread up to 45cm (1½ft)
☐ Flowers late spring to early summer
☐ Well-drained soil
☐ Sunny site
☐ Evergreen sub-shrubby perennial

Globe daisy is a delightful little plant, bearing fluffy puffballs of lavender-blue flowers in early summer. Some species grow in rosettes of glossy, leathery and paddle-shaped leaves; others grow as tangled stems covered with minute spear-shaped leaves. When well established the plants form useful ground-covering mats.

Popular species
Globularia cordifolia grows 5cm (2in) high, spreading its woody stems to 20cm (8in). It is an evergreen shrubby species with small dark green oval leaves, notched at their tips. The round, fluffy, lavender-blue flowers appear on short stems during early summer.
Globularia meridionalis, syn. *G. bellidifolia*, grows 23cm (9in) high and wide, in tangled mats of woody stems with glossy dark green leaves. The flowers are blue to lavender-purple and carried on short stems in early summer.
Globularia nudicaulis is an herbaceous species with tufts of leathery green leaves. Almost leafless stems, 15-23cm (6-9in) high, rise from the centre of the leaf rosettes, carrying round heads of clear blue flowers in early summer.
Globularia punctata forms rosettes of rounded leathery leaves. The pale blue, bell-shaped flowers are borne on 23-30cm (9-12in) high stems in early summer.
Globularia repens, syn. *G. nana*, is similar to *G. cordifolia* but even

Gypsophila
baby's breath

Gypsophila aretioides

Gypsophila cerastioides

Globularia nudicaulis

smaller. It spreads to a dense mat of tangled stems, covered with minute, dark green, leathery leaves. It creeps attractively as an evergreen carpet over rocks, walls and ledges. The flower heads, almost stemless, are pale blue fading to lilac.

Globularia trichosantha grows about 23cm (9in) high. It is herbaceous and very similar to *G. nudicaulis*, with leafless stems and fairly large mid blue flower heads. It is rather coarser in growth.

Cultivation
Plant globe daisies during early to mid autumn or in early to mid spring in full sun and any well-drained soil. They thrive on chalky soil and do well in scree beds and in pockets of soil.

Propagation Divide clumps in autumn or spring. Alternatively, take stem cuttings in summer and root in a cold frame.

Pests and diseases Generally trouble free.

☐ Height 5-15cm (2-6in)
☐ Spread 15-60cm (6-24in)
☐ Flowers late spring to late summer
☐ Any well-drained soil
☐ Sunny site
☐ Hardy perennial

Dwarf species of *Gypsophila* are perfect for carpeting rock gardens, walls and sunny banks with their semi-evergreen foliage and delicate clouds of pink or white flowers.

Popular species
Gypsophila aretioides grows only 5cm (2in) high, but spreads to a 23cm (9in) wide cushion of minute oval, grey-green leaves. The white or pale pink flowers are borne in early summer.

Gypsophila cerastioides grows 7.5cm (3in) high and wide, with clumps of oval, grey leaves. Saucer-shaped, white flowers marked with purple veins are borne in late spring and early summer.

Gypsophila repens, 15cm (6in) high, forms a 60cm (2ft) wide mat of many-branched wiry stems and narrow grey-green leaves. Sprays of flowers, from white to deep pink, appear from early to late summer. 'Rosea' is pink.

Cultivation
Plant baby's breath in early spring or early autumn in well-drained soil, and in a sunny site. *G. repens* is best planted where it can trail over rocks or walls. *G. aretioides* thrives in an alpine house.

Propagation Root young shoots of *G. aretioides* in a cold frame in spring. Divide and replant *G. cerastioides* in spring or autumn. Take basal shoot cuttings of *G. repens* in spring and root in a cold frame.

Pests and diseases Trouble free.

Haberlea

haberlea

Haberlea rhodopensis

☐ Height 7.5-15cm (3-6in)
☐ Spread 15-23cm (6-9in)
☐ Flowers late spring
☐ Enriched well-drained soil
☐ Shaded site
☐ Hardy perennial

Haberlea is a useful rock garden plant, being one of the few that prefers a shady site. It thrives in crevices in north-facing rocks or walls. The plant has proportionally large leaves, with prominent veins and toothed edges. They contrast well with the delicate primrose-like flowers with frilled petals.

Popular species

Haberlea ferdinandi-coburgii grows 10-15cm (4-6in) high and spreads to 15-23cm (6-9in). It forms a rosette of thick, dark green, oval leaves. The lilac-pink flowers have frilled lobes and are about 2.5cm (1in) across; the long throats are white inside, spotted with gold. The flowers are carried three or four to a spray on 10-15cm (4-6in) high stems during late spring.

Haberlea rhodopensis grows only 7.5cm (3in) high but spreads to 15-23cm (6-9in). It is similar to *H. ferdinandi-coburgii* but smaller and lavender-pink. 'Virginalis' is a pure white variety.

Cultivation

Plant haberleas in early autumn or early spring in well-drained soil, preferably enriched with organic matter. They flourish in cool, shady sites. Ideally, plant them in vertical rock crevices so that rain is prevented from accumulating in the rosettes and rotting the plants. If necessary, wedge small pieces of turf around the plants, grass-side in, to keep them in place.

Propagation Mature plants can be divided in spring, but the most rapid method of obtaining new plants is by leaf cuttings taken in early to mid summer. Gently remove whole mature leaves from the plants and insert to one-third of their length in potting compost in a cold frame. Pot up in early spring and keep in the frame. Plant out in early autumn.

Alternatively, seeds can be sown in spring and germinated in a cold frame.

Pests and diseases Slugs may eat leaves and flower stems.

x *Halimiocistus*

halimiocistus

x *Halimiocistus ingwersenii*

☐ Height up to 30cm (1ft)
☐ Spread up to 90cm (3ft)
☐ Flowers late spring to mid summer
☐ Any well-drained soil, preferably containing lime
☐ Sunny site
☐ Evergreen shrub

Halimiocistus is a member of the rock rose family, an intergeneric hybrid between *Cistus* and *Halimium*. The few species in the genus are low-growing shrubs and one, x *Halimiocistus ingwersenii*, is of dwarf habit and suitable for a rock garden. It is semi-prostrate, growing up to 30cm (1ft) high and spreading to 90cm (3ft). Like the rock roses, it is also an excellent ground cover plant and is hardy in all but the coldest areas. It has hairy stems and narrow lance-shaped, dark green and hairy leaves. The saucer-shaped, white flowers, 2.5cm (1in) across, with five papery petals and a golden centre, are borne for a long period during late spring and early summer. The individual flowers last only one day, but are freely produced in succession.

Cultivation

Plant halimiocistus during mid and late spring in sharply-drained soil, preferably containing lime, in full sun. The plants resent root disturbance, and container-grown specimens establish themselves better than bare rooted plants.

Little pruning is required – just pinch back young stems to keep the plant bushy, and cut out old stems in spring.

Propagation Take semi-ripe cuttings in mid to late summer and root in a cold frame.

Pests and diseases Generally trouble free, but shoots may die back because of frost damage.

Haplopappus

haplopappus

Haplopappus coronopifolius

- ☐ Height 30cm (1ft)
- ☐ Spread 30cm (1ft)
- ☐ Flowers early to late summer
- ☐ Any well-drained soil
- ☐ Sunny site
- ☐ Evergreen perennial

Haplopappus is a member of the daisy family and bears typical rayed flowers with a central boss, in a delightful golden colour. It is rather large for the rock garden, but the 30cm (1ft) high sub-shrubby perennial is compact and neat-looking. The plants are useful for winter interest as well as summer colour, as they are fully hardy, with evergreen foliage.

Popular species

Haplopappus coronopifolius grows up to 30cm (1ft) high, forming a compact mound of dark green, leathery and toothed leaves. A profusion of golden yellow daisy flowers is produced in early to late summer, carried on upright wiry stalks.

Haplopappus lyallii is very similar to *H. coronopifolius* and probably synonymous with it.

Cultivation

Plant haplopappus during early to mid autumn or mid to late spring in any sharply-drained soil in a sunny position.

Propagation Divide and replant mature plants during spring. Alternatively, take stem cuttings in summer and root in a cold frame.

Pests and diseases Generally trouble free.

HAREBELL – see *Campanula*
HAWKWEED – see *Crepis, Hieracium*

Hebe

hebe

Hebe 'Carl Teschner'

- ☐ Height 5-30cm (2-12in)
- ☐ Spread 15-60cm (6in-2ft)
- ☐ Flowers late spring to late summer
- ☐ Any well-drained soil
- ☐ Sunny site
- ☐ Evergreen shrub

Dwarf hebes are ideal for sunny rock gardens, brightening them through the summer with lilac, purple or white spikes and clusters and throughout the year with their neat foliage. Many species are only moderately hardy, but those described here thrive in southern and western seaside gardens.

Popular species and hybrids

Hebe buchananii grows only 5cm (2in) high and spreads to 15cm (6in). It is a hardy, cushion-forming species, consisting of dense wiry twigs with tiny green, round leaves. The white flowers in summer are small, stemless and rather sparse.

Hebe 'Carl Teschner', syn. *H.* 'Youngii', is hardy and grows up to 30cm (1ft) high, spreading for up to 60cm (2ft), with grey-green leaves and purple flowers. It is suitable for ground cover.

Hebe 'Pagei' grows 15-23cm (6-9in) high and spreads to 60cm (2ft) or more. It is hardy and bears grey-green leaves and white flowers.

Cultivation

Plant hebes in early to mid autumn or mid to late spring. They thrive in most well-drained

Hebe 'Pagei'

soils, including chalk, in full sun. In inland gardens, grow hebes in the protection of warm sheltered walls. Dead-head all species immediately flowering is finished. If a plant becomes leggy cut it back hard in mid spring; new shoots usually break freely from the base.

Propagation Take tip cuttings of non-flowering shoots in summer and root in a cold frame.

Pests and diseases Downy mildew and leaf spot may discolour leaves. Honey fungus may kill the plants.

HEDGEHOG BROOM – see *Erinacea*

Helianthemum

rock rose, sun rose

- ☐ Height 7.5-15cm (3-6in)
- ☐ Spread 30-60cm (1-2ft)
- ☐ Flowers early to mid summer
- ☐ Any well-drained soil
- ☐ Sunny site
- ☐ Evergreen shrub

The hardy free-flowering rock or sun roses are useful in large rock gardens if sited where they do not swamp less vigorous plants. They are also suitable for growing on sunny banks and retaining walls.

Popular species and varieties

Helianthemum alpestre, syn. *H. oelandicum*, grows only 7.5-10cm (3-4in) high but spreads to about 30cm (1ft). It has oval mid green

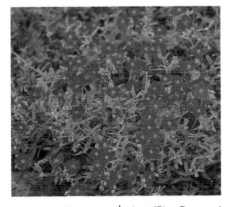

H. nummularium 'Fire Dragon'

Helianthemum nummularium 'The Bride'

leaves. The bright yellow flowers are borne in abundance.

Helianthemum lunulatum forms a dainty cushion, 15cm (6in) high and 23cm (9in) wide. It has grey-green leaves and a profusion of bright golden orange-eyed flowers.

Helianthemum nummularium is the most widely grown species. It grows 10-15cm (4-6in) high and spreads for about 60cm (2ft). The oval leaves are deep green above, paler beneath. The flowers appear

H. nummularium 'Wisley Pink'

in profusion in early and mid summer. The species is superseded by numerous named varieties, including the 'Ben' series, such as 'Ben Dearg' (deep bronze gold) and 'Ben Hope' (carmine-pink). Other varieties include 'The Bride' (white); 'Mrs. Croft' (pink and orange); 'Fire Dragon' (vermilion); 'Wisley Pink'; and 'Wisley Primrose'.

Cultivation

Plant rock roses between early autumn and spring in any well-drained soil in a sunny spot. Cut *H. nummularium* hard back after flowering to maintain a neat shape. Trim all rock roses after flowering to encourage fresh blooms.

Propagation Take heel cuttings of non-flowering lateral shoots in summer and root in a cold frame. Set out in permanent positions the following spring.

Pests and diseases Powdery mildew and leaf spot may occur on the leaves.

Helianthemum nummularium 'Ben Dearg'

Helichrysum
strawflower

Helichrysum milfordiae

☐ Height 5-25cm (2-10in)
☐ Spread 15-30cm (6-12in)
☐ Flowers early to late summer
☐ Any sharply-drained soil
☐ Sunny site
☐ Evergreen perennial or sub-shrub

The alpine species of strawflower are grown mainly for their handsome grey-green or woolly white evergreen foliage, though some also have attractive flowers.

Popular species
Helichrysum bellidioides grows 7.5cm (3in) high, with matted, slender, branching stems forming a half-hardy, prostrate shrublet. The oval leaves are dark green

Helichrysum selago

above, woolly white beneath. Clusters of white, everlasting flowers are borne from late spring to mid summer.
Helichrysum coralloides is a striking foliage plant with small, scale-like, overlapping grey-green leaves. It is half-hardy, growing 25cm (10in) high and only 15cm (6in) wide. It rarely flowers.
Helichrysum milfordiae, syn. *H. marginatum*, forms a dense cushion only 5cm (2in) high but 23cm (9in) wide. The oblong leaves are soft silver; crimson buds open to white flowers in summer.
Helichrysum selago is a compact wiry shrublet with a height and spread of 15-23cm (6-9in). It has closely overlapping, scale-like, silver-grey leaves and, in summer, small buff-white flowers.

Cultivation
Plant in early autumn, or late spring, in any sharply-drained soil. *H. milfordiae* is best grown in an alpine house. Other species need a sheltered sunny site; protect from cold and wet in winter.
Propagation Take heel cuttings of side-shoots in early summer.
Pests and diseases Downy mildew may occur.

Hepatica
hepatica

Hepatica transsylvanica

☐ Height 10-15cm (4-6in)
☐ Spread 15-30cm (6-12in)
☐ Flowers late winter to mid spring
☐ Rich moist soil
☐ Partial shade
☐ Semi-evergreen perennial

Hepatica was formerly classified as *Anemone,* and resembles it closely. It thrives in shady woodland conditions and flowers in late winter, before the tri-lobed mid green leaves have fully developed.

Popular species
Hepatica × media 'Ballard's Variety' grows 15cm (6in) high and carries anemone-like, soft lavender-blue flowers in early spring.
Hepatica nobilis, syn. *H. triloba, Anemone hepatica,* grows about 10cm (4in) high. The flowers range from white to red and purple; double-flowered forms are also available.
Hepatica transsylvanica, syn. *H. angulosa,* grows 10cm (4in) high. The saucer-shaped flowers are pale mauve-blue.

Cultivation
Plant hepaticas in early to mid autumn. They do best in partial shade and in any deep and moist soil containing plenty of organic matter.
Propagation Divide plants in early autumn and replant at once in permanent positions.
Pests and diseases Generally trouble free.

Hieracium

hawkweed

Hieracium aurantiacum

☐ Height 10-45cm (4-18in)
☐ Spread 30cm (1ft)
☐ Flowers early to mid summer
☐ Any well-drained soil
☐ Sunny or partially shaded position
☐ Perennial

Most hawkweeds resemble dandelions and like them are weeds inhabiting grassy and rocky areas. A few species are suitable for garden borders and rock gardens. They flourish anywhere, even in poor dry soil, and are useful for problem areas where little else will grow.

Some species are grown mainly for their rosettes of silver-grey leaves, but most hawkweeds also produce dandelion-like, orange or yellow flowers with strap-shaped petals throughout summer.

Hieracium villosum

Popular species

Hieracium aurantiacum grows 23-30cm (9-12in) high, with mid green leaves. The flowers are rich orange-red. Plants are invasive and spread freely by runners; they also self-seed from airborne fluffy seeds.

Hieracium bombycinum grows 15cm (6in) high, with silvery hairy leaves and yellow flowers.

Hieracium lanatum, syn. *H. tomentosum*, grows 10-45cm (4-18in) high, producing ground-hugging rosettes of leaves covered in snow-white hairs. Attractive woolly bracts surround the flower buds, but these are best removed to allow the leaves to give their best show.

Hieracium villosum (shaggy hawkweed) forms rosettes of grey white-felted leaves, about 15cm (6in) across. Wiry stems, 30cm (1ft) high, rise from the centres of the rosettes, bearing orange-yellow, slightly cup-shaped flowers in summer.

Cultivation

Plant hawkweed from mid autumn to mid spring in any well-drained soil, including poor and shallow types, in sun or partial shade.

Propagation Divide plants between autumn and spring and replant in their permanent positions.

Pests and diseases Generally trouble free.

Horminum

horminum

Horminum pyrenaicum

☐ Height 15-23cm (6-9in)
☐ Spread up to 30cm (1ft)
☐ Flowers in summer
☐ Any well-drained soil
☐ Sunny, open position
☐ Perennial

Horminum is a modest but hardy plant, related to sage, but worth growing for its spikes of rich purple tubular flowers. It makes good ground cover. There is only one species, *Horminum pyrenaicum*, which grows wild from the Pyrenees to the Tyrol. It produces basal rosettes of rough, toothed leaves with puckered surfaces, similar to those of *Ramonda*. During early to late summer the plant produces sturdy 15-23cm (6-9in) high flower stems carrying numerous clusters of blooms with slightly protruding stamens.

The variety 'Roseum' has pink flowers.

Cultivation

Plant horminum between mid autumn and early spring in any well-drained soil, in an open sunny position.

Propagation Divide and replant established clumps in spring, or sow seed in autumn.

Pests and diseases Generally trouble free.

HORNED RAMPION – see
Phyteuma
HOUSELEEK – see
Sempervivum

Houstonia

bluets

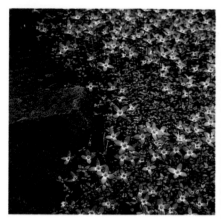

Houstonia caerulea

☐ Height 7.5cm (3in)
☐ Spread 30-45cm (1-1½ft)
☐ Flowers mid spring to mid summer
☐ Moist lime-free soil
☐ Partial shade
☐ Evergreen perennial

Houstonia, known as bluets in its native North America, is a useful carpeting plant for shady areas, but it requires lime-free soil. It bears a profusion of yellow-centred, porcelain blue flowers.

Popular species

Houstonia caerulea grows up to 7.5cm (3in) high and spreads 30-45cm (1-1½ft). It resembles chickweed, forming bright green carpets of tiny spoon-shaped leaves. Cross-shaped, four-petalled flowers are borne in profusion from mid spring to mid summer. 'Millard's Variety' has deeper blue flowers; 'Alba' is white.

Houstonia serpyllifolia (creeping bluets) is a prostrate species, forming a mat up to 7.5cm (3in) high and 30-45cm (1-1½ft) across. It is similar to *H. caerulea*, but has darker flowers and rounded leaves.

Cultivation

Plant bluets in early to mid spring in moist, lime-free soil in a semi-shaded position.
Propagation Divide mature plants in early to mid spring, or immediately after flowering, and replant straight away. Alternatively, sow seed every year – bluets tend to die away after two years.
Pests and diseases Trouble free.

Hutchinsia

chamois cress

Hutchinsia alpina

☐ Height 7.5-10cm (3-4in)
☐ Spread 25cm (10in)
☐ Flowers early summer
☐ Any well-drained soil
☐ Open but cool site
☐ Evergreen perennial

Chamois cress, *Hutchinsia alpina*, forms low mounds of dark green, finely cut ferny leaves and bears tiny white flowers which cover the plant in early summer. It is related to *Draba*, and very similar to it.

Chamois cress comes from the mountains of central and southern Europe.

Cultivation

Plant chamois cress during early to mid spring in any well-drained soil in a well-lit site out of direct sun. It looks well growing in crevices between rocks, in a sink garden, or in tufa blocks. It is also suitable for planting in crevices between paving stones, or on scree.
Propagation Divide and replant clumps in spring; alternatively, sow seeds in spring in pots of compost or directly where the plants are to grow.
Pests and diseases Generally trouble free.

Hylomecon

hylomecon

Hylomecon japonicum

☐ Height 20-30cm (8-12in)
☐ Spread up to 30cm (1ft)
☐ Flowers early spring
☐ Rich well-drained soil
☐ Partial shade
☐ Perennial

Hylomecon japonicum, syn. *Stylophorum japonicum*, is a Japanese woodland plant grown for its poppy-like, bowl-shaped, bright yellow flowers borne on slender stems early in the spring.

The elegant foliage is bright lush green in colour, each leaf divided into two or three pairs of leaflets. The plants become dormant by late summer.

Cultivation

Plant hylomecon during early to mid spring in rich moist soil with plenty of organic matter, in a shady or woodland position. Lift and divide plants every few years – hylomecon has fleshy roots which soon become congested, reducing the flowering vigour of the plant.
Propagation Take root cuttings or divide plants in spring, replanting strong-growing sections immediately.
Pests and diseases Generally trouble free.

Hypericum

St. John's wort

Hypericum cerastioides

- ☐ Height 7.5-30cm (3-12in)
- ☐ Spread 30-45cm (1-1½ft)
- ☐ Flowers mid summer to autumn
- ☐ Any well-drained soil
- ☐ Sunny site
- ☐ Evergreen and deciduous shrubs

Dwarf species of St. John's wort are carpeting shrubs for sunny banks and large rock gardens. They add bright colour with their golden flowers conspicuous for their distinctive tufts of long stamens. The species described are generally hardy, and evergreen unless otherwise stated.

Popular species

Hypericum balearicum is a half-hardy species growing 30cm (1ft) or more high. It is closely covered in small, puckered leaves, and produces fragrant flowers from early summer onwards.

Hypericum cerastioides, syn. *H. rhodoppeum*, is semi-prostrate, 15cm (6in) high and 30cm (12in) across, with hairy, oval, grey-green leaves. The flowers appear in small clusters in mid summer.

Hypericum coris grows 15cm (6in) high and thrives in poor and limy soil. The foliage is grey-green and heather-like. Golden flowers are borne in clusters in mid summer.

Hypericum empetrifolium forms a low mat, 7.5cm (3in) high and 30cm (12in) across, of heather-like foliage. The golden-yellow flowers are borne in small clusters. Half-hardy, the species needs a sheltered site.

Hypericum olympicum grows as a 23-30cm (9-12in) high hummock. It is a hardy deciduous shrub with grey-green oval leaves. Golden flowers are borne in profusion at the tips of the shoots in summer. 'Citrinum' has pale lemon-yellow flowers.

Hypericum repens is a tufted herbaceous plant only 15cm (6in) high, with narrow grey-green leaves. The flowers are borne in loose terminal clusters.

Hypericum reptans is a mat-forming, hardy species only 7.5cm (3in) high, but spreading to 30-45cm (1-1½ft). It has rounded light green leaves that turn red-brown in autumn. Scarlet buds open to orange-yellow flowers from mid summer to early autumn.

Cultivation

Plant St. John's worts in mid spring in any, even poor but well-drained soil in a sunny site.

Propagation Take cuttings of soft basal shoots in late spring and root in a cold frame. Plant out the following spring.

Pests and diseases Rust disease may infest the leaves.

Hypericum olympicum 'Citrinum'

Hypsela

hypsela

Hypsela reniformis

☐ Height 2.5cm (1in)
☐ Spread 23cm (9in) or more
☐ Flowers in summer
☐ Moist soil
☐ Semi-shaded site
☐ Perennial

Hypsela is a useful creeping plant which makes good ground cover in shady rock gardens. It flourishes in peaty soil where it can become invasive and is more manageable in ordinary soil provided it is moisture-retentive.

Only one species is in general cultivation, *Hypsela reniformis*, syn. *H. longiflora*, a native of South America. This grows 2.5cm (1in) high and spreads 23cm (9in) or more. The bright green, rather fleshy leaves are round or heart-shaped. Small starry pale pink flowers are produced during summer on very short stems growing from the axils of the leaves.

Cultivation
Plant hypsela between mid autumn and early spring in a cool, sheltered, semi-shaded spot in moist soil. The plant is fully hardy.
Propagation Divide mature plants in early spring and replant in the growing positions.
Pests and diseases Generally trouble free.

Iberis

candytuft

Iberis sempervirens

☐ Height 7.5-30cm (3-12in)
☐ Spread 30-60cm (1-2ft)
☐ Flowers late spring and early summer
☐ Any well-drained soil
☐ Sunny site
☐ Perennial and sub-shrub

The perennial species of hardy candytuft make ideal rock garden plants, forming neat mounds of dark green foliage, smothered in dense clusters of snow-white or pink flowers in late spring and early summer. The plants thrive almost anywhere and are tolerant of urban pollution. *Iberis sempervirens* spreads quite widely, and is often planted on banks or walls where it can tumble freely.

Popular species
Iberis gibraltarica grows up to 30cm (1ft) high, spreading to 30-45cm (1-1½ft). It is an evergreen sub-shrub but not reliably hardy, though easily replaced as it self-seeds freely. The dark green, narrowly oblong leaves are thick-textured. Pink flowers are borne in dense flattened clusters during mid and late spring.
Iberis saxatilis, an herbaceous perennial, has slender, fleshy, dark green leaves. It grows about 7.5cm (3in) high with a spread of 30cm (1ft). The white flowers are borne in flat-topped clusters from late spring to mid summer.
Iberis sempervirens is a perennial evergreen species, growing up to 23cm (9in) high and spreading to 60cm (2ft) or more, with dark green, narrow oblong leaves. Dense heads of snow-white flowers appear from late spring to early summer.

'Little Gem' is a more compact variety growing only 10cm (4in) high; 'Snowflake' is larger and more vigorous, to 30cm (12in) high and wide.

Cultivation
Plant candytuft between early autumn and early spring in ordinary, even poor soil in a sunny site. Dead-head after flowering.
Propagation Take cuttings from non-flowering shoots in early to late summer and root in a cold frame.
Pests and diseases Flea beetles may eat small holes in the leaves.

Iberis gibraltarica

Inula

inula

Inula ensifolia 'Compacta'

☐ Height 5-25cm (2-10in)
☐ Spread up to 30cm (1ft)
☐ Flowers mid to late spring and late summer
☐ Moist fertile soil
☐ Sunny site
☐ Perennial

The golden, finely-rayed, daisy-like flowers of inula are familiar in borders, and two compact species are suitable for growing in rock gardens.

Popular species

Inula acaulis grows 5-10cm (2-4in) high, forming a flat mat of spoon-shaped, mid green leaves. The flowers, each up to 5cm (2in) across, are borne on short stems from mid to late spring.

Inula ensifolia is represented in cultivation by the variety 'Compacta'. This grows 25cm (10in) high, spreading to 30cm (12in). It is clump-forming, with slender, lance-shaped leaves and a profusion of yellow flowers in late summer.

Cultivation

Plant inula from mid autumn to early spring in any moisture-retentive, fertile soil in a sunny position.

Propagation Divide and replant mature plants between early spring and mid autumn.

Pests and diseases Generally trouble free.

Ipheion

ipheion

Ipheion uniflorum 'Froyle Mill'

☐ Height 10-15cm (4-6in)
☐ Spread 5-7.5cm (2-3in)
☐ Flowers mid and late spring
☐ Any well-drained soil
☐ Sheltered site, sun or partial shade
☐ Hardy bulb

Ipheion is a genus of about 20 species of hardy bulbs native to Mexico and southwards as far as Chile. Only one species is in cultivation, *Ipheion uniflorum*, syn. *Brodiaea uniflora, Triteleia uniflora*. It is ideal for growing in sheltered pockets in a rock garden. The leaves and bulbs smell faintly of garlic.

Ipheion grows 10-15cm (4-6in) high, with grass-like, pale green leaves. The scented, star-like flowers are white to violet-blue and produced in mid to late spring. Several named varieties include 'Album' (white); 'Caeruleum' (pale blue); 'Froyle Mill' (violet-blue); and 'Wisley Blue' (deep blue).

Cultivation

Plant ipheion bulbs 5-7.5cm (2-3in) deep in early or mid autumn. Choose a sheltered spot in sun or partial shade, with good well-drained soil. Keep free from weeds and remove dead leaves and flower stems in late summer.

Divide and replant regularly to

Ipheion uniflorum

maintain a good show of flowers.

Propagation Offsets are freely produced, and the plants spread of their own accord. Every two or three years lift the bulbs as the leaves die down, separate the bulblets and replant at once. If the bulbs must be kept until the autumn before replanting, keep them cool and do not allow them to dry out or get wet.

Pests and diseases Trouble free.

Iris

iris

Iris reticulata 'Clairette'

- ☐ Height 10-30cm (4-12in)
- ☐ Spread up to 38cm (15in)
- ☐ Flowers late winter to early summer
- ☐ Well-drained soil
- ☐ Sunny site
- ☐ Rhizomatous or bulbous-rooted perennials

The beauty and variety of the flowers of the iris family can be enjoyed as much in the rockery as elsewhere in the garden, as there are numerous enchanting dwarf species and hybrids, all fully hardy. Their dainty flowers have the characteristic iris shape, with upright inner petals (standards) and downward-curving lower petals (falls). So-called bearded irises have a small tuft of hair on each of the fall petals.

Iris leaves are sword-shaped or grassy, and mainly evergreen. In some species they are tiny or non-existent at flowering time.

Iris innominata

Iris danfordiae

Iris tectorum

Popular species and varieties

Iris chamaeiris is a variable species of dwarf bearded iris, with flowers which may be white, yellow or purple, produced in spring. It grows 15-25cm (6-10in) high and thrives in limy soil. Although similar to *I. pumila*, it is distinguished by having a real stem and sometimes more than one flower to a stem. The variety 'Campbellii', which has large deep indigo-blue flowers, is more reliable.

Iris cristata, a crested iris, grows 15cm (6in) high. It produces its main flush of flowers in mid to late spring, usually in pairs. They are striking lilac and orange, with a white orange-tipped crest.

Iris danfordiae is a bulbous iris. It grows 10cm (4in) high, and flowers in mid to late winter before the leaves have developed. The blooms are bright lemon yellow with a honey-like scent; the falls are dusted with black spots.

Iris gracilipes, a crested iris, grows about 23cm (9in) high. It bears rather flat lavender-pink flowers in mid and late spring. This species needs acid soil.

Iris graminea belongs to the Spuria group of beardless irises and grows 20cm (8in) high, with dense tufts of grassy leaves which can sometimes obscure the fragrant flowers. Produced in early summer, they are red-purple with white falls veined blue-purple.

Iris histrioides 'Major' is a bulbous iris, only 10cm (4in) high. It is among the earliest to flower, often starting in early winter, and survives all weathers – even snow. The leaves are only 2.5cm (1in) high at flowering time but eventually reach 45cm (1½ft). The flowers are bright royal blue with a yellow ridge on the falls.

Iris innominata, one of the beardless Pacific coast irises, forms small clumps of grassy leaves about 15cm (6in) high. Flowers appear singly or in pairs in spring and early summer. They are usually cream, beige, yellow or orange, with tawny brown veins, but there are also deep pink and blue-purple forms.

Iris pumila is a bearded dwarf iris growing up to 10cm (4in) high. Most forms are stemless; the flowers have recurved falls in shades of purple, white, yellow and brown-tinted yellow. They appear in mid spring.

Iris reticulata grows about 15cm (6in) high, and belongs to the bulbous group. The flowers are purple with golden patches on the falls. They appear in late winter to early spring, accompanied by leaves. Popular varieties include 'Cantab' (pale blue, orange-marked falls); 'Clairette' (sky blue, deep royal blue and white falls); 'Harmony' (sky blue, falls marked yellow); 'Joyce' (sky blue, falls marked light red); 'J.S. Dijt' (red-purple, marked orange); 'Pauline' (red violet marked white); and 'Violet Beauty' (deep violet).

Iris ruthenica is a spring-flowering beardless iris, ultra-hardy but unreliable: in some years it is smothered in flowers, in others it produces none. The upper petals are purple, the falls white veined with blue. It has deciduous grass-like leaves and grows 15-23cm (6-9in) high.

Iris tectorum is a crested species, growing about 30cm (1ft) high and flowering in late spring and early summer. The flowers are lavender, the falls being mottled with darker spots, and the crest white. 'Alba' has white flowers.

Iris winigradowii is a bulbous iris growing only 10cm (4in) high. It resembles *I. histrioides* 'Major' but bears lemon-yellow flowers in late winter and early spring.

Popular hybrids

Miniature dwarf irises include a number of hybrids growing 10-15cm (4-6in) high and ideal for rock gardens. They include 'Bee Wings' (yellow with brown-spotted falls); 'Bibury' (cream-white); 'Katharine Hodgkin' (pale blue, yellow markings); 'Moonlight' (light yellow); 'Natasha' (blue and white, orange markings); 'Promise' (red, yellow-striped falls); and 'Ritz' (yellow, falls marked maroon).

Cultivation

Position most iris rhizomes (except crested and Spuria types) with the tops just showing above ground, all facing the same way to receive the maximum sunshine. Plant iris bulbs 5-7.5cm (2-3in) deep for the species, and 10-15cm (4-6in) deep for the hybrids.

Iris chamaeiris 'Campbellii'

Iris histrioides 'Major'

□ Dwarf bearded irises: plant from early to late summer in rich, well-drained soil in full sun. Replant every 2-3 years.

□ Dwarf beardless Pacific coast irises: plant in late autumn in sun or partial shade. *I. innominata* benefits from neutral or acid soil with added leaf-mould.

□ Beardless Spuria irises: plant rhizomes 5cm (2in) deep in any fertile soil in a sunny spot in mid to late autumn. Avoid lifting as they resent disturbance.

□ Crested irises: plant rhizomes just below soil level in late spring to early summer in slightly moist soil with plenty of leaf-mould, in a sheltered spot. *I. tectorum* tolerates limy soil.

□ Bulbous irises: plant bulbs in early and mid autumn in light well-drained alkaline soil in sun.

Propagation To increase bearded irises dig up the rhizomes after flowering, cut off pieces with a strong fan of foliage and replant. Divide and replant rhizomes of beardless irises in early and mid autumn. To increase bulbous irises lift after the leaves die down, grade the bulbs according to size and store until planting time in autumn.

Pests and diseases Generally trouble free.

JACOB'S LADDER – see
Polemonium

Jasione
jasione

Jasione laevis

□ Height 10-23cm (4-9in)
□ Spread up to 23cm (9in)
□ Flowers in summer
□ Any well-drained soil
□ Sunny site
□ Perennial

The small neat species of jasione are grown in the rock garden for their fluffy, blue globular flowers, rather similar to those of scabious. They are fully hardy and easy to grow.

Popular species
Jasione humilis forms neat basal rosettes of narrow leaves. Bright blue flower heads are borne on 10cm (4in) stems in summer.
Jasione laevis, syn. *J. perennis*, is a tufted plant up to 23cm (9in) high and 20cm (8in) across. The narrowly oblong, grey-green leaves are covered with rough hairs. In summer deep blue flowers are carried on wiry branching stems.

Cultivation
Plant jasione in autumn or early spring, in any well-drained soil, including chalk, in an open sunny position.
Propagation Divide established clumps in spring and replant in permanent positions.
Pests and diseases Generally trouble free.

Jasminum

dwarf jasmine

Jasminum parkeri

☐ Height 20-30cm (8-12in)
☐ Spread up to 60cm (2ft)
☐ Flowers early summer
☐ Any well-drained soil
☐ Sheltered sunny site
☐ Evergreen shrub

Jasminum parkeri is the one species of jasmine suitable for the rock garden. Dwarf and almost prostrate, it is a hardy shrub, forming a dome of crowded woody stems. It grows 20-30cm (8-12in) high, with small dark green leaves. Fragrant pale yellow, tubular flowers are borne in early summer.

Cultivation

Plant dwarf jasmine in mid autumn or mid spring in any well-drained but moist soil in a sheltered and sunny position.
Propagation Take heel cuttings in late summer to early autumn.
Pests and diseases Generally trouble free.

JONQUIL – see *Narcissus*
KNAPWEED – see *Centaurea*
KNOTWEEK – see *Polygonum*
LADYBELLS – see *Adenophora*
LADY'S MANTLE – see *Alchemilla*
LADY'S SMOCK – see *Cardamine*
LAMB'S TAIL – see *Chiastophyllum*

Leontopodium

edelweiss

Leontopodium alpinum

☐ Height up to 20cm (8in)
☐ Spread up to 23cm (9in)
☐ Flowers early and mid summer
☐ Good well-drained soil
☐ Sunny site
☐ Perennial

Edelweiss is one of the best known alpine plants, with its clumps of lance-shaped, woolly-haired leaves, and short stems bearing flower heads composed of white bracts densely covered with hairs. The bracts form a star shape and surround the true silvery flower.

Edelweiss (*Leontopodium alpinum*) grows 20-23cm (8-9in) high and wide. It is fully hardy – but susceptible to winter wet – and easy to grow though usually short-lived. It thrives in rock crevices where rapid drainage can be ensured by a deep collar of grit around the crowns of the plants.

Cultivation

Plant edelweiss in early spring in an open sunny site in good and sharply-drained soil.
Propagation Divide and replant mature clumps in spring, before they flower. Or sow seeds in spring in a cold frame; plant out the following spring.
Pests and diseases Trouble free.

Leptospermum

dwarf tea tree

Leptospermum scoparium 'Nanum'

- ☐ Height 15-30cm (6-12in)
- ☐ Spread up to 90cm (3ft)
- ☐ Flowers late spring to early summer
- ☐ Lime-free, well-drained soil
- ☐ Sunny site
- ☐ Evergreen shrub

Dwarf tea trees are handsome shrubs, reliably hardy only in mild coastal districts and even here they need a sheltered spot by a south-facing rock. Elsewhere, the shrubs are better grown in an alpine house.

Popular species

Leptospermum humifusum is a mat-forming species, 15cm (6in) high and spreading to 90cm (3ft). The dark green leaves are narrowly oblong and pointed. Saucer-shaped, white flowers are borne in great profusion in early summer.
Leptospermum scoparium itself grows up to 3m (10ft) high, but 'Nanum' is a compact dwarf shrub only 25-30cm (10-12in) high, with tiny deep green leaves and deep pink flowers.

Cultivation

Plant container-grown tea trees in mid to late spring in good, sharply-drained lime-free soil in sunny and sheltered sites.
Propagation Take half-ripe cuttings in summer and root in a heated propagator.
Pests and diseases Trouble free.

Leucojum

snowflake

Leucojum vernum

- ☐ Height 20-25cm (8-10in)
- ☐ Spread 7.5-10cm (3-4in)
- ☐ Flowers spring or autumn
- ☐ Good moist soil
- ☐ Sun or partial shade
- ☐ Bulb

Snowflake produces its graceful bell-shaped white flowers in spring, summer or autumn, according to species; spring and autumn-flowering species are small enough for growing in the rock garden. They are hardy bulbous plants, with narrow, strap-shaped leaves and flowers that are similar to those of the snowdrop (*Galanthus*), but more

Leucojum autumnale

rounded, with all six petals the same size. They are also carried on taller stems.

Popular species

Leucojum autumnale (autumn snowflake) grows 20-25cm (8-10in) high, with slender, almost grass-like, mid green leaves. White flowers with a pink flush are borne from mid summer to early autumn. Best in a sunny site.
Leucojum vernum (spring snowflake) grows 20cm (8in) high, with strap-shaped mid green leaves. White, green-tipped flowers appear from late winter to early spring. The species naturalizes freely in moist shady places.

Cultivation

Plant the bulbs as soon as they become available in late summer or early autumn. Put *L. autumnale* bulbs 5cm (2in) deep in free-draining soils, those of *L. vernum* 10cm (4in) deep in moisture-retentive soil. Space both types 15-20cm (6-8in) apart. Leave undisturbed for several years.

When the clumps become overcrowded and produce more leaves than flowers, lift, divide and replant the bulbs as soon as the leaves die down.
Propagation The bulbs produce offsets which can be detached when the clumps are lifted, and grown on in a nursery bed; they quickly reach flowering size.
Pests and diseases Generally trouble free.

Lewisia

lewisia

Lewisia cotyledon 'Heckneri'

Lewisia rediviva

Lewisia 'Sunset' strain

- ☐ Height 7.5-30cm (3-12in)
- ☐ Spread 7.5-25cm (3-10in)
- ☐ Flowers mid spring to late summer
- ☐ Rich, well-drained soil
- ☐ Sunny site
- ☐ Semi-succulent perennial

Lewisias are choice plants for rock garden crevices, sink gardens and alpine houses. Many are evergreens and cannot tolerate water in their fleshy leaf rosettes.

Popular species

Lewisia cotyledon grows up to 30cm (1ft) high, in a dense rosette of evergreen fleshy leaves. The saucer-shaped flowers are pink with white veins. 'Heckneri' is rose-pink; 'Howellii' is pink striped carmine. The 'Sunset' strain comes with pink, apricot and red flowers.

Lewisia rediviva (bitter root) grows 7.5cm (3in) high with narrow red-green leaf rosettes which die down in summer as the stemless rose-pink or white flowers appear.

Lewisia tweedyi grows 15cm (6in) high, with evergreen leaf rosettes. The flowers are borne in spring and vary in colour from pale pink to soft apricot.

Cultivation

Plant lewisias in early to mid spring in humus-rich, neutral to acid, sharply-drained soil in a sunny position. Protect them from winter wet or, ideally, grow in an alpine house.

Propagation Detach and pot up offsets in early summer.

Pests and diseases Excessive moisture may cause collar rot.

LILY TURF – see *Ophiopogon*

Linaria
alpine toadflax

Linaria alpina

☐ Height 7.5-20cm (3-8in)
☐ Spread up to 25cm (10in)
☐ Flowers throughout summer
☐ Any well-drained soil
☐ Sunny site
☐ Perennial

Alpine toadflax are easily grown plants valued for their colourful flower spikes that resemble spurred snap-dragons and are produced all summer long. They are ideal for trailing over rocky ledges, in dry-stone walls and between paving. Often short-lived, they seed themselves freely.

Popular species
Linaria alpina grows 7.5-15cm (3-6in) high forming compact mats of trailing stems with slender blue-grey leaves. Violet flowers with orange-striped lower lips are produced in numerous sprays.

Linaria origanifolia forms mats of dark green, rounded leaves. It grows 20cm (8in) high, with spikes of rich purple flowers with a paler throat.

Linaria tristis 'Lurida' resembles *L. alpina*, but bears waxy blue-green leaves and yellowish flowers veined with red-purple and large maroon-purple blotches. It is best grown on a sunny scree or in an alpine house.

Cultivation
Plant alpine toadflax between mid autumn and early spring in any well-drained soil in a sunny site.

Propagation Sow seed directly in the flowering site.

Pests and diseases Trouble free.

Linaria tristis 'Lurida'

Linum
dwarf flax

Linum 'Gemmell's Hybrid'

☐ Height 5-30cm (2-12in)
☐ Spread 23-30cm (9-12in)
☐ Flowers late spring to autumn
☐ Any well-drained soil
☐ Open, sunny site
☐ Herbaceous or shrubby perennial

Linum, or flax, is a large genus which includes several dwarf species suitable for the rock garden. The golden yellow, white or blue, funnel-shaped flowers are borne in profusion throughout summer and autumn. Dwarf flaxes are short-lived but easily grown from seed or cuttings.

Popular species
Linum arboreum grows 30cm (1ft) high and wide, with blue-green, narrowly triangular leaves. The flowers are golden yellow and borne in late spring and early summer. The species needs warmth and shelter and is not hardy in cold districts.

Linum 'Gemmell's Hybrid' is semi-evergreen, with a woody rootstock. It is hardy and grows about 15cm (6in) high as a dome of fleshy grey-green leaves. The short stems carry clusters of large golden-yellow flowers in early summer.

Linum perenne grows 30cm (1ft) or more high, with grey-green, grass-like leaves. It produces an abundance of sky-blue flowers throughout summer. *L. perenne*

Lithospermum

lithospermum

Linum perenne alpinum

alpinum is a dwarf form growing only 15cm (6in) high.

Linum salsoloides, syn. *L. suffruticosum salsoloides*, is semi-prostrate, growing 5cm (2in) high and spreading to 23cm (9in). It has tiny needle-like leaves on woody stems and bears sprays of pearly white flowers flushed blue or pink. 'Nanum' is a more widely grown variety, reaching about 7.5cm (3in) high.

Cultivation

Plant dwarf flax in mid to late autumn or early to mid spring in any fertile, well-drained soil, in an open sunny position. Trim the plants back in mid to late autumn.

Propagation Dwarf flax is easily grown from seed but named varieties do not come true to type. Sow seeds of the species in early to mid spring in a cold frame. Alternatively, take cuttings of basal shoots in mid to late spring and root in a cold frame. Transfer to nursery rows and grow on until autumn or the following spring before planting out in their permanent positions.

Pests and diseases Generally trouble free.

Lithospermum 'Heavenly Blue'

- ☐ Height 10-15cm (4-6in)
- ☐ Spread up to 60cm (2ft)
- ☐ Flowers early summer to mid autumn
- ☐ Good well-drained soil
- ☐ Sunny site
- ☐ Evergreen sub-shrub

Mat-forming and evergreen, hardy lithospermum, now correctly known as *Lithodora* species, makes excellent ground cover, with a bonus of freely produced, funnel-shaped flowers in beautiful shades of blue.

Popular species

Lithospermum diffusum, syn. *Lithodora diffusa*, grows 10cm (4in) high and spreads up to 60cm (2ft). The prostrate stems bear oval dark green leaves. Deep blue flowers, with five rounded spreading lobes, are produced from early summer to mid autumn. 'Grace Ward' is an outstanding variety, more vigorous than the species and with larger blooms of a more intense shade of blue. 'Heavenly Blue' is the long-established form commonly grown, with profuse deep blue flowers.

Lithospermum oleifolium, syn. *Lithodora oleifolia*, grows 15cm (6in) high, with rounded silvery haired leaves. It bears nodding clusters of pink buds which turn sky blue as they open, from late spring to late summer.

Cultivation

Plant lithospermum in mid spring in any fertile, well-drained soil, in a sunny site. *L. diffusum* and its varieties need lime-free soil; other species will tolerate lime.

Propagation Take cuttings of lateral shoots, preferably with a heel, in mid summer. Root in a cold frame; water *L. diffusum* plentifully, other species moderately until cuttings have rooted; overwinter under glass and plant out in mid spring.

Pests and diseases Generally trouble free.

LIVINGSTONE DAISY – see *Mesembryanthemum*

Lithospermum oleifolium

Lotus

lotus, alpine pea

Lotus berthelotii

- ☐ Trails or scrambles to 30cm (1ft)
- ☐ Spread up to 90cm (3ft)
- ☐ Flowers early summer to early autumn
- ☐ Any well-drained soil
- ☐ Sunny site
- ☐ Perennial

A member of the pea family, lotus can be grown as ground cover or trailing from baskets. Half-hardy only, the species described are suitable for an alpine house.

Popular species

Lotus berthelotii (parrot's beak) grows about 30cm (1ft) high, with woody, trailing stems and intensely silver, hairy leaves. It bears clusters of scarlet, beak-like flowers in early summer.

Lotus corniculatus (bird's foot trefoil) is a British wild plant, but a double-flowered form, 'Plenus', is cultivated. This is a prostrate and spreading plant, with heads of bright yellow flowers appearing from early summer to early autumn. Those of 'Alpinus' are tinted red.

Cultivation

Grow lotus in any well-drained soil in a warm, sunny and sheltered site, or in pans in the alpine house.

Propagation Take softwood cuttings in early summer and root in a propagator unit.

Pests and diseases Generally trouble free.

Lychnis

campion

Lychnis flos-jovis

- ☐ Height 10-60cm (4-24in)
- ☐ Spread 10-30cm (4-12in)
- ☐ Flowers late spring to late summer
- ☐ Any well-drained soil
- ☐ Sun or light shade
- ☐ Perennial

Different species of campion offer a wide range of flower colour, from white through pink, red and orange to purple. Campions are easy plants, with low-growing types suitable for edging and rock gardens, taller species for borders.

Popular species

Lychnis alpina, syn. *Viscaria alpina*, grows up to 10cm (4in) high and 5cm (2in) across, forming a tuft of dark green strap-shaped leaves. Short stems bear dense flower clusters, usually deep rose-pink, from late spring onwards. It is excellent as a trough plant.

Lychnis flos-jovis (flower of Jove) is rather large – up to 60cm (2ft) high – with its thick, silvery or grey spear-shaped leaves, and rich red or purple flowers. 'Hort's Variety', with pink flowers, grows only 30cm (12in) high.

Lychnis viscaria (German catchfly), syn. *Viscaria vulgaris*, *V. viscosa*, grows 30cm (1ft) high, with tufts of grassy leaves. It bears tight clusters of carmine-pink flowers in early summer. 'Splendens Plena' is a showier form with double, carnation-like flowers.

Lychnis alpina

Cultivation

Plant campion between mid autumn and early spring, in any well-drained soil and in full sun or light shade. Dead-head to prevent self-seeding.

Propagation Sow seeds in a cold frame in late spring or early summer. Named varieties do not come true and should be propagated from cuttings taken in late spring and rooted in a cold frame.

Pests and diseases Aphids and froghoppers may attack and stunt flowering shoots.

Lysimachia

creeping Jenny, moneywort

Lysimachia nummularia

☐ Height 2.5-5cm (1-2in)
☐ Spread 45cm (1½ft) or more
☐ Flowers early to mid summer
☐ Moist soil
☐ Sun or partial shade
☐ Perennial

Lysimachia nummularia (creeping Jenny, moneywort) is, like other species of *Lysimachia*, highly invasive. However, it makes admirable ground cover in moist soil and creeps easily over stones in the rock garden. Creeping Jenny forms a dense carpet of mid green, rounded, evergreen leaves. In early to mid summer it bears bright yellow, cup-shaped flowers. The variety 'Aurea' has golden yellow leaves.

Cultivation
Plant creeping Jenny between mid autumn and mid spring in sun or partial shade in moist soil. In the wild it is a waterside plant, and will grow in as little as 5cm (2in) of soil. However, it adapts easily to dry soil – even chalk is acceptable provided the soil does not dry out in hot weather.
Propagation Divide and replant at any time between mid autumn and early spring. Alternatively take 7.5-10cm (3-4in) long stem cuttings in mid spring or early autumn and plant directly in the growing positions.
Pests and diseases Trouble free.

Mazus

mazus

Mazus reptans

☐ Height 2.5-5cm (1-2in)
☐ Spread 30cm (1ft) or more
☐ Flowers late spring to late summer
☐ Any moist soil
☐ Sunny site
☐ Perennial

Mazus is a hardy, little-known plant, but makes useful ground cover, with tiny flowers resembling flattened snapdragons. It grows well in paving cracks.

Popular species
Mazus pumilio is the most compact species, forming neat mats only 2.5cm (1in) high, but 30cm (12in) wide. The flowers are lavender-blue and white.
Mazus radicans grows 5cm (2in) high forming a 23cm (9in) wide mat of toothed oval leaves. The flowers are white blotched purple.
Mazus reptans grows up to 5cm (2in) high. The creeping mat of spear-shaped toothed leaves spreads 30cm (12in) or more. The flowers are lilac with lips speckled gold and white.

Cultivation
Plant in early spring in a sunny site in any soil that does not dry out.
Propagation Divide and replant in spring or autumn.
Pests and diseases Trouble free.

MEADOW RUE – see *Thalictrum*

Mesembryanthemum

Livingstone daisy

Mesembryanthemum 'Lunette'

☐ Height up to 15cm (6in)
☐ Spread 15-30cm (6-12in)
☐ Flowers early to late summer
☐ Any well-drained soil
☐ Sunny site
☐ Succulent half-hardy annual

Mesembryanthemum is a large genus of plants, commonly called Livingstone daisies, though this name strictly refers only to *M. criniflorum*, a popular half-hardy annual. This and similar species of *Mesembryanthemum* bear a profusion of brilliantly coloured, large daisy-like flowers which open wide in full sun. They make good fillers in rock gardens.

Many species formerly included in this genus are now classified as *Dorotheanthus*.

Popular species and varieties
Mesembryanthemum criniflorum, syn. *Dorotheanthus bellidiformis* (Livingstone daisy), grows 15cm (6in) high and spreads for up to 30cm (1ft). The narrow, almost cylindrical, succulent pale green leaves have a glistening, almost sugary appearance. Given bright sun, it carries a succession of brightly coloured, dark-eyed and zoned flowers from early to late summer. Colours include white, crimson to pink and orange-gold to buff.

Popular varieties include 'Lunette', also known as 'Yellow Ice', with lemon-yellow petals and a rust-red central disc; and 'Magic

Mimulus
monkey flower

Mimulus x *hybridus* 'Scarlet Bee'

Mesembryanthemum criniflorum

Carpet Mixed', with yellow, orange, pink, red and lavender flowers, the darker colours showing a white band around the central disc.

Mesembryanthemum crystallinum (ice plant, sea fig) grows 15cm (6in) high and can spread for up to 1m (3ft); it makes good ground cover for larger rock gardens. It has white or rose-pink flowers and self-seeds readily.

Mesembryanthemum tricolor grows 7.5cm (3in) high and spreads for about 30cm (1ft). It is a hardy annual, with dark green, slender cylindrical leaves. The flowers are dark-centred white, rose or deep purple. They are produced from early to late summer.

Cultivation
Plant Livingstone daisies in full sun in any well-drained soil; they thrive on sandy soil.

Propagation Sow seeds in early spring at a temperature of 15°C (59°F). Prick out into boxes and harden off seedlings before planting out in late spring. Alternatively, sow directly in the flowering sites in mid spring and thin out the seedlings as necessary.

Pests and diseases Plants may collapse at ground level due to foot rot disease.

MILKWORT – see *Polygala*

- ☐ Height 7.5-30cm (3-12in)
- ☐ Spread 23cm (9in)
- ☐ Flowers late spring to early autumn
- ☐ Any moist soil
- ☐ Sun or light shade
- ☐ Perennial

In the wild *Mimulus* species are bog plants, but they adapt well to any moist soil. Low-growing types are suitable for rock gardens and for edging; they are generally hardy, but short-lived. The flowers resemble open-mouthed snapdragons, with vivid ground colours, blotched in bright contrasting hues.

Popular species
Mimulus x *burnetti* grows 15-23cm (6-9in) high, and spreads to 30cm (1ft), with mats of mid green, oval leaves. The coppery-coloured flowers are produced from late spring to late summer.

Mimulus cupreus grows 23-30cm (9-12in) high, with a 23cm (9in) spread. The leaves are mid green, oblong ovals. The flowers, which are borne from early summer to early autumn, open yellow and change to coppery-orange spotted brown.

Mimulus x *hybridus* is a group of moderately hardy hybrids derived in part from *M. cupreus*; they are sometimes treated as annuals. They include: 'Andean Nymph' (pink-and-yellow); 'Malibu' series (red, orange or yellow flowers);

'Red Emperor' (bright crimson and scarlet); 'Scarlet Bee' (deep scarlet); and 'Whitecroft Scarlet' (10cm/4in high, orange-scarlet).

Cultivation
Plant monkey flowers between early and late spring in sun or light shade, in any moisture-retentive soil. In cold districts protect the plants with cloches.

Propagation Increase by division, stem cuttings or seed in early to mid spring.

Pests and diseases Trouble free.

Mimulus x *hybridus* 'Andean Nymph'

Minuartia

minuartia

Minuartia verna

☐ Height 12mm-10cm (½-4in)
☐ Spread up to 30cm (1ft)
☐ Flowers late spring to early summer
☐ Well-drained soil
☐ Sunny site
☐ Evergreen perennial

Minuartias are tiny, almost moss-like plants ideal for growing in troughs and sinks and in cracks between paving stones. They are covered in starry white flowers from late spring to early summer. Minuartias are sometimes listed as *Arenaria*, a closely related genus.

Popular species

Minuartia laricifolia, syn. *Arenaria laricifolia*, forms loose grassy mats, about 10cm (4in) high, of slender grey-green leaves. The flowers are milky white and borne in loose clusters.
Minuartia stellata forms hard flat pads of bright green leaves, only about 12mm (½in) high, with stemless white flowers.
Minuartia verna, syn. *Arenaria verna*, forms a neat rounded dome of minute narrow, emerald green leaves. In spring, it is smothered with white flowers on thread-like, 2.5cm (1in) high stems.

Cultivation

Plant minuartia in early to mid autumn in an open sunny position and in well-drained soil.
Propagation Divide established plants after flowering, or take semi-ripe cuttings in mid summer and root in a cold frame.
Pests and diseases Trouble free.

Moltkia

moltkia

Moltkia petraea

☐ Height 23-38cm (9-15in)
☐ Spread up to 30cm (1ft)
☐ Flowers early to late summer
☐ Any well-drained soil
☐ Sunny site
☐ Evergreen sub-shrub

Moltkia is closely related to *Lithospermum* and was formerly included in that genus. The species are hardy, low-growing shrubs, of compact habit. They are grown for their drooping clusters of funnel-shaped blue or purple flowers. Most species have narrow greyish leaves.

Popular species

Moltkia coerulea grows 30cm (1ft) high and wide, its woody stems set with pointed, rather silky leaves. It produces short clusters of sky blue flowers.
Moltkia doerfleri grows up to 38cm (15in) high, with slightly hairy leaves. Purple flowers are borne in rounded clusters.
Moltkia x *intermedia* is a hybrid between *M. petraea* and *M. suffruticosa*. It grows 30cm (12in) high, with a spread of 20cm (8in). It bears evergreen narrow, dark green leaves. The flowers are a deep clear blue and borne in profuse clusters throughout summer.
Moltkia petraea grows 30cm (1ft) high and as much or more across; the narrow leaves are hairy. It bears an abundance of soft blue flowers from pinkish buds.
Moltkia suffruticosa grows up to 23cm (9in) high, with tufts of long

Moltkia doerfleri

slender, grassy, softly hairy leaves that are semi-evergreen or deciduous. Pale blue flowers are borne in clusters from the tips of the stems.

Cultivation

Plant moltkia in spring or autumn, in any well-drained, even lime-rich, soil, in full sun.
Propagation Take semi-ripe cuttings in mid summer and root in a cold frame.
Pests and diseases Trouble free.

MONEYWORT – see *Lysimachia*
MONKEY FLOWER – see *Mimulus*

Morisia

morisia

Morisia monanthos

☐ Height 2.5-5cm (1-2in)
☐ Spread up to 15cm (6in)
☐ Flowers during spring
☐ Sharply-drained soil
☐ Sunny site
☐ Perennial

Morisia monanthos, syn. *M. hypogaea*, is a tiny tufted plant with conspicuous golden yellow flowers, ideal for growing in a sink garden or trough or on a scree slope. It is fully hardy and has tooth-edged, glossy dark green and fern-like leaves; the stemless flowers appear from early spring into summer.

Cultivation

Plant morisias in early to mid autumn in any sharply-drained soil, in a sunny position.
Propagation Take 2.5-5cm (1-2in) long cuttings from thick roots in late winter or early spring and root in a cold frame. Pot up singly when small rosettes have formed and grow on in the frame. Plant out in permanent positions in autumn.
Pests and diseases Generally trouble free.

MOUNT ATLAS DAISY – see *Anacyclus*
MOUNTAIN AVENS – see *Dryas*
MOUNTAIN HEATH – see *Phyllodoce*
MOUNTAIN TOBACCO – see *Arnica*
MOUSE-EAR CHICKWEED – see *Cerastium*
MULLEIN – see *Verbascum*

Muscari

grape hyacinth

Muscari armeniacum

☐ Height 15-30cm (6-12in)
☐ Spread 7.5-10cm (3-4in)
☐ Flowers early spring to early summer
☐ Any well-drained soil
☐ Sunny site
☐ Bulb

Common grape hyacinth (*Muscari*) is a familiar springtime sight with its attractive heads of tightly packed flowers resembling small blue grapes. More unusual species have purple and green, or yellow and brown, flower spikes. All bring welcome spring colour to rock gardens and window boxes.

The species described have mid green, strap-shaped leaves with a channelled inner surface. The upper flowers are sterile and do not open; except for *Muscari comosum* they are paler than the lower urn-shaped ones.

Popular species

Muscari armeniacum grows 20-25cm (8-10in) high, carrying densely packed cobalt blue flowers with white rims. Named varieties include 'Blue Spike' (scented mid blue double flowers in densely packed spikes); 'Cantab' (bright blue); 'Early Giant' (strongly scented, cobalt-blue); and 'Heavenly Blue' (bright sky blue).

Muscari comosum (tassel hyacinth) grows 30cm (1ft) or more high; the lower flowers are olive green, the sterile upper ones purple. *M. c.* 'Monstrosum', syn. 'Plumosum' (feather hyacinth), produces only sterile flowers, violet-blue or reddish purple, with petals cut into a tangle of fine filaments.

Muscari macrocarpum grows 15-23cm (6-9in) high and is a robust species with semi-prostrate, grey-

Muscari macrocarpum

Myosotis
alpine forget-me-not

Myosotis alpestris 'Blue Ball'

- ☐ Height 10-15cm (4-6in)
- ☐ Spread 10-15cm (4-6in)
- ☐ Flowers late spring to early summer
- ☐ Any well-drained soil
- ☐ Sunny site
- ☐ Perennial

Unlike the forget-me-nots grown in borders, alpine versions are true, hardy perennials. They may be short-lived, but seed themselves almost as readily as the biennial species. More compact in habit, alpine forget-me-not is suitable for rock gardens as well as sinks and troughs.

Myosotis alpestris, syn. *M. sylvatica alpestris*, is a compact little plant, up to 15cm (6in) high and wide, forming clumps of hairy, green, spear-shaped leaves. The fragrant flowers, produced in dense clusters, are azure-blue with a distinctive yellow eye. The variety 'Blue Ball' has deep blue flowers.

Cultivation
Alpine forget-me-not grows in any soil and position, but for best results plant in a sunny site, in well-drained gritty soil during early and mid autumn.

Propagation Sow seeds in mid to late spring in a cold frame or an outdoor seed bed.

Pests and diseases Generally trouble free, but in cold wet conditions grey mould may cause flowers to rot and become covered in grey furry mould.

Narcissus
dwarf daffodil

Narcissus triandrus 'Hawera'

- ☐ Height 5-30cm (2-12in)
- ☐ Spread up to 20cm (8in)
- ☐ Flowers late winter to mid spring
- ☐ Good well-drained soil
- ☐ Sun or partial shade
- ☐ Bulb

Dwarf narcissi have all the charm of their larger cousins, the trumpet daffodils, and are just as easy to grow. They are ideal in rock and sink gardens, and in raised beds, where their delicate beauty can be appreciated.

Popular species
Narcissus asturiensis, syn. *N. minimus*, is a tiny yellow trumpet narcissus 7.5cm (3in) high. The flowers are 2.5cm (1in) long, on weak stems, and borne in late winter.

Narcissus bulbocodium (hoop petticoat daffodil) grows 5-15cm (2-6in) high. The wide-open, 2.5cm (1in) long, yellow trumpets, which appear in late winter, dominate the very narrow yellow petals.

Narcissus jonquilla (wild jonquil) grows 30cm (1ft) high. The strongly scented deep yellow flowers are 4-5cm (1½-2in) wide with a small central cup; they appear in mid spring.

Narcissus minor grows 20cm (8in) high and bears pale yellow flowers with slightly deeper yellow trumpets in early spring.

Narcissus triandrus is usually represented in cultivation by varieties characterized by pendent flowers with funnel-shaped

---

Muscari comosum

green leaves. The fragrant flowers are bright rich yellow with a brown mouth, shading to blue-grey at the top.

Muscari neglectum grows 23cm (9in) high with dark blue, white-edged flowers.

Muscari racemosum (musk hyacinth) grows 20cm (8in) high and bears dark purple, white-rimmed flowers fading to yellowish green. It is often regarded as a sub-species of *M. neglectum*.

Muscari tubergenianum, syn. *M. aucheri* (Oxford and Cambridge grape hyacinth), grows about 23cm (9in) high. The almost round flower clusters are dark (Oxford) blue at the top, fading to paler (Cambridge) blue at the base of the spike.

Cultivation
Plant grape hyacinth bulbs from late summer to late autumn in any well-drained soil in full sun. If planted in shade they will produce plenty of leaves and few flowers. Set the bulbs 7.5cm (3in) deep, in small groups.

Lift and divide the plants every three years.

Propagation Many species spread readily on their own by means of bulbils or self-sown seed. Divide congested clumps after three years, waiting until the leaves are yellow before lifting. Replant straight away in the flowering positions.

Pests and diseases Generally trouble free, though flowers can be affected by smut fungus.

Narcissus bulbocodium

cups and backswept petals. 'Albus' is 7.5-10cm (3-4in) high, with creamy white flowers. 'Hawera' grows to 20cm (8in), with lemon-yellow flowers; and 'Ice Wings', 25cm (10in) high, is pure white.

Cultivation
Plant dwarf narcissi in fertile soil in sun or partial shade, as soon as the bulbs are available in early autumn. Plant in small groups, spacing the bulbs 5-7.5cm (2-3in) apart, in flat-bottomed holes three times the depth of the bulbs. Leave undisturbed and let the leaves turn brown before removing them.
Propagation Lift overcrowded bulbs in early autumn, remove any offsets and plant in a nursery bed. They will reach flowering size in two to three years.
Pests and diseases Root or basal rot may stunt growth.

NASTURTIUM – see
Tropaeolum
NAVELWORT – see *Omphalodes*
NEW ZEALAND BURR – see
Acaena
NEW ZEALAND DAPHNE – see
Pimelea

Narcissus minor

Nierembergia

nierembergia

Nierembergia repens

☐ Height 5-20cm (2-8in)
☐ Spread up to 60cm (2ft)
☐ Flowers early to late summer
☐ Moist soil
☐ Sunny site
☐ Perennial

The small nierembergias, with their funnel- or cup-shaped summer flowers, are suitable for edging, rock gardens and alpine houses.

Popular species

Nierembergia caerulea var. *violacea*, syn. *N. hippomanica* (cup flower), is a moderately hardy perennial usually grown as an annual. It reaches a height and spread of 15-20cm (6-8in). Slender branching stems form a hummock of linear, mid green leaves. The flowers are pale lavender with a yellow throat. The variety 'Purple Robe' has deep purple flowers.
Nierembergia repens, syn. *N. rivularis* (white-cup), grows only 5cm (2in) high, but spreads to 45-60cm (1½-2ft). It forms a low mat of rooting stems set with light green, spoon-shaped leaves. The flowers are white with a yellow centre.

Cultivation

Plant nierembergias in spring, in moist but well-drained soil in a sunny and sheltered position.
Propagation Divide and replant *N. repens* in early to mid spring. Sow seed of *N. caerulea* under glass in late winter; or take cuttings in summer.
Pests and diseases Generally trouble free.

Oenothera

evening primrose, sundrops

Oenothera missouriensis

☐ Height 7.5-30cm (3-12in)
☐ Spread up to 45cm (1½ft)
☐ Flowers late spring to mid autumn
☐ Any well-drained soil
☐ Sunny site
☐ Perennial

Most evening primroses open their short-lived, faintly scented flowers in the evening. They are hardy plants, the shorter-growing species suitable for rock gardens.

Popular species

Oenothera acaulis, syn. *O. taraxacifolia*, grows 15cm (6in) high and 20cm (8in) across. It forms rosettes of dandelion-like, toothed, mid green leaves on prostrate zigzag branches. Stemless flowers, off white but turning rose-pink, open in the evening from late spring onwards.
Oenothera caespitosa grows 7.5-10cm (3-4in) high and spreads to 20cm (8in) by underground runners. It has narrowly oval, sometimes toothed mid green leaves, and white fragrant flowers. They open on summer evenings.
Oenothera missouriensis (Ozark sundrops) grows 10-15cm (4-6in) high, with spear-shaped mid green leaves. The near-prostrate stems spread to 45cm (1½ft). Buds, often red-spotted on the outside, open in the evening to yellow flowers throughout the summer.
Oenothera perennis, syn. *O. pumila* (dwarf sundrops), grows 30cm (1ft) or more high and wide, but has a floppy growth habit. The leaves are mid green and lance-shaped. Loose leafy spikes of yellow flowers open in the evening from early summer to early autumn.

Cultivation

Plant evening primroses in mid autumn or mid spring in any well-drained soil, in a sunny but sheltered position. Protect *O. caespitosa* from winter wet.
Propagation Take half-ripe cuttings of lateral shoots in late summer and root in a cold frame. Or divide and replant mature clumps in spring.
Pests and diseases Trouble free.

Oenothera perennis

Omphalodes

navelwort

Omphalodes verna

☐ Height 10-23cm (4-9in)
☐ Spread up to 60cm (2ft)
☐ Flowers late winter to early autumn
☐ Moist or well-drained soil
☐ Partial shade or sun
☐ Perennial

Navelworts have five-petalled blue flowers resembling large forget-me-nots. They are hardy rock-garden plants.

Popular species

Omphalodes cappadocica grows 15-23cm (6-9in) high, forming clumps up to 60cm (2ft) across, with bright green, hairy leaves. Sprays of azure-blue flowers appear in late spring and early summer.

Omphalodes luciliae grows 10-15cm (4-6in) high and wide, with blue-green leaves. Loose sprays of soft blue flowers are borne from late spring to early autumn. It resents winter wet.

Omphalodes verna (blue-eyed Mary) grows 15cm (6in) high and spreads for up to 30cm (1ft). Sprays of bright blue white-eyed flowers are freely borne from late winter to late spring.

Cultivation

Plant in mid spring, *O. cappadocica* and *O. verna* in acid soil in a partly shaded site. Plant *O. luciliae* in any well-drained soil and in full sun.

Propagation Divide and replant in mid spring or after flowering.

Pests and diseases Trouble free.

ONION (ORNAMENTAL) – see *Allium*

Onosma

golden drop

Onosma albo-roseum

☐ Height 15-20cm (6-8in)
☐ Spread up to 25cm (10in)
☐ Flowers late spring to late summer
☐ Any well-drained soil
☐ Full sun
☐ Evergreen sub-shrub

Golden drops are named for their pendent tubular flowers, typically golden yellow and fragrant. The leaves are rough-textured and hairy. They are hardy plants, thriving in sunny rock gardens and wall crevices.

Popular species

Onosma albo-roseum grows 15cm (6in) or more high and 25cm (10in) across. It bears tufts of silver-haired leaves and clusters of white flowers in summer; they age to pink.

Onosma tauricum (sometimes listed as *O. echioides*) grows 15cm (6in) high and 23cm (9in) wide, with narrow, grey-green bristly leaves. Clusters of yellow flowers are borne from late spring to late summer.

Cultivation

Plant golden drops in mid spring, in any well-drained soil in full sun.

Propagation Take softwood cuttings in summer and root in a cold frame.

Pests and diseases Trouble free.

Onosma tauricum

Origanum

origanum, dittany

Origanum amanum

Origanum rotundifolium

☐ Height 5-30cm (2-12in)
☐ Spread 15-30cm (6-12in)
☐ Flowers early summer to early autumn
☐ Any well-drained soil
☐ Sheltered sunny site
☐ Perennial and sub-shrub

Some species of *Origanum* are culinary herbs (marjoram and oregano), others are grown for their ornamental value in borders and rock gardens or as ground cover. Those described here are hardy in sunny and sheltered positions, in spite of their Mediterranean origin; they are deciduous sub-shrubs or woody-stemmed perennials, suitable for trailing over rock ledges and walls and for carpeting sunny banks.

Popular species

Origanum amanum grows 5-10cm (2-4in) high and spreads to 15cm (6in), forming a mat of slen-der stems with closely set pale green, heart-shaped leaves. It bears tubular rose-pink flowers that are surrounded by showy purple bracts, from mid summer to early autumn. It dislikes wet conditions.

Origanum dictamnus, syn. *Amaracus dictamnus* (Cretan dittany), reaches 30cm (1ft) in height and spread; it is of rounded habit with arching stems that die back in winter. The rounded, aromatic leaves are covered in dense white woolly hairs. The true pale pink flowers are almost hidden by purple-pink bracts giving a hop-like appearance. They are borne from early to late summer.

Origanum laevigatum grows 25-30cm (10-12in) high and spreads to 20cm (8in) or more. It forms a neat shrubby mat of grey-green aromatic leaves that contrast with the maroon stems. Throughout summer the plant bears a profu-sion of small pink flowers sur-rounded by red-purple bracts.

Origanum rotundifolium grows 20-23cm (8-9in) high, with a spread of 30cm (12in). It is a woody-stemmed, rhizomatous perennial spreading by under-ground runners. The small and rounded leaves are mid green with a bluish tinge. Nodding whorls of tiny pale pink flowers, surrounded by conspicuous yel-low-green bracts, are freely pro-duced in summer.

Cultivation

Plant origanums in early to mid spring in a sunny sheltered site in any well-drained soil. It is advis-able to protect the plants with raised panes of glass during the winter months.

Propagation Take cuttings of non-flowering basal shoots between mid summer and early autumn and root in a cold frame. Plant out the following early to mid spring.

Pests and diseases Generally trouble free.

Ornithogalum
star of Bethlehem

Ornithogalum nutans

- ☐ Height 10-38cm (4-15in)
- ☐ Spread 10-20cm (4-8in)
- ☐ Flowers early to late spring
- ☐ Good well-drained soil
- ☐ Sun or partial shade
- ☐ Bulb

The best-known species of *Ornithogalum* is the popular cut flower chincherinchee (*O. thyrsoides*), with its beautiful clusters of star-like, white or cream flowers. It is a tender species which can only be grown under glass in Britain. Those described here are hardy and suitable for the rock garden. Their dazzling white starry flowers have broad green stripes on the back, visible when

Ornithogalum umbellatum

they are in bud or half open; they close up at night. Mid to dark green, slender strap-shaped leaves are carried at the base of the plants.

Popular species
Ornithogalum balansae grows 10-15cm (4-6in) high. The flowers are borne in early to mid spring and associate well with late-flowering crocuses and scillas.

Ornithogalum nutans grows about 38cm (15in) high and produces stems of nodding, bell-shaped flowers in mid to late spring. The species thrives in semi-shaded sites.

Ornithogalum umbellatum (star of Bethlehem) grows 30cm (1ft) high. The stout stems carry clusters of glistening white flowers in mid to late spring.

Cultivation
Plant ornithogalums in autumn, in fertile well-drained soil, setting the bulbs 5cm (2in) deep in irregular groups. *O. balansae* needs full sun but the other species will thrive in partial shade. All can remain undisturbed for years.

Propagation The plants self-seed readily; or lift established clumps when the leaves die down and detach bulbils.

Pests and diseases Generally trouble free.

Ourisia
ourisia

Ourisia macrophylla

- ☐ Height 15-30cm (6-12in)
- ☐ Spread 45-60cm (1½-2ft)
- ☐ Flowers late spring to early autumn
- ☐ Moist preferably acid soil
- ☐ Partial shade
- ☐ Evergreen perennial

Ourisias are low-growing woodland plants thriving in gentle shade and acid soil. They spread widely from creeping rootstocks and are ideal for raised peat beds.

Popular species
Ourisia coccinea grows 15-30cm (6-12in) high and spreads to 60cm (2ft). It forms dense mats of mid green, shallowly toothed, oval leaves. Upright stems bear tubular to trumpet-shaped, scarlet flowers, from late spring through to early autumn.

Ourisia macrophylla grows 20-30cm (8-12in) high and spreads up to 45cm (1½ft). It is a sturdy plant with rounded, toothed, mid green leaves. Dense clusters of tubular white flowers with yellow centres are produced in mid summer.

Cultivation
Plant ourisias in early to mid spring in a partially shaded site, in moist, acid soil.

Propagation Divide established clumps in mid spring and replant at once.

Pests and diseases Generally trouble free.

Oxalis

wood sorrel

Oxalis enneaphylla

Oxalis deppei

- ☐ Height 5-25cm (2-10in)
- ☐ Spread 15-30cm (6-12in)
- ☐ Flowers late spring to late autumn
- ☐ Rich well-drained soil
- ☐ Sun or partial shade
- ☐ Perennial

Wood sorrel (*Oxalis*) is a large and diverse genus and includes pernicious weeds as well as plants of delicate charm. All are characterized by shamrock-like leaves. Those described here are hardy perennials excellent for the rock garden and attractive in leaf and flower. The funnel-shaped flowers open in sun and close up at night.

Popular species

Oxalis adenophylla grows 7.5cm (3in) high and 10cm (4in) wide, with rosettes of elaborately folded grey-green foliage. The flowers are satin-pink with maroon eyes and appear from late spring onwards.

Oxalis chrysantha grows 5cm (2in) high and spreads to a 30cm (12in) mat of pale green, three-lobed leaves. The flowers are golden-yellow and borne in summer.

Oxalis deppei grows up to 25cm (10in) high and 15cm (6in) across. The four-lobed leaves are marked with brown blotches; the flowers are carmine-pink to purplish red and borne in loose sprays in late spring and summer.

Oxalis enneaphylla is a bulbous species growing 7.5cm (3in) high, with deeply folded grey-green leaves, and large fragrant, white flowers in summer.

Oxalis inops, syn. *O. depressa*, grows 10cm (4in) high. It forms a mat of light green, three-lobed leaves and bears pink flowers in summer. Not fully hardy, it does best in an alpine house.

Oxalis laciniata grows 5-10cm (2-4in) high, with grey-green, crinkly-edged leaves. The fragrant flowers are lavender-blue to pale purple with darker veins and are borne in summer.

Cultivation

Plant oxalis in early spring or early autumn in sun or partial shade in any well-drained soil enriched with organic matter. *O. chrysantha* needs a sheltered site and is best planted where the roots can spread under a rock and survive if top growth is killed.

Propagation Divide and replant in early spring.

Pests and diseases Trouble free.

Oxalis adenophylla

Papaver

alpine poppy

Papaver pyrenaicum

- ☐ Height 10-25cm (4-10in)
- ☐ Spread 10-25cm (4-10in)
- ☐ Flowers early summer
- ☐ Well-drained soil
- ☐ Sunny site
- ☐ Perennial

Alpine poppies are miniature relations of the glamorous oriental poppy grown in herbaceous borders. They have similar large, broad-petalled and bowl-shaped flowers in glowing colours, opening from attractive furry buds and followed by shapely seed heads.

Popular species

Papaver alpinum has a height and spread of 10-25cm (4-10in). Although perennial it is short-lived, and usually raised annually from seed. It forms a low mound of deeply dissected grey-green leaves, from which the slender leafless flower stems arise. The flowers are 2.5-5cm (1-2in) across and range from white and yellow to red and orange in colour.
Papaver pyrenaicum is a similar plant but slightly taller and sturdier, with greener leaves.

Cultivation

Plant alpine poppies in any well-drained soil, in rock gardens, crevices between paving stones or on retaining walls, in full sun.
Propagation The plants self-seed freely. Alternatively, sow seed where the plants are to flower, in early spring.
Pests and diseases Yellow blotches on the leaves are caused by downy mildew; the undersurfaces develop a grey fungal growth.

Parahebe

parahebe

Parahebe catarractae

- ☐ Height up to 20cm (8in)
- ☐ Spread up to 30cm (12in)
- ☐ Flowers early summer
- ☐ Any well-drained soil
- ☐ Sunny site
- ☐ Evergreen perennial

Parahebes are closely related to the shrubby *Hebe* and *Veronica* species. Their small size makes them suitable for the rock garden.

Popular species

Parahebe catarractae is a shrubby plant 20cm (8in) high and 30cm (12in) across, with oval, toothed leaves. It bears funnel-shaped, white flowers veined crimson.
Parahebe decora, syn. *Veronica bidwillii*, grows 20cm (8in) high and 30cm (12in) or more across, with semi-prostrate stems and tiny rounded leaves. The flowers are white or pale lilac, veined pink.
Parahebe lyallii is a semi-prostrate shrubby species; the branches root on touching the soil. It bears thick, leathery, smooth leaves and, in early summer, loose sprays of white flowers, striped pink.

Cultivation

Plant parahebes in any good well-drained soil in a sunny site.
Propagation Take softwood cuttings in early summer and root in a cold frame.
Pests and diseases Trouble free.

PARTRIDGE-BERRY – see *Gaultheria*
PASQUE FLOWER – see *Pulsatilla*
PEARLWORT – see *Sagina*

Penstemon

alpine penstemon

Penstemon pinifolius

- ☐ Height 7.5-45cm (3-18in)
- ☐ Spread 23-45cm (9-18in)
- ☐ Flowers late spring to early summer
- ☐ Any well-drained but moist soil
- ☐ Sunny site
- ☐ Perennial or sub-shrub

Unlike the larger border species, which need protection to survive winter cold and wet, alpine penstemons are perfectly hardy. This makes them popular rock-garden plants, valued for their long-lasting showy spikes of brightly coloured tubular flowers.

Popular species

Penstemon alpinus forms a clump up to 25cm (10in) high and 15cm (6in) across, with broad leaves. Blue or purplish flowers, with white throats, appear in early summer.
Penstemon confertus is a prostrate, semi-evergreen species growing about 15cm (6in) high and 45cm (18in) across, with lance-shaped, mid green leaves. The cream-white or pale yellow flowers appear in mid summer.
Penstemon cristatus, syn. *P. eriantherus*, is a bushy species about 25cm (10in) high. The leaves are lance-shaped to oval; red-purple flower spikes are borne in mid summer.
Penstemon davidsonii is a low sub-shrub, about 7.5cm (3in) high and spreading to 23cm (9in), with broadly oval, grey-green leaves. Ruby-red flowers are borne in short spikes in late spring and early summer.
Penstemon heterophyllus is a semi-evergreen shrubby species, up to 30cm (12in) high and across.

Petrophytum

rock spiraea

Petrophytum hendersonii

☐ Height 7.5-10cm (3-4in)
☐ Spread up to 15cm (6in)
☐ Flowers in summer
☐ Sharply-drained alkaline soil
☐ Sunny site
☐ Evergreen shrub

Petrophytum is a small genus of alpine sub-shrubs, closely related to *Spiraea* and known as rock spiraea. They are suitable for growing in rock crevices and tufa blocks; they are fully hardy.

Popular species

Petrophytum caespitosum, syn. *Spiraea caespitosa*, grows up to 7.5cm (3in) high, forming dense mats, up to 15cm (6in) across, of small silky-hairy, grey-green leaves. Numerous short spikes of tightly packed, fluffy white flowers are borne in mid summer.

Petrophytum hendersonii forms compact hummocks up to 10cm (4in) high and 15cm (6in) across. The leaf rosettes are dark blue-green, sometimes tinged bronze. Fluffy creamy white flower spikes appear during mid summer.

Cultivation

Plant rock spiraea between autumn and spring, in sharply-drained, gritty, preferably alkaline soil and in full sun.

Propagation Take softwood cuttings in early summer and root in a cold frame.

Pests and diseases Aphids and red spider mites may attack the foliage.

Penstemon scouleri

It bears blue, sometimes pink-flushed flowers in early to mid summer. 'Blue Gem' has deep azure-blue flowers.

Penstemon menziesii grows 23cm (9in) or more high and 38cm (15in) across. It is a semi-erect, evergreen sub-shrub with mid green, oblong to oval leaves. Clusters of violet-purple flowers appear in early summer.

Penstemon newberryi is similar to *P. menziesii* but shorter and with pink or rose-purple flowers.

Penstemon pinifolius grows 15-23cm (6-9in) high, spreading to neat clumps up to 15cm (6in) wide, with narrow, grey-green leaves. Loose spikes of orange-red flowers appear in profusion from early summer to early autumn.

Penstemon roezlii is a 10-23cm (4-9in) high sub-shrub, spreading 30cm (12in) or more. The mid green leaves are narrowly spear-shaped. Sprays of lavender to violet-blue flowers appear in mid summer.

Penstemon rupicola is a prostrate sub-shrub, only 7.5-10cm (3-4in) high but spreading to 23cm (9in). The leaves are oval and mid green; rose-carmine flowers are borne during late spring.

Penstemon scouleri grows up to 30cm (1ft) high and wide, with leathery, spear-shaped mid green leaves. Clusters of lilac flowers are borne in early and mid summer.

Cultivation

Plant penstemons from mid autumn to early spring in good well-drained but moist soil in full sun.

Propagation Take cuttings of non-flowering side-shoots in mid to late summer and root in a cold frame. Overwinter in the frame before planting out in late spring.

Pests and diseases Trouble free.

Penstemon newberryi

PERIWINKLE – see *Vinca*

Phlox
rock phlox

Phlox subulata 'Scarlet Flame'

Phlox douglasii 'Boothman's Variety'

- ☐ Height 5-25cm (2-10in)
- ☐ Spread up to 45cm (1½ft)
- ☐ Flowers late spring and early summer
- ☐ Fertile well-drained or moist soil
- ☐ Sun or partial shade
- ☐ Evergreen perennial

Rock phlox is so thickly smothered in blooms in early summer that hardly a leaf can be seen. The generally hardy species are mat-forming, with mid green, lance-shaped evergreen leaves. They are ideal for rock gardens and walls. The five-petalled flowers come in shades of pink, red, purple and blue as well as white.

Popular species and varieties
Phlox adsurgens is 20cm (8in) high with salmon-pink flowers. 'Wagon Wheels' has deeply cut petals and resembles a cartwheel. Both are best in light shade and acid soil.

Phlox bifida (sand phlox) forms a mound up to 20cm (8in) high, with lilac or lavender flowers.

Phlox 'Chattahoochee' grows 20cm (8in) high, with violet, purple-eyed flowers through summer and into autumn.

Phlox douglasii is a sub-shrubby species forming a dense prostrate mat, 5-10cm (2-4in) high and 45cm (1½ft) across. It bears a mass of pale lavender flowers. Popular varieties include 'Boothman's Variety' (mauve); 'Crackerjack' (crimson-red); 'Daniel's Cushion' (rose-pink); 'Mabel' (clear lilac-mauve); 'May Snow' (white); and 'Red Admiral' (crimson).

Phlox subulata forms a mat of needle-like, mid green leaves. It grows 5-10cm (2-4in) high and up to 45cm (1½ft) across with purple or pink flowers. Popular varieties include 'Alexander's Surprise' (rich salmon-pink); 'Benita' (lavender-blue); 'Oakington Blue' (sky blue); and 'Scarlet Flame' (magenta with red eye).

Cultivation
Plant alpine phlox between early autumn and early spring. Most flourish in rich well-drained soil in full sun, though *P. adsurgens* and *P.* 'Chattahoochee' prefer a moist acid soil and partial shade. Trim back all plants after flowering.
Propagation Take cuttings of non-flowering side-shoots in early summer and root in a cold frame.
Pests and diseases Trouble free.

Phlox bifida

Phyllodoce
mountain heath

Phyllodoce caerulea

☐ Height 7.5-30cm (3-12in)
☐ Spread 10-30cm (4-12in) or more
☐ Flowers mid spring to early summer
☐ Moist, lime-free soil
☐ Semi-shade
☐ Evergreen sub shrub

The species of *Phyllodoce* or mountain heath are fully hardy evergreens and suitable for the rock garden and as ground cover provided they can be given cool, moist lime-free conditions. They do especially well in areas of high rainfall. The plants are related to heathers, but daintier and more compact, with typically narrow, heath-like, pale or dark green leaves arranged in whorls. The urn- or bell-shaped flowers appear from mid spring to early summer, and sometimes again in the autumn.

Popular species
Phyllodoce aleutica grows 15-30cm (6-12in) high. White to green-yellow flowers are borne in loose clusters. The variety *glanduliflora* is taller, with hairy, yellow flowers.
Phyllodoce breweri grows up to 23cm (9in) high. The saucer-shaped flowers are purplish pink and borne in loose sprays.
Phyllodoce caerulea, syn. *P. taxifolia*, is ultra hardy and cushion forming, growing 7.5-15cm (3-6in) high, with pale pink-mauve to purplish flowers.
Phyllodoce empetriformis grows 7.5-30cm (3-12in) high, with purple flowers in spring. The species is tolerant of dry soils.
Phyllodoce x intermedia is a tufted, mat-forming species growing 15-25cm (6-10in) high and spreading widely. The flowers are mauve to purple. Popular varieties include 'Fred Stoker' (bright red-purple flowers).
Phyllodoce nipponica is a compact species only 10-15cm (4-6in) high and wide. The flowers are white, often tinged pink.

Cultivation
Plant mountain heath in spring or autumn, in moist acid soil and in semi-shade. Shear the plants after flowering.
Propagation Take heel cuttings of young side-shoots from mid summer to mid autumn and root in a cold frame.
Pests and diseases Die-back and honey fungus may occur.

Phyteuma
horned rampion

Phyteuma comosum

☐ Height 5-20cm (2-8in)
☐ Spread 15-23cm (6-9in)
☐ Flowers early to mid summer
☐ Sharply-drained soil
☐ Sun
☐ Perennial

Horned rampion (*Phyteuma*) bears curious claw-shaped, tubular flowers, densely packed into globular or oval heads. The species can be grown in rock gardens, scree beds, tufa blocks and alpine houses.

Popular species
Phyteuma comosum, syn. *Physoplexis comosa*, grows 5-10cm (2-4in) high, as a tuft of coarsely toothed, pointed-oval mid green leaves. The purple, almost stemless flowers rise from the leaf clusters in mid summer. Ideal for wall crevices but dislikes winter wet.
Phyteuma scheuchzeri grows 15-20cm (6-8in) high, with grass-like mid green leaves. The spiky globular flower heads are deep blue.

Cultivation
Plant phyteumas in early spring in a scree bed, rock garden or drystone wall in sun or partial shade and in sharply-drained, preferably alkaline soil; or in gritty compost in the alpine house. Sun or light shade is equally acceptable. Protect from winter wet.
Propagation Divide and replant after flowering or in spring.
Pests and diseases Stems and leaves may be eaten by slugs.

Picea

dwarf spruce

Picea abies 'Reflexa'

- ☐ Height 20cm-1.2m (8in-4ft)
- ☐ Spread 90cm (3ft) or more
- ☐ Foliage plant
- ☐ Moist, acid soil
- ☐ Sun or partial shade
- ☐ Dwarf conifer

The spruce family contains a number of dwarf forms which look most attractive in an alpine setting. They have short needle-like, generally mid green leaves and are mainly conical in shape.

Popular species

Picea abies 'Gregoryana' has dense sea-green foliage on a rounded, flat-topped shrub reaching 20cm (8in) high. 'Little Gem' is dense, bun-shaped and up to 30cm (1ft) high. 'Nidiformis' is a popular, flat-topped form, 30cm

Picea mariana 'Nana'

(1ft) high and spreading to 90cm (3ft). 'Pygmaea', extremely slow-growing, is globular to dome-shaped, about 20cm (8in) high. 'Reflexa' is a prostrate variety, forming a low wide-spreading dome of rigid stems with upward-swept tips.

Picea glauca 'Alberta Globe', of dense bun shape, grows up to 25cm (10in) high. 'Conica' very slowly forms a cone-shaped shrub 1.2m (4ft) high; 'Lilliput' is a dwarf version of 'Conica', no more than 30cm (1ft) high. 'Echiniformis', a dense miniature globe, has grey-green leaves.

Picea mariana 'Nana' is a slow-growing miniature, never reaching much more than 30cm (1ft) high. It forms a neat rounded shrub with fine grey-green foliage. *Picea pungens* 'Glauca Globosa' is a dense and flat-topped rounded shrub, up to 60cm (2ft) high, and silvery blue.

Cultivation

Plant dwarf spruces in moist soil, preferably acid, from late autumn onwards. Delay planting until spring on heavy soils. Give them a sheltered sunny position.

Propagation Home propagation is inadvisable; buy new stock.

Pests and diseases Adelgids may produce pineapple-like galls on young shoots.

Pimelea

New Zealand daphne

Pimelea prostrata

- ☐ Height 10-15cm (4-6in)
- ☐ Spread up to 30cm (1ft)
- ☐ Flowers in summer
- ☐ Well-drained neutral to acid soil
- ☐ Sun and shelter
- ☐ Evergreen sub-shrub

Most New Zealand daphnes are too tender for the British climate, but one species will survive outdoors in frost-free regions. The shrubs are closely related to the true daphnes and best grown in scree beds.

Pimelea prostrata forms a prostrate, spreading mat of tangled stems bearing tiny grey-green leaves. The fragrant flowers in summer are waxy-white and followed by white berries.

Cultivation

Plant New Zealand daphne in well-drained, lime-free soil in mid to late autumn or mid to late spring. Protect from winter wet and winds with raised panes of glass.

Propagation Take half-ripe cuttings with a heel in mid summer and root in a propagator unit.

Pests and diseases Generally trouble free, though die-back may suddenly occur.

PINE (MOUNTAIN) – see *Pinus*
PINKS – see *Dianthus*

Pinus

mountain pine

Pinus mugo 'Mops'

☐ Height 40-50cm (16-20in)
☐ Spread up to 1.2m (4ft)
☐ Foliage plant
☐ Any well-drained soil
☐ Sunny site
☐ Dwarf conifer

The only species of pine with dwarf varieties suitable for the rock or scree garden is *Pinus mugo*, the ultra-hardy mountain pine. Like all pines it has a gnarled, rugged appearance, with bottlebrush-like sprays of stiff, dark green needle-like foliage.

The species itself is too large for rock gardens, forming a medium to large shrub of dense bushy habit, but the varieties described are slow-growing and naturally dwarf and maintain their neat shape without pruning.

Popular varieties

'Gnom', one of the most widely grown dwarf mountain pines, is of compact habit, with dark green foliage. It eventually grows 50cm (20in) high.
'Humpy', densely compact and of rounded shape, grows some 40cm (16in) high.
'Mops' is a compact, globular type reaching about 40cm (16in) high.
'Winter Gold' is of spreading habit, with yellow foliage in winter.

Cultivation

Plant dwarf mountain pines during late autumn in any well-drained soil, in a sunny site; they are tolerant of lime.
Propagation Buy new plants.
Pests and diseases Generally trouble free.

Plantago

plantain

Plantago nivalis

☐ Height 2.5-13cm (1-5in)
☐ Spread up to 30cm (1ft)
☐ Foliage plant
☐ Sharply-drained soil
☐ Sunny site
☐ Evergreen perennial

The genus *Plantago* includes the curse of the perfect lawn, common plantain, as well as several species which are grown for their attractive rosettes of silver and grey-haired, sometimes rich beet-red leaves. They are suitable for sunny scree beds.

Popular species

Plantago argentea forms rosettes of long, narrow, densely felted leaves covered in long silvery hairs. It grows 13cm (5in) high and spreads to 23cm (9in).
Plantago major 'Rosularis' (rose plantain) forms a silvery leaf rosette; instead of flower spikes, it produces a central rosette of curly bracts like a small posy.
Plantago nivalis has neat rosettes of thick, narrow leaves densely felted with a covering of fine silver hairs. In summer it bears insignificant black and yellow flowers. Of prostrate habit, it rarely exceeds 5cm (2in) in height or 13cm (5in) in spread.

Cultivation

Plant plantains in spring or autumn, in any very well-drained soil in full sun. Protect rosettes from winter wet with raised panes of glass.
Propagation Divide and replant established rosettes in autumn or spring.
Pests and diseases Generally trouble free.

PLANTAIN – see *Plantago*

Pleione

pleione

Pleione bulbocodioides 'Snow White'

☐ Height 15-20cm (6-8in)
☐ Spread 10cm (4in)
☐ Flowers mid winter, spring or autumn
☐ Rich, well-drained soil
☐ Sheltered partially shaded site, or alpine house
☐ Orchid

Pleiones are beautiful orchids, deciduous and terrestrial and almost hardy. A few species can be grown in the open though they are better in pans in an alpine house; they can be moved outside in a shady site for the summer months. Like many other orchids, pleiones grow from pseudobulbs, each of which produces one or two long-stalked, narrowly lance-shaped leaves, usually after the flowers.

The large blooms, with narrow spreading petals surrounding a frilled trumpet or lip, are white, yellow, pink or lilac, usually with attractive markings in contrasting colours. Under glass, the flowers are borne from late winter onwards, outdoors in mid and late spring. The foliage begins to turn yellow in early autumn as the pseudobulbs become dormant.

Popular species

Pleione bulbocodioides, syn. *P. limprichtii*, is the hardiest species and can be grown in sheltered rock gardens. It grows 20cm (8in) high and bears flowers up to 10cm (4in) across, either singly or in pairs, on short stalks. They are variable but typically have long narrow petals and sepals, white to pale or deep lilac in colour, with a trumpet-shaped fringed lip, usually spotted red or yellow. Quite large, spear-shaped, heavily-ribbed leaves develop after the flowers are finished. Named varie-

Polemonium
Jacob's ladder

Polemonium carneum

☐ Height 15-38cm (6-15in)
☐ Spread up to 30cm (1ft)
☐ Flowers mid to late summer
☐ Rich well-drained soil
☐ Sun or partial shade
☐ Perennial

Dwarf Jacob's ladders, with their bowl-shaped blue or purple flowers and delicate feathery foliage, thrive in sunny rock gardens. They are hardy but often short-lived.

Popular species
Polemonium carneum is a clump-forming species, about 38cm (15in) high, with many-branched stems bearing finely divided, mid green leaves, and pinkish flowers.
Polemonium confertum grows 15-20cm (6-8in) high and wide. It has woody stems with sticky leaves divided into fine leaflets. Dense heads of clear blue flowers are borne in summer.
Polemonium reptans grows 15cm (6in) high, forming spreading matted clumps of deep green leaves. It bears sprays of bright blue flowers in late spring to mid summer.

Cultivation
Plant dwarf Jacob's ladder from mid autumn to early spring in rich well-drained soil in sun or partial shade. Cut flowering stems back to basal growth when flowering has finished.
Propagation Divide and replant in mid autumn or early spring.
Pests and diseases Trouble free.

Pleione bulbocodioides 'Versailles'

ties include 'Blush of Dawn' (pale lilac petals and white lip tinted pale mauve); 'Limprichtii' (red-purple flowers and crimson-freckled lip, fringed with white); 'Oriental Grace' (purple-red to violet petals and white, yellow-lined white lip); 'Polar Sun' (pure white, lip with lemon-yellow markings); 'Snow White' (all white); and 'Versailles' (lilac petals with an orange-spotted lip).
Pleione hookeriana grows 7.5-15cm (3-6in) high and has rose-purple flowers with a yellow-throated white lip, marked with red or brown. A single lance-shaped leaf later appears from each pseudobulb. The species is near-hardy.
Pleione humilis, only 5-7.5cm (2-3in) high, has flagon-shaped pseudobulbs and large white flowers tinged pink. The lip is marked with brown-purple stripes and blotches and heavily fringed. Spear-shaped leaves appear after flowering. Although generally hardy, the species is best grown in an alpine house.
Pleione praecox is a near-hardy species, 7.5-13cm (3-5in) high. In spite of its name, it flowers in autumn, with pairs of rose-pink, fragrant blooms on each stalk; they have violet markings and fringed lips.

Cultivation
Plant pleiones outdoors in mid to late spring in well-drained soil enriched with plenty of organic matter. Choose a sheltered partially shaded site. Protect from winter wet with cloches.

In the alpine house, pot pleiones in late winter or early spring, in humus-rich compost containing plenty of fine grit. Set three to five pseudobulbs in a 15cm (6in) half-pot, covering the bottom third of each bulb with compost. Water carefully until growth is well advanced, then more generously with a fine spray until the foliage dies down. Thereafter withhold water and store the bulbs in their pots in a cool but frost-free cold frame or greenhouse. In early spring, start the growth cycle again with renewed watering; repot every other year.

Shade the house from hot sun and ventilate freely throughout the year, except in frosty weather.
Propagation Detach offsets when repotting and pot up separately, repotting them as necessary until they reach flowering size. Or pot up the little bulbils that form on top of mature bulbs; treat them as offsets.
Pests and diseases Outdoors, slugs feed on shoots and flowers; glasshouse red spider mites attack under glass. Brown blotches on the foliage are usually due to over-watering.

Polygala

milkwort

Polygala chamaebuxus

☐ Height 5-15cm (2-6in)
☐ Spread 23-30cm (9-12in)
☐ Flowers mid spring to late summer
☐ Well-drained, fertile soil
☐ Sun or partial shade
☐ Evergreen perennial

Milkworts are useful ground-cover plants, with glossy leaves and attractive pea-like flowers. They are excellent plants for rock and trough gardens and for scree beds.

Popular species

Polygala calcarea (milkwort) is an evergreen prostrate plant growing only 5-7.5cm (2-3in) high but spreading to 30cm (1ft). It forms a mat of mid to dark green spreading branches covered with small oval leaves. Sprays of lilac-blue flowers are borne in profusion from late spring onwards.
Polygala chamaebuxus (ground box) has woody 15cm (6in) high stems with hard, box-like evergreen leaves. The flowers are yellow-and-cream, with a purple base. The variety *P. c. grandiflora*, syn. *P. c. rhodoptera*, has striking magenta-and-gold flowers.

Cultivation

Plant milkwort between early autumn and early spring. Both species grow in ordinary well-drained soil but do better in fertile soil enriched with organic matter. *P. chamaebuxus* prefers partial shade.

Propagation Take softwood cuttings of lateral or basal shoots, preferably with a heel, between early and late summer and root in a cold frame. *P. chamaebuxus* may also be divided and replanted in early spring.

Pests and diseases Generally trouble free.

Polygala calcarea

Polygonum

knotweed

Polygonum tenuicaule

☐ Height 10-23cm (4-9in)
☐ Spread 30-60cm (1-2ft)
☐ Flowers early spring to mid autumn
☐ Well-drained soil
☐ Sun or partial shade
☐ Perennial

Knotweeds belong to a diverse genus that includes rampant climbers, common weeds and decorative garden plants. Several ground-hugging, mat-forming species are suitable for the rock garden and alpine house.

Popular species

Polygonum affine grows 15-23cm (6-9in) high and spreads up to 45cm (1½ft). It makes good ground cover for larger rock gardens. Two varieties are commonly grown. 'Darjeeling Red' forms a dense mat of narrow lance-shaped, dark green leaves, which turn russet brown in winter until replaced by new ones. Spikes of deep pink flowers, 15cm (6in) long, are produced from mid summer to early autumn. 'Donald Lowndes' is more compact, with larger leaves. The rose-red flower spikes are 15-20cm (6-8in) long and appear in early summer, though young plants flower for a longer period.
Polygonum tenuicaule grows 10cm (4in) high and spreads to 30-45cm (1-1½ft). It has ovate, mid green leaves and white flower spikes borne in early to mid spring, before the leaves expand.
Polygonum vacciniifolium grows 15cm (6in) high and spreads to 60cm (2ft). It forms a close mat of

Polygonum affine 'Darjeeling Red'

shining evergreen, oval and leathery leaves; it is ideal trailing over a wall. Upright, pale rose-red flower spikes are produced from late summer to mid autumn.

Cultivation
Plant knotweed between mid autumn and early spring in any well-drained soil in a sunny position. Choose the site carefully as the plants are invasive. Plant *P. tenuicaule* in moist soil in partial shade, or in shallow pans in an alpine house.

Propagation Divide and replant in early spring or autumn.

Pests and diseases Trouble free.

POPPY – see *Papaver*

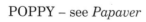
Polygonum affine, autumn foliage

Potentilla
cinquefoil

Potentilla cinerea

☐ Height 5-7.5cm (2-3in)
☐ Spread up to 45cm (1½ft)
☐ Flowers in summer
☐ Any well-drained soil
☐ Sunny site
☐ Perennial

The hardy herbaceous potentillas, or cinquefoils, include a number of mat-forming species. They are valued for their saucer-shaped flowers.

Popular species
Potentilla cinerea, syn. *P. tommasiniana*, grows as neat mats up to 7.5cm (3in) high and 45cm (1½ft) wide, with grey, softly hairy leaves and yellow flowers.

Potentilla eriocarpa forms clumps, 7.5cm (3in) high and 15cm (6in) across, of grey-green leaves and pale yellow flowers.

Potentilla nitida grows 7.5cm (3in) high and 30cm (12in) wide, with silvery, hairy leaves and pale pink crimson-centred flowers.

Potentilla x *tonguei* is prostrate, 5cm (2in) high and 25cm (10in) across, with dark green leaves. It bears soft apricot-coloured flowers with crimson centres.

Cultivation
Plant cinquefoils from mid autumn to early spring in any well-drained soil in full sun. *P. nitida* thrives in poor soil.

Propagation Divide and replant in autumn or spring. Or take basal cuttings in spring and root in a cold frame.

Pests and diseases Trouble free.

Pratia

pratia

Pratia treadwellii

☐ Height up to 5cm (2in)
☐ Spread 30cm (1ft) or more
☐ Flowers late spring and summer
☐ Moist soil
☐ Semi-shade
☐ Evergreen perennial

With a prostrate habit, a mass of lobelia-shaped flowers and handsome autumn berries, pratia is an ideal ground-cover plant for a partially shaded rockery.

Popular species

Pratia angulata bears rounded dark green leaves on slender, branching pinkish stems. The star-shaped, white flowers, usually streaked with purple, are followed by purplish seed pods. Probably a selected garden form of *P. angulata*, *Pratia treadwellii* is similar, but has larger leaves and brighter fruit. Both plants bloom from late spring onwards.
Pratia repens is very similar, but has kidney-shaped leaves, and flowers flushed with purple. It blooms from early summer to mid autumn.

Cultivation

Plant pratia in spring in a semi-shaded position in moist but well-drained soil.
Propagation Divide in spring, or detach and replant rooted sections from the outer edges of mature plants.
Pests and diseases Generally trouble free.

PRICKLY HEATH – see
Acantholimon
PRIMROSE – see *Primula*

Primula

primula

Primula sieboldii 'Chinese Mountains'

☐ Height 5-30cm (2-12in)
☐ Spread 10-30cm (4-12in)
☐ Flowers mid winter to early summer
☐ Well-drained or moist fertile soil
☐ Sun or partial shade
☐ Herbaceous and evergreen perennials

The well-loved primulas come in a bewildering range of shapes, sizes and colours, and varying growing needs. The Alpine types, suitable for edging, raised beds and rock gardens, are generally less exacting and fully hardy. They are often grouped in sections according to botanical affinities:
Auricula (A) Rounded flower clusters; fleshy leaves usually covered with a mealy powder.
Cortusoid (C) Clustered flowers; lobed, crinkled, hairy leaves.
Farinose (F) Clustered flowers; leaves usually mealy.
Muscarioid (M) Flower spikes held like grape hyacinth.
Nivalis (N) Flower clusters on tall stems; strap-shaped leaves.
Petiolaris (P) Clustered, short-stemmed flowers; dense rosettes.
Soldanelloid (S) Clustered bell-shaped flowers, usually pendent; soft, hairy leaves.
Vernalis (V) Single primrose flowers; leaves crinkled and hairy.

Popular species

Primula allionii (A), no more than 5cm (2in) tall, forms a tight, 15cm (6in) wide, sticky-leaved hummock hidden by purple, or rose-red to white, flowers during

Primula auricula 'Candida'

early and mid spring. Best grown in an alpine house.
Primula amoena (V) is a primrose-like plant about 20cm (8in) tall and 10cm (4in) wide, with pink flowers carried in clusters during mid to late spring.
Primula auricula (A) has bright yellow, scented flowers on 15cm (6in) tall stems in spring. Varieties include 'Blossom' (crimson-red, golden centres); 'Candida' (bold eye markings and white or greenish grey picotee margins); and 'Mark' (pink, pale yellow eye).
Primula edgeworthii (P) is 7.5-10cm (3-4in) tall with pale mauve, white-eyed blooms from mid winter to mid spring above grey-green leaf rosettes.
Primula x *juliana* (V) hybrids resemble the primrose, but with flowers in various colours. They appear from mid winter to spring on 7.5-15cm (3-6in) high plants. They include 'Blue Riband' (deep blue, red centre); 'Gigha White'; and 'Wanda' (wine-purple, and purple-green foliage).

Primula nutans

Primula x juliana 'Wanda'

Primula marginata (A), with silver-edged, toothed leaves, is a woody-based species some 10cm (4in) tall. Fragrant, pale lavender to violet flowers appear in spring.

Primula minima (A) is mat-forming and spring-flowering, up to 5cm (2in) tall, and best grown in a crevice or trough. The rose-pink petals are deeply notched.

Primula nutans (S) has spikes of nodding lavender-violet flowers on 30cm (1ft) tall stems in early summer, and velvety leaves in 30cm (1ft) wide rosettes.

Primula reidii (S) is about 10cm (4in) tall with rosettes of soft hairy leaves, and clusters of semi-pendent, bell-shaped, ivory-white flowers in late spring.

Primula rosea (F) is about 15cm (6in) tall and wide with clusters of carmine-rose flowers that begin to appear in early spring before the leaves have fully developed.

Primula sieboldii (C) is up to 23cm (9in) high and rather wider. Umbels of rose-purple flowers appear in late spring. 'Chinese Mountains' has white flowers.

Primula vialii (M) has the appearance of a miniature red-hot poker. It has erect rosettes of leaves and dense spikes of pinkish to lavender-blue flowers, crimson in bud, on 30cm (1ft) tall stems.

Cultivation

Plant from early autumn to early spring. The best sites and soils vary according to section:

□ Auricula: well-drained soil;

Primula sieboldii

Primula vialii

semi-shade in warm areas, full sun in cool gardens.

☐ Cortusoid: moist fertile soil; semi-shade.

☐ Farinose: moist, cool soil; sun or partial shade.

☐ Muscarioid: lime-rich, well-drained soil; partial shade.

☐ Nivalis: moist but well-drained soil; semi-shade.

☐ Petiolaris: well-drained, humus-rich soil; cool, humid shade; protect from winter wet.

☐ Soldanelloid: moist, acid, gritty soil; cool semi-shade.

☐ Vernalis: cool humus-rich soil; light shade; divide regularly.

Propagation Divide primulas after flowering. Cuttings can be taken during summer and rooted in a cold frame. Alternatively, sow ripe seed from late spring.

Pests and diseases Aphids, caterpillars and cutworms may damage and weaken top growth. Rots, grey mould, leaf spot, rust and several virus diseases may disfigure growth.

Primula rosea

Prunella
self-heal

Prunella x webbiana 'Pink Loveliness'

☐ Height 15-30cm (6-12in)
☐ Spread up to 45cm (1½ft)
☐ Flowers late spring to early autumn
☐ Any slightly moist soil
☐ Sun or partial shade
☐ Perennial

Self-heals are hardy, easy-going plants which, although not falling into the category of 'choice' rock garden plants, provide good ground cover and a long season of colour from their dense spikes of lipped flowers. Vigorously spreading, they are best confined to the wilder parts of a rock garden.

Popular species
Prunella grandiflora is a spreading species, up to 45cm (1½ft), with dense spikes, 15cm (6in) tall, of hooded tubular flowers, and oval, somewhat diamond-shaped, mid green leaves. The flowers, which appear during summer and early autumn, are purple or violet-blue.
Prunella vulgaris is a British native flower – often a weed on lawns. Its spikes of violet flowers are 23cm (9in) tall. This can be an invasive plant, but more decorative white, pink and rose-red varieties are available. 'Rubra', sometimes listed as *P. incisa*, has rich violet-purple flower spikes and rarely spreads more than 38cm (15in).
Prunella x *webbiana* comprises a range of hybrids, of which *P. grandiflora* is one parent and which they all closely resemble.

They are generally taller, reaching 30cm (1ft) when in bloom. Available varieties include 'Loveliness', which has flowers of pale violet, and 'Blue Loveliness', 'Pink Loveliness', 'White Loveliness' and 'Little Red Riding Hood', all with flowers of the colours indicated by their names.

Cultivation
Self-heals will grow in any reasonable, moist but well-drained soil in sun or semi-shade. Plant in early spring and, because of their self-seeding nature, dead-head them frequently to prevent unwanted seedlings. It is advisable to keep these spreading plants away from slower-growing, more choice neighbours.
Propagation The spreading habit makes division easy; this can be done at any time from early autumn to early spring. Alternatively, sow seed in spring; named varieties do come true to type.
Pests and diseases Generally trouble free.

Pterocephalus
pterocephalus

Pterocephalus perennis

☐ Height up to 10cm (4in)
☐ Spread up to 30cm (1ft)
☐ Flowers in summer
☐ Any well-drained soil
☐ Full sun
☐ Evergreen perennial

Pterocephalus perennis, syn. *P. parnassii, Scabiosa pterocephalus*, is a low, cushion-forming plant with grey-green, usually toothed leaves covered with dense, soft hairs. During most of the summer it bears 2.5cm (1in) wide scabious-like flower heads of purplish pink held on short stems just above the foliage; they are followed by fluffy seed heads.

Cultivation
Plant in early autumn or mid spring in a position in full sun. These small plants flower best in poor soils, well-drained and alkaline, in rich soils they make excessive leaf growth instead of flowers. Rock crevices, paving cracks, dry-stone walls and sunny scree beds are ideal sites.
Propagation Divide and replant in early spring or mid autumn. Or take 5cm (2in) soft basal cuttings in mid spring and root in a propagator unit. Alternatively, propagate from seed sown in late summer and overwintered in a cold frame.
Pests and diseases Generally trouble free.

Pulsatilla vulgaris

Pulsatilla

pasque flower

Pulsatilla vulgaris 'Rubra'

☐ Height 15-23cm (6-9in)
☐ Spread 15-25cm (6-10in)
☐ Flowers mid spring to early summer
☐ Well-drained rich soil
☐ Open sunny position
☐ Perennial

Pasque flowers are excellent for an open rock garden. Long-lived, hardy and reliable, they look charming with their cup-shaped nodding flowers, each with a central boss of golden stamens, their ferny leaves, softly hairy buds and silky seed heads.

Popular species

Pulsatilla alpina is the tallest species, up to 30cm (12in), and 15cm (6in) across. The flowers, which open in late spring and early summer, are white, sometimes flushed bluish-purple on the outside and up to 6cm (2½in) across. There is an attractive subspecies, *P. alpina apiifolia*, syn. *P. alpina sulphurea*, with pale yellow flowers.

Pulsatilla vernalis, syn. *Anemone vernalis*, is small and almost prostrate, with a height and spread of 15cm (6in). Hairy buds open in mid spring to reveal pearl-white flowers, some 5cm (2in) across, flushed with pink or purple-blue on the outside.

Pulsatilla vulgaris, syn. *Anemone pulsatilla* (true pasque flower), is the best-known species. Up to 23cm (9in) tall, its purple flowers can be as much as 7.5cm (3in) across. Several delightful forms with flowers of different colours are available, including: 'Alba' (white); 'Barton's Pink' (shell pink); and 'Rubra' (red).

Cultivation

Pasque flowers resent root disturbance. Set out young container-grown plants in early autumn, in a sunny open position and in rich, well-drained soil. They thrive on alkaline soil, except *P. alpina apiifolia*, which prefers acid soil.

Propagation Sow seed in mid summer in pans or boxes of seed compost in a cold frame. When the seedlings are large enough to handle, prick them off and overwinter them in the frame; pot up when the new leaves make their appearance and grow on; plant out in permanent positions in early autumn.

Pests and diseases Generally trouble free.

Pulsatilla alpina apiifolia

Puschkinia

striped squill

Puschkinia scilloides

☐ Height 10-15cm (4-6in)
☐ Spread up to 7.5cm (3in)
☐ Flowers early to late spring
☐ Well-drained humus-rich soil
☐ Sun or light shade
☐ Bulb

The small striped squill, *Puschkinia scilloides*, syn. *P. libanotica*, is the only species generally available. It is a delightful, hardy bulbous plant, ideal for sink and trough gardens and for small pockets near the front of a rock garden.

Blooming during spring, striped squill has strap-shaped leaves and slender stems bearing clusters of icy-blue, bell-shaped flowers, each petal with a central darker blue stripe. 'Album' is white.

Cultivation

Plant in autumn in an open or lightly shaded position in well-drained, but moisture retentive, fertile soil. The bulbs can be left undisturbed for several years.

Propagation The bulbs readily produce offsets. Lift overcrowded plants when the foliage has died down in late summer. Separate the offsets from mature bulbs and grow them on separately. Plant larger bulbs at once where they are to flower.

Pests and diseases Generally trouble free, although slugs feed on bulbs, stems and leaves.

Ramonda

ramonda

Ramonda myconi

- ☐ Height 10-15cm (4-6in)
- ☐ Spread up to 23cm (9in)
- ☐ Flowers mid to late spring
- ☐ Moist rich soil
- ☐ Shade
- ☐ Evergreen perennial

Long-lived plants suitable for north-facing positions, ramondas have African violet-like flowers in mid and late spring. The attractive evergreen leaf rosettes are deep green and deeply toothed.

Popular species

Ramonda myconi, syn. *R. pyrenaica*, has mauve or blue-violet flowers with yellow stamens. It grows up to 15cm (6in) high. Varieties are available with white, blue or pink flowers.
Ramonda nathaliae, 10cm (4in) high, has pale green leaves and, in late spring, clusters of white or lavender flowers.
Ramonda serbica resembles *R. nathaliae*, but with cup-shaped, lilac-blue flowers.

Cultivation

Plant in early spring in well-drained soil, enriched with organic matter, in north-facing rock crevices or walls.
Propagation Divide and replant the rosettes in early spring. Or take leaf cuttings in mid to late summer and root in a cold frame. Alternatively, sow seeds in early spring or autumn in a cold frame.
Pests and diseases Slugs may feed on the foliage.

Ranunculus

alpine buttercup

Ranunculus gramineus

- ☐ Height 10-30cm (4-12in)
- ☐ Spread 10-30cm (4-12in)
- ☐ Flowers early spring to mid summer
- ☐ Well-drained, moisture-retentive soil
- ☐ Sunny site
- ☐ Perennial

Alpine buttercups are hardy, clump-forming plants. They are easy to grow, lack the invasive habit of other buttercups and deserve a place in the rockery.

Popular species

Ranunculus alpestris is evergreen, 10cm (4in) tall, with glossy dark green, heart-shaped, toothed leaves. It bears cup-shaped white flowers from late spring to mid summer.
Ranunculus amplexicaulis, up to 20cm (8in) tall, has lance-shaped blue-grey leaves. White flowers appear in late spring, and by late summer the whole plant has died down.
Ranunculus calandrinioides is about 15cm (6in) tall and fleshy rooted. Its long, oval, blue-green leaves are present during autumn and winter, but disappear in summer. Poppy-like flowers, white flushed pink and up to 5cm (2in) in diameter, appear during winter or early spring. It is perfectly hardy, but, because of its early flowering, it is best grown in an alpine house.
Ranunculus crenatus, 10cm (4in) high and wide, is semi-evergreen with toothed and heart-shaped leaves. White flowers with golden stamens are borne just above the foliage in early summer.
Ranunculus ficaria (lesser celandine) is a native wild species with glossy heart-shaped leaves and 5cm (2in) wide golden yellow flowers from early to late spring. The species grows 30cm (12in) and is invasive, but selected garden forms rarely exceed 10cm (4in) and are compact in habit. They include: 'Albus' (white); 'Aurantiacus' (copper-orange); 'Brazen Hussey' (bronzed leaves, yellow flowers); and 'Flore Pleno' (double, yellow).
Ranunculus gramineus has grass-like leaves, and bright yellow flowers from late spring to mid summer. It grows 30cm (12in) tall.
Ranunculus montanus has round dark green lobed leaves; it bears shiny, bright yellow flowers from late spring to summer and grows about 15cm (6in) tall. 'Molten Gold' is a free-flowering form.

Cultivation

Plant from early autumn to mid spring in a sunny site and in any well-drained but moisture-retentive soil.
Propagation Divide and replant in autumn or spring.
Pests and diseases Trouble free.

Raoulia

raoulia

Raoulia lutescens

☐ Height 6mm-7.5cm (¼-3in)
☐ Spread 30-45cm (1-1½ft)
☐ Foliage plant
☐ Well-drained, gritty soil
☐ Full sun
☐ Evergreen perennial

Raoulias are slowly spreading carpeting or cushion-forming plants useful for ground cover, in paving cracks and for softening rocky outlines. They have tiny hairy evergreen leaves, often in rosettes. Minute, stemless daisy flower heads are borne in spring or summer on some species.

Popular species
Raoulia glabra forms a slow-growing mat, 15cm (6in) wide, of pale green leaves. It has fluffy white flowers.
Raoulia hookeri, syn. *R. australis*, grows 12mm (½in) high and 30cm (12in) wide as a carpet of tight silver rosettes. It sometimes bears pale yellow fluffy flower heads.
Raoulia lutescens, syn. *R. subsericea*, forms a film of tiny grey-green leaves and yellow flowers from late spring to early summer.
Raoulia tenuicaulis, the easiest species, makes a grey-green carpet 6mm (¼in) high and 30cm (12in) wide, with yellow flowers in late spring.

Cultivation
Outdoors, plant raoulias in mid spring, in gritty, well-drained soil in full sun. During winter, protect with raised panes of glass. In an alpine house, plant in April in pans of a proprietary compost with an equal amount of grit; repot every second or third year in mid spring. Always water from the bottom.
Propagation Divide and replant between mid summer and early autumn. Or, detach small portions from the edges of mature plants in spring and pot up.
Pests and diseases Trouble free.

Raoulia glabra

Rhododendron

rhododendron

Rhododendron scintillans

☐ Height 90cm-1.2m (3-4ft)
☐ Spread 90cm-1.5m (3-5ft)
☐ Flowers late winter to early summer
☐ Moist, humus-rich acid soil
☐ Partial shade
☐ Shrub

Dwarf, compact and creeping forms of rhododendron are perfect specimen shrubs for large rock gardens with acid soil. They add vibrant colour for several months, and the neat evergreen foliage is attractive throughout the year.

Popular species
Rhododendron campylogynum grows 45cm (1½ft) or more high and wide. In late spring and early summer it bears bell-shaped, waxy flowers in shades of purple, rose and pink. *R. c. myrtilloides* is only 15cm (6in) tall and has plum-purple flowers.
Rhododendron 'Chikor', 30-60cm (1-2ft) high and wide, has clusters of yellow flowers in late spring.
Rhododendron ferrugineum (alpen rose) bears trusses of rose-red flowers in early summer. It forms a dome-shaped shrub 1-1.2m (3-4ft) wide and high; the leaves are red on the undersides.
Rhododendron forrestii, syn. *R. repens*, up to 30cm (1ft) tall, has a creeping habit, spreading to 1.5m (5ft). It has rounded leaves and large crimson, bell-shaped flowers in mid and late spring.
Rhododendron keleticum, syn. *R.*

Rhodohypoxis
rhodohypoxis

Rhodohypoxis baurii 'Douglas'

☐ Height up to 7.5cm (3in)
☐ Spread 10-15cm (4-6in)
☐ Flowers summer to early autumn
☐ Well-drained acid soil
☐ Full sun
☐ Perennial

Rhododendron campylogynum myrtilloides

calostrotum keleticum, forms hummocks up to 30cm (1ft) high and 45cm (1½ft) wide. In late spring and early summer it carries wide-open flowers of crimson-purple with darker markings.

Rhododendron leucaspis is up to 60cm (2ft) high and 1.2m (4ft) wide; its white saucer-shaped flowers, about 5cm (2in) across, with brown anthers, appear from late winter to early spring. It is best grown in a sheltered site.

Rhododendron pemakoense is a true alpine species of suckering habit, only about 5cm (2in) high but 90cm (3ft) wide. It has small

rounded leaves and, in early and mid spring, large pink-mauve, funnel-shaped flowers. Avoid sites where early morning sun after frost can damage the buds.

Rhododendron scintillans makes a twiggy little shrub, about 60cm (2ft) high and wide, with small clusters of funnel-shaped, lavender to violet flowers in mid spring.

Cultivation
Plant dwarf rhododendrons between mid autumn and mid spring in a moist but well-drained, acid and rich soil in partial shade, or in full sun in cool areas. Ensure that the roots do not dry out.

Propagation Take cuttings from young growths in mid to late summer. Root in a cold frame.

Pests and diseases Weevils and caterpillars may damage flowers and leaves.

The rhizomatous *Rhodohypoxis baurii* is the only species generally available. Hardy except in severe winters, it grows only 7.5cm (3in) high, with tufts of narrow, pale green, hairy leaves. Rose-pink, six-petalled flowers are borne from late spring to early autumn. Varieties include: 'Dawn' (pale pink); 'Douglas' (rose-red); and 'Margaret Rose' (palest pink).

Cultivation
Plant in early autumn in lime-free well-drained soil and a sunny site. Do not let the plants dry out in hot summers. In winter, protect with panes of glass. In the alpine house, keep them dry from mid autumn to mid spring.

Propagation Divide and replant the rhizomes in spring.

Pests and diseases Trouble free.

ROCK CRESS – see *Arabis*
ROCK JASMINE – see *Androsace*
ROCK PINK – see *Dianthus*
ROCK ROSE – see *Helianthemum*
ROCK SPIRAEA – see *Petrophytum*

Rhododendron forrestii

Roscoea

roscoea

Roscoea cautleoides

Roscoea purpurea var. *procera*

- ☐ Height 15-30cm (6-12in)
- ☐ Spread 10-20cm (4-8in)
- ☐ Flowers early and mid summer
- ☐ Rich, moisture-retentive soil
- ☐ Sun or partial shade
- ☐ Perennial

The hardy tuberous-rooted roscoeas bear spikes of orchid-like flowers in summer. They grow naturally in woodland conditions and thrive in cool pockets in the rock garden and the front of borders. The leaves are lance-shaped and erect.

Popular species

Roscoea alpina is a miniature species, no more than 15cm (6in) high and wide. Soft pink-purple flowers are borne among the leaves.

Roscoea 'Beesiana' is similar to *R. cautleoides* and is possibly a hybrid with that and another species. It has yellow flowers, the lower pair of petals flushed and streaked with purple.

Roscoea cautleoides is a robust plant 30cm (12in) high and 15cm (6in) across, with long sheath-like leaves. In summer it bears handsome soft yellow flowers.

Roscoea purpurea var. *procera*, about 30cm (12in) high and 20cm (8in) across, bears spikes of long-tubed rich violet-purple flowers with prominent lower lips.

Cultivation

Plant roscoeas in good, moisture-retentive and cool soil in early spring, choosing sheltered, sunny or partially shaded sites; set the tuberous roots at a depth of 7.5-10cm (3-4in). Mark the site, as growth does not begin until late spring, and the plants die down in early autumn.

Propagation Divide and replant the crowns in early spring. Alternatively, sow ripe seed in a cold frame in late summer or early autumn.

Pests and diseases Generally trouble free.

Sagina

pearlwort

Sagina glabra 'Aurea'

- ☐ Height 12-25mm (½-1in)
- ☐ Spread to 25cm (10in)
- ☐ Foliage plant
- ☐ Well-drained moist soil
- ☐ Sun or partial shade
- ☐ Evergreen perennial

Most pearlworts are weedy plants, but a few species are well enough behaved for a place in the rock garden. Although their greenish or white summer flowers are fairly insignificant, their mat- or hummock-forming habit makes them useful for ground cover, in paving cracks and for softening rocky edges.

Popular species

Sagina boydii is slow-growing, forming tight rosettes of stiff, narrow, dark green leaves in domed hummocks. Insignificant greenish flowers are borne in summer. The species is suitable for troughs or the alpine house.

Sagina glabra spreads to pale green carpets with tiny white flowers. Its golden-leaved form, 'Aurea', is more decorative.

Cultivation

Plant pearlwort between autumn and spring in well-drained but moist soil in sun or semi-shade.

Propagation Divide and replant clumps in autumn or spring.

Pests and diseases Generally trouble free, but red spider mites and aphids can be troublesome.

ST. JOHN'S WORT – see *Hypericum*

Salix
dwarf willow

Salix reticulata

☐ Height 10-30cm (4-12in)
☐ Spread 25-60cm (10-24in)
☐ Catkins in spring
☐ Moist loamy soil
☐ Sun or partial shade
☐ Deciduous shrub

Several dwarf willows are neat enough for associating with rock plants. Some are miniature gnarled trees, others are prostrate creepers, moulding themselves to the contours of rock and ground. Male plants, which have prominent catkins in spring, are the ones to grow.

Popular species
Salix apoda spreads to 60cm (2ft)

Salix apoda

and is about 25cm (10in) high. Upright silvery catkins covered in yellow anthers appear in spring before the glossy green leaves.
Salix x boydii is a slow-growing pygmy tree, about 30cm (1ft) high and wide, with insignificant catkins but with handsome, silver-grey leaves, netted with veins. Ideal for a trough.
Salix herbacea is a ground-hugging species, only 10cm (4in) high and 25cm (10in) wide. Catkins with yellow anthers appear at the same time as the glossy green leaves.
Salix reticulata is slow-growing and prostrate, eventually reaching 15cm (6in) in height and spreading to 60cm (2ft). Upright catkins appear after the oval, netted leaves.
Salix retusa is prostrate, forming a carpet up to 25cm (10in) wide of oblong, notched leaves. The catkins are small, grey and upright.

Cultivation
Plant between mid autumn and late winter in good moist soil and in sun or light shade. Prune away any dead wood during winter.
Propagation Take hardwood cuttings in autumn and root in a nursery bed of moist soil. Plant out rooted cuttings after one year.
Pests and diseases Caterpillars, beetle larvae, aphids and scale insects can damage leaves. Galls may be a problem.

SANDWORT – see *Arenaria*

Sanguinaria
bloodroot

Sanguinaria canadensis 'Plena'

☐ Height 15-20cm (6-8in)
☐ Spread 30cm (1ft)
☐ Flowers mid to late spring
☐ Rich, moist acid soil
☐ Partial shade
☐ Perennial

Bloodroot (*Sanguinaria canadensis*), the only species in its genus, obtained its common name from the red colour of its sap.

Palmate, grey-green leaves, which push up through the soil in early spring, unfurl to reveal the flower buds, which open in mid spring. The leaves continue to develop, but by late summer they have died down. Each cup-shaped flower, about 4cm (1½in) wide, is carried on a single stem, and consists of eight to ten waxy white petals and a central boss of golden stamens. The variety 'Plena' is a beautiful double-flowered form with long-lasting blooms.

Disliking lime, bloodroot is a good plant for a shady peat bed.

Cultivation
Plant bloodroot in autumn, in dappled shade in rich moisture-retentive, acid soil.
Propagation Divide and replant after flowering, taking care not to damage the brittle rhizomes.
Pests and diseases Generally trouble free.

Saponaria
soapwort

Saponaria 'Bressingham Hybrid'

☐ Height 5-15cm (2-6in)
☐ Spread 10-60cm (4-24in)
☐ Flowers late spring to early autumn
☐ Well-drained, fertile soil
☐ Full sun
☐ Perennial

The hardy, low-growing soap-worts are colourful, sun-loving plants, ideal for trailing over walls and banks and for growing in troughs and scree beds.

Popular species
Saponaria 'Bressingham Hybrid' forms a cushion of hairy leaves, about 5cm (2in) tall and 10cm (4in) wide, with bright pink flowers in late spring and summer. Ideal for a trough.
Saponaria ocymoides is a vigorous plant, up to 15cm (6in) tall and 60cm (2ft) wide, useful for trailing over rocks and walls. It carries prolific pink flowers from late spring to early autumn.
Saponaria x *olivana* forms a near-evergreen cushion about 5cm (2in) tall and 20cm (8in) wide, with bright pink flowers in summer.

Cultivation
Plant soapworts from early autumn to spring in a sunny site in any well-drained, gritty soil.
Propagation Divide and replant in autumn or spring; or take cuttings of non-flowering shoots in early summer.
Pests and diseases Trouble free.

Saxifraga
saxifrage

Saxifraga Mossy Hybrid

☐ Height 5-60cm (2-24in)
☐ Spread 15-45cm (6-18in)
☐ Flowers spring and summer; handsome foliage
☐ Well-drained, alkaline soil
☐ Sun or partial shade
☐ Evergreen perennial

Saxifrages are neat in habit, mainly hardy and evergreen and come in a wide range of shapes and sizes, leaf and flower colours. They are indispensable in rock gardens, wall crevices, troughs and alpine houses. The genus is divided into several sections according to growth habits and needs, plus a Miscellaneous section (Misc); the most commonly grown saxifrages belong to just three:
Cushion (C) or Kabschia saxifrages have hard rosettes of silvery leaves, usually lime-encrusted, and form small cushions; they flower in spring.
Encrusted (E), Euaizoonia or Aizoon saxifrages have rosettes of strap-shaped, lime-encrusted leaves of silvery appearance. Sprays of flowers appear in early summer, usually white and often spotted; the rosettes die after flowering but more are produced on runners for the next season.
Mossy (M) or Dactyloides saxifrages form dense hummocks of deeply divided leaves and bear loose sprays of starry flowers in mid to late spring.

Popular species and hybrids
Saxifraga x *apiculata* (C) makes a green cushion, 40cm (16in) across, with primrose-yellow flowers on 7.5cm (3in) stems.
Saxifraga x *borisii* (C) has citron-yellow flowers on reddish stems above grey-green cushions that spread to 30cm (12in).
Saxifraga burseriana (C) bears large white flowers above grey-green spiny cushions up to 15cm (6in) across. Early-flowering, in late winter and spring.
Saxifraga callosa (E) bears arching sprays, 38cm (15in) tall, of white flowers, often spotted red, in summer. The leaves form blue-green rosettes with a spread of about 30cm (1ft).
Saxifraga cochlearis (E), to 20cm (8in) tall and 30cm (1ft) wide, has silvery rosettes and sprays of milky white flowers in summer.
Saxifraga cotyledon (E) has large rosettes to 23cm (9in) wide, and 60cm (2ft) tall sprays of white flowers; in 'Southside Seedling' the flowers are spotted with red.
Saxifraga 'Elizabethae' (C) forms dark green cushions up to 7.5cm (3in) high and 30cm (1ft) across, with short-stemmed yellow flowers in spring.
Saxifraga granulata (Misc) is deciduous; kidney-shaped, grey-green leaves, in loose rosettes about 20cm (8in) across, die down in early summer. White flowers on 25cm (10in) stems appear in mid spring. Bulbils, useful for propagating, are formed around the underground part of the stem. 'Flore Pleno' has double flowers.

Saxifraga oppositifolia

Saxifraga x apiculata

Saxifraga grisebachii (C), 15-23cm (6-9in) high and 23-30cm (9-12in) wide, has lime-encrusted rosettes, with bract-like leaves in a central boss that turns red, and elongates to a stem with pinkish red flowers in spring.

Saxifraga Kabschia hybrids (C) include: 'Harlow Car' (crimson) and 'Myra' (rich pink).

Saxifraga longifolia (E) produces a large, long-lived rosette, 30cm (12in) across, that eventually produces a 45cm (1½ft) long, arching spray of white flowers, and then dies; plenty of seed is set. 'Tumbling Waters' has white flowers.

Saxifraga moschata (M) forms a bright green hummock up to 7.5cm (3in) high and 45cm (1½ft) or more across, with yellow or white flowers in spring. 'Cloth of Gold' is golden-leaved.

Saxifraga oppositifolia (Misc) makes a dark green mat 5cm (2in) high and 45cm (1½ft) wide. Almost stemless crimson to red-purple flowers appear in early spring. 'Florissa' is a lilac-pink form.

Cultivation

Plant saxifrages in early autumn or early spring. The encrusted types do best in well-drained, limy soil; in the south and west they require partial shade, elsewhere they tolerate full sun. Kabschia saxifrages need the same conditions, but shade from midday sun. Mossy types grow best in moist soil and light shade.

Propagation Divide and replant after flowering. Or, detach non-flowering rosettes in late spring and early summer and root as cuttings.

Pests and diseases Trouble free.

Saxifraga callosa

Scabiosa

scabious

Scabiosa alpina

- ☐ Height 15-23cm (6-9in)
- ☐ Spread 20-25cm (8-10in)
- ☐ Flowers mid summer to mid autumn
- ☐ Any well-drained soil
- ☐ Sunny position
- ☐ Perennial

Dwarf scabious, with their elegant, finely cut foliage and large flowers, are perfect for rock garden pockets.

Popular species

Scabiosa alpina is the name used in catalogues for dwarf forms of *S. columbaria*. They grow up to 15cm (6in) tall and 23cm (9in) wide. Lavender-blue flowers are borne from mid summer to mid autumn above grey-green leaves.

Scabiosa graminifolia forms a clump, about 23cm (9in) tall and 25cm (10in) or so wide, of grassy silvery leaves, which make an attractive setting for the pinkish-purple flower heads in mid and late summer. The foliage is evergreen in all but severe winters.

Cultivation

Scabious is fully hardy. Plant in early autumn or mid spring in a sunny position in any well-drained soil. Scabious thrives on lime.

Propagation Divide and replant in early spring or mid autumn; or sow seed in late summer and overwinter in a cold frame.

Pests and diseases Trouble free.

Scilla

squill

Scilla peruviana

- ☐ Height 7.5-30cm (3-12in)
- ☐ Spread 7.5-20cm (3-8in)
- ☐ Flowers late winter to early summer
- ☐ Well-drained, moist soil
- ☐ Sun or partial shade
- ☐ Hardy bulb

Glossy, strap-shaped leaves and graceful bell-shaped or starry flowers, in many different shades of blue, make these hardy dwarf bulbs an attractive choice for small rock garden pockets and for naturalizing.

Popular species

Scilla bifolia usually has only two leaves per bulb. Star-shaped flowers in gentian-blue are carried in early spring on spikes up to 20cm (8in) high. 'Alba' has white flowers; in 'Rosea' they are shell pink.

Scilla peruviana is up to 30cm (1ft) high with dense clusters, up to 15cm (6in) across, of some 100 deep blue, starry flowers during late spring and early summer.

Scilla sibirica produces 15cm (6in) tall stems of brilliant blue, nodding star-shaped flowers in early spring. 'Alba' is a white form, and 'Atrocoerulea' ('Spring Beauty') has earlier, larger and deeper blue flowers.

Scilla tubergeniana, 10cm (4in) tall, bears open bell-like flowers from late winter to early spring; they are coloured pale blue with darker stripes.

Cultivation

Plant in autumn in sun or dappled shade in any well-drained but moisture-retentive soil. Set the bulbs at a depth of three times their size.

Propagation When the leaves have died down, lift congested clumps and replant. Remove offsets at the same time and plant them out; they will flower after a couple of years. Sow ripe seed in early summer in a cold frame. Seedlings usually reach flowering size after three years.

Pests and diseases Stem and bulb eelworms weaken growth, and rust may infect the leaves.

Scilla sibirica 'Atrocoerulea'

Scutellaria
skullcap

Scutellaria alpina

☐ Height 15-23cm (6-9in)
☐ Spread 30-45cm (1-1½ft)
☐ Flowers summer and early autumn
☐ Well-drained soil
☐ Sunny position
☐ Perennial

Skullcaps, named from the shape of the upper part of their two-lipped, tubular flowers, are hardy plants for rock gardens and scree beds.

Popular species
Scutellaria alpina is about 23cm (9in) high with a spread of 45cm (1½ft) of toothed oval leaves. In late summer clusters of purple flowers are borne at the tips of ground-hugging stems.
Scutellaria indica is similar, but 15cm (6in) tall, with grey-green hairy leaves, and purple-blue flowers into early autumn.

Cultivation
Plant between early autumn and early spring in a sunny position in well-drained soil.
Propagation Sow seed of *S. alpina* in early autumn or take soft cuttings in summer. Propagate *S. indica* by seed in spring, by soft cuttings in late spring to early summer, or by division of the rhizomes in spring.
Pests and diseases Generally trouble free.

SEA HEATH – see *Frankenia*

Sedum
stonecrop

Sedum acre

☐ Height 12mm-20cm (½-8in)
☐ Spread 10-45cm (4-18in)
☐ Flowers late spring to early autumn
☐ Ordinary well-drained soil
☐ Full sun
☐ Evergreen and herbaceous perennials

Stonecrops belong to a large genus of easily grown and hardy succulents, many perfectly suited to rock gardens, raised beds, paving and walls in full sun. They have small but profuse star-like flowers in a broad range of colours; fleshy, often evergreen leaves are a feature in themselves.

Popular species
Sedum acre is the floriferous and rather invasive common stonecrop with bright yellow flowers in early to mid summer. No more than 5cm (2in) tall but spreading to more than 30cm (1ft), it makes a mat of egg-shaped leaves. The golden-leaved form 'Aureum', is less vigorous.
Sedum album grows up to 15cm (6in) high and spreads to 38cm (15in) wide mats of evergreen, egg-shaped leaves on pink stems. Loose clusters of white flowers are freely borne in mid summer.
Sedum cauticolum is a woody-based herbaceous species, 10-15cm (4-6in) high and 30cm (12in) across. The floppy, purple-red stems are set with ovate, grey-green leaves. Flat, branched heads of crimson-cerise flowers are produced in late summer.

Sedum dasyphyllum has a spread of about 30cm (1ft) and is only 12mm (½in) tall. Small, blue-green oval leaves are the background for flat clusters of minute white flowers in early summer.
Sedum ewersii has rounded grey-ish blue leaves on trailing stems that grow to about 15cm (6in) tall. The plant has a 30-45cm (1-1½ft) spread and in late summer to mid autumn carries rounded heads of pink or red flowers.
Sedum kamtschaticum is ever-green and about 10cm (4in) tall and 20cm (8in) wide. From mid summer to early autumn golden-yellow flowers in flattish clusters are held above tufts of spoon-shaped leaves. It grows well in semi-shade. 'Variegatum' has white-margined leaves and bears flowers that turn red in autumn.
Sedum oreganum, syn. *S. obtusatum*, grows only 7.5cm (3in) high but spreads to 23cm (9in). It forms loose evergreen rosettes of glossy green, rounded leaves suffused with red. Bright yellow flower heads on pink stems appear in summer.
Sedum pilosum, 7.5cm (3in) tall and 10cm (4in) wide, forms softly hairy rosettes covered with rose-pink flowers in late spring and early summer. It takes two or three years to flower and then dies, leaving plenty of seed.
Sedum pulchellum forms tufts of narrow lance-shaped, rich green leaves on erect, reddish stems up

123

Sedum spurium

Sempervivum
houseleek

Sempervivum montanum

Sedum kamtschaticum

to 7.5cm (3in) tall; it spreads to 15cm (6in). Rosy purple flowers are carried in branched sprays in mid and late summer.

Sedum reflexum, stone orpine, is an evergreen, mat-forming species, about 20cm (8in) high and 30cm (12in) or more wide, with egg-shaped, grey-green leaves. Wide, flat heads of bright yellow flowers are borne in mid summer.

Sedum sieboldii, much used in hanging baskets, is half-hardy and usually grown in an alpine house. It bears pink flowers during early and mid autumn, but the foliage is the chief attraction. Blue-grey rounded leaves are car-

ried in threes along spreading stems, making the plant some 7.5cm (3in) tall and 40cm (16in) wide. In the form 'Medio-Variegatum' the leaves are splashed with creamy yellow. The plants die down in winter.

Sedum spurium forms a tangled mat of evergreen, slightly toothed, oval, mid green leaves on reddish stems. Up to 10cm (4in) tall it spreads to 40cm (16in) and has flat heads of rich pink flowers in mid and late summer.

Cultivation
Plant from mid autumn to mid spring in ordinary, well-drained soil in a sunny, open position; *S. ewersii* tolerates semi-shade, and *S. pulchellum* prefers semi-shade and moist soil. Do not dead-head after flowering but leave the faded stems intact until the following spring when they can be easily snapped off.

Propagation Seed can be sown in a cold frame in spring, but division is easy and can be done from autumn to early spring.

Pests and diseases Generally trouble free, although slugs may attack large-leaved sedums.

SELF-HEAL – see *Prunella*

☐ Height 12mm-30cm (½-12in)
☐ Spread 20-30cm (8-12in)
☐ Foliage plants
☐ Well-drained soil
☐ Sunny position
☐ Evergreen perennial

Houseleeks have succulent leaves arranged in tight, perfectly symmetrical rosettes. Slowly spreading by means of short runners, the rosettes make low mounds and, being hardy and evergreen, provide all-year interest in a rock garden, dry wall or trough, or in pans in an alpine house.

Star-shaped flowers, with ten or more petals, are carried on a stout leafy stem from the centre of each rosette. After flowering the rosette dies, but is replaced by offsets. A few species have bell-shaped flowers and are often classified in the genus *Jovibarba*.

Popular species
Sempervivum arachnoideum (cobweb houseleek) has a covering of silvery, woolly hairs that stretch between the tips of the green, often red-flushed leaves. Bright pink flowers are carried on 15cm (6in) tall stems from early summer to early autumn. 'Laggeri' has deep pink flowers; 'Royal Ruby' bears ruby red leaves.

Sempervivum arenarium, syn. *Jovibarba arenaria*, is only 12mm (½in) high, with pale green and red leaf rosettes. It bears yellow flowers from mid summer onwards.

Shortia

shortia

Shortia uniflora 'Grandiflora'

□ Height 10-15cm (4-6in)
□ Spread 30-38cm (12-15in)
□ Flowers early to late spring
□ Neutral or acid moist soil
□ Partial shade
□ Evergreen perennial

Suitable for cool semi-shaded sites in a rock garden, shortias spread by creeping roots and runners. They are hardy, with evergreen leaves and fringed, funnel- or bell-shaped flowers.

Popular species

Shortia galacifolia, 15cm (6in) tall and 30cm (1ft) wide, has rounded, wavy-edged, pale green leaves, bronzing in autumn and winter. In mid and late spring, it bears white funnel-shaped flowers, fading to pink.

Shortia soldanelloides, up to 12.5cm (5in) high, has dark green, toothed leaves which are reddish in autumn, and sprays of deep rose, pendent flowers in mid and late spring.

Shortia uniflora forms a clump 10cm (4in) tall and 38cm (15in) wide. In early and mid spring it bears pale pink, funnel-shaped flowers. In 'Grandiflora' they are frilled and up to 5cm (2in) wide.

Cultivation

Plant in spring or autumn in rich well-drained but moist, neutral or acid soil and in partial shade. Dead-head after flowering.
Propagation Divide and replant in early summer. Softwood cuttings of basal shoots, taken in early summer, can be rooted in a cold frame.
Pests and diseases Trouble free.

Sempervivum tectorum

Sempervivum x *funckii* has rosettes up to 2.5cm (1in) high and 23cm (9in) across, with green, white-hairy, purple tipped leaves. Rose-purple flowers are borne on 15cm (6in) stems in mid summer.
Sempervivum grandiflorum has rosettes of densely hairy, purple-tipped, dark green leaves. They grow up to 10cm (4in) high and 20cm (8in) wide. Loose clusters of yellow-green, purple-stained flowers are borne in summer.
Sempervivum heuffelii, syn. *Jovibarba heuffelii*, has yellowish flowers on 15cm (6in) stems from mid summer to early autumn. Instead of having runners, the green or blue-green, sometimes red-flushed, rosettes split into two.
Sempervivum montanum has 2.5cm (1in) high rosettes of dark

Sempervivum tectorum calcareum

green, finely hairy leaves; pale red-purple flowers on 15cm (6in) stems are borne in summer.
Sempervivum soboliferum (hen-and-chickens houseleek), syn. *Jovibarba sobolifera*, takes its common name from the many small offset rosettes surrounding the main one. They are bright green, often flushed with red. Yellow, bell-shaped flowers sometimes appear in summer.
Sempervivum tectorum (common houseleek) has deep pink flowers on stems up to 30cm (1ft) tall from mid summer to early autumn. The bright green leaf rosettes, up to 7.5cm (3in) high and 30cm (1ft) across, are tinged and tipped with maroon. Numerous forms and hybrids with colourful rosettes include: *calcareum* (grey-green, tipped brownish purple); 'Commander Hay' (glossy purple red, green tipped); and 'Othello' (ruby red).

Cultivation

Plant in well-drained soil in a sunny position from early autumn to mid spring; *S. grandiflorum* dislikes lime.
Propagation Detach and replant rooted offsets in autumn or spring.
Pests and diseases Trouble free.

SHOOTING STAR – see
Dodecatheon

Silene

dwarf campion

Silene schafta

☐ Height 5-20cm (2-8in)
☐ Spread 15-45cm (6-18in)
☐ Flowers late spring to mid autumn
☐ Any well-drained soil
☐ Sunny position
☐ Perennial

Dwarf campions are tufted or clump-forming, hardy plants with mats of narrow leaves. The flowers are star or saucer shaped.

Popular species

Silene acaulis (moss campion) has pale green leaves and forms cushions about 5cm (2in) tall and up to 45cm (1½ft) wide. Almost stemless bright pink flowers appear during late spring and early summer.
Silene alpestris forms tufts 15cm (6in) tall and 15cm (6in) wide. In summer, sprays of white flowers with fringed petals are carried on wiry stems. 'Plena' ('Flore Pleno') is double-flowered.
Silene maritima (sea campion) has somewhat fleshy, grey-green leaves and lax stems on plants 15cm (6in) tall and 30cm (1ft) wide. White flowers appear in profusion from mid summer to early autumn. The larger-flowered double form, 'Plena' ('Flore Pleno'), is more commonly seen; 'Rosea' has pink, smaller flowers.
Silene schafta forms a green-leaved clump up to 15cm (6in) tall and about 30cm (1ft) wide. Magenta-pink flowers are borne from mid summer to mid autumn.

Silene maritima

Cultivation

Plant in early autumn to early spring in any good well-drained soil in a sunny position. Once planted, campions resent root disturbance. *S. acaulis* thrives in the gritty conditions of a scree bed or in a pan in the alpine house.
Propagation Take cuttings of basal shoots in summer and root in a cold frame.
Pests and diseases Trouble free.

Sisyrinchium

sisyrinchium

Sisyrinchium angustifolium

☐ Height 15-30cm (6-12in)
☐ Spread 15-30cm (6-12in)
☐ Flowers early spring to early autumn
☐ Well-drained soil
☐ Sunny position
☐ Herbaceous and evergreen perennials

These generally hardy little plants have a creeping rootstock, and six-petalled, often starry, flowers borne in clusters amid tufts of iris-like leaves. Each flower lasts no more than a day but is quickly replaced by others.

Popular species

Sisyrinchium angustifolium, syn. *S. gramineum* (blue-eyed grass), reaches 25cm (10in) tall with a spread of about 23cm (9in). It is semi-evergreen and clump-forming with tufts of grassy leaves. Iris-like, blue-violet flowers with a yellow eye open from mid summer to early autumn.
Sisyrinchium bermudiana resembles *S. angustifolium* though slightly taller and with profuse pale violet-blue flowers.
Sisyrinchium californicum (golden-eyed grass) is semi-evergreen and 30cm (1ft) or more high, with a spread of up to 30cm (1ft). It bears bright yellow flowers with darker veins during the summer.
Sisyrinchium douglasii (grass widow, spring bell), syn. *S. grandiflorum*, is up to 25cm (10in) tall. It is a herbaceous species that

Soldanella

soldanella, snowbell

Soldanella montana

Sisyrinchium bermudiana

grows in a neat clump of grassy foliage sheathing short-stalked, pendent bell flowers of rich purple in early spring. After flowering, it dies down completely to rest under the soil until early winter. *Sisyrinchium macounii*, syn. *S. idahoense* of gardens, rarely grows more than 10cm (4in) high and 15cm (6in) across. It bears grey-green narrow leaf fans and large violet-blue flowers throughout summer. 'May Snow' is a white-flowered form. Both plants do best in a sunny scree bed.

Cultivation

Plant from early autumn to early spring in good well-drained soil – *S. douglasii* dislikes lime and, because it becomes completely dormant from mid spring to early winter, it is advisable to mark the site. *S. californicum* prefers moist soil, and all species do best in sunny open sites; they resent root disturbance.

Propagation Overgrown clumps can be divided and replanted between autumn and spring. Alternatively, sow seeds in a cold frame during autumn or early spring. Several species will self-sow and may become a nuisance.

Pests and diseases Trouble free.

SKULLCAP – see *Scutellaria*
SLIPPER FLOWER – see *Calceolaria*
SNOWBELL – see *Soldanella*
SNOWFLAKE – see *Leucojum*
SNOW-IN-SUMMER – see *Cerastium*
SOAPWORT – see *Saponaria*

☐ Height 5-7.5cm (2-3in)
☐ Spread 15-30cm (6-12in)
☐ Flowers early and mid spring
☐ Cool, well-drained acid soil
☐ Partial shade
☐ Perennial

With charming pendent, bluish, bell-shaped and fringed flowers, soldanellas are among the best-loved alpine plants. They flower from early spring onwards, and although the plants are fully hardy, the flower buds, which form in autumn, are often damaged without a cover of snow. Soldanellas thrive in rock garden pockets, troughs and peat beds.

Popular species

Soldanella alpina (alpine snowbell) is 7.5cm (3in) tall and 23cm (9in) wide with kidney-shaped, rich green leaves and lavender-purple flower clusters in early spring.

Soldanella minima is only 5cm (2in) tall and forms a prostrate mat 15cm (6in) wide of tiny round, glossy green leaves. Minute pale violet or white flowers with narrow fringes appear during spring.

Soldanella montana resembles *S. alpina*, but is more robust, up to 15cm (6in) tall and with a spread of 30cm (1ft). It has clusters of lavender flowers on sturdy stems in early and mid spring.

Soldanella pindicola grows up to 15cm (6in) high and 30cm (12in) across. It bears rounded deep green leaves and lavender-blue, pendent bell flowers in spring.

Soldanella pusilla is about 7.5cm (3in) tall and 15cm (6in) wide. Pale lavender flowers are carried singly rather than in a cluster.

Soldanella villosa is probably a variant of *S. montana* but with leathery leaves on hairy stalks. The flowers are similar.

Cultivation

Plant in early and mid autumn or in late spring, in well-drained acid soil. It is advisable to surround the plants with stone chippings to ensure perfect drainage, and to raise panes of glass as protection from winter rain.

Propagation Divide and replant in mid summer. Alternatively, take cuttings of basal shoots in late spring or early summer and root in a cold frame.

Pests and diseases Slugs may eat the flower buds and destroy succulent young growth.

Solidago
golden rod

Solidago virgaurea nana

- ☐ Height 15-23cm (6-9in)
- ☐ Spread up to 15cm (6in)
- ☐ Flowers late summer to early autumn
- ☐ Any well-drained soil
- ☐ Sun or partial shade
- ☐ Perennial

Forming bushy little clumps, dwarf golden rods bear golden-yellow, daisy-like flower heads in erect, leafy pyramids. They bloom late in the season, at a time when rock gardens are bereft of colour. Plants are usually listed as *Solidago virgaurea brachystachys*, *S. virgaurea nana* or *S. v. minuta*.

Cultivation
Plant between autumn and spring in any well-drained soil in a sunny or slightly shaded site.
Propagation Divide and replant in spring.
Pests and diseases Powdery mildew may disfigure growth.

Teucrium
germander

Teucrium pyrenaicum

- ☐ Height 5-20cm (2-8in)
- ☐ Spread 30-45cm (1-1½ft)
- ☐ Flowers early summer to early autumn
- ☐ Well-drained soil
- ☐ Sunny, sheltered position
- ☐ Evergreen sub-shrub

These small creeping sub-shrubs bear short terminal spikes or flattened whorls of tubular flowers with a prominent lower lip. The evergreen foliage is often aromatic. Generally hardy, germanders are suitable for ground cover in rock gardens, troughs and scree beds.

Popular species
Teucrium aroanium is 10cm (4in) tall and about 30cm (1ft) wide. Oval silver-grey leaves on rooting stems contrast with the grey-blue flowers in mid and late summer.
Teucrium chamaedrys (wall germander) is up to 20cm (8in) tall and 30cm (12in) wide. Its oak-like, aromatic leaves are bright green above and greyish below. Spikes of pinkish flowers are borne from mid summer to early autumn.
Teucrium pyrenaicum forms a creeping mat, 5cm (2in) high and up to 38cm (15in) across. The hairy, rounded leaves are silver-green. From early to late summer it bears dense heads of small mauve and cream flowers.
Teucrium rosmarinifolium, syn. *T. creticum*, is 7.5cm (3in) tall and spreads its trailing stems to 30cm (1ft). White hairs on the narrow, oblong leaves give them a silver-grey appearance. Clusters of rose-purple flowers, with a white woolly calyx, are borne from early summer to autumn.

Cultivation
Plant from autumn to spring in any, even poor, well-drained soil, in full sun. Trim the plants to shape after flowering.
Propagation Take cuttings of basal or lateral shoots in summer and root in a cold frame.
Pests and diseases Generally trouble free.

Teucrium chamaedrys

Thalictrum

dwarf meadow rue

Thalictrum orientale

- ☐ Height 15cm (6in)
- ☐ Spread 15-20cm (6-8in)
- ☐ Flowers early summer to early autumn
- ☐ Moist but well-drained soil
- ☐ Sun or partial shade
- ☐ Perennial

Like the tall border forms, dwarf meadow rues have elegant fern-like leaves and sprays of fluffy flowers.

Popular species

Thalictrum coreanum is about 15cm (6in) tall and wide with bronze-tinted leaves. Lilac flowers are borne on wiry stems in mid summer and early autumn.
Thalictrum kiusianum is a tufted species, 15cm (6in) high and wide, with deeply divided, grey to bronzy leaves and lilac-purple flowers in early and mid summer.
Thalictrum orientale, up to 15cm (6in) tall, spreads slowly by underground runners. Fern-like leaves contrast handsomely with the rich pink flowers in summer.

Cultivation

Plant in early or mid spring in rich, moist, but well-drained soil in a semi-shaded position.
Propagation Divide and replant in spring. Or sow seeds in early spring in a cold frame.
Pests and diseases Trouble free.

THISTLE (STEMLESS) – see *Carlina*
THRIFT – see *Armeria*
THYME – see *Thymus*

Thymus

thyme

Thymus praecox 'Albus'

- ☐ Height 5-15cm (2-6in)
- ☐ Spread 25-60cm (10-24in)
- ☐ Flowers early to late summer
- ☐ Well-drained soil
- ☐ Sunny position
- ☐ Evergreen sub-shrub

Thymes are hardy mat-formers or bushy sub-shrubs with evergreen aromatic leaves. Small tubular two-lipped flowers are carried in dense spikes or heads. They are invaluable for ground cover on banks and in rock gardens, for planting in troughs and in crevices in dry walls and paving.

Popular species

Thymus x *citriodorus* grows 15-20cm (6-8in) high, with a similar spread. The green foliage is lemon-scented, and is often used for culinary purposes; small clusters of pale lilac flowers are borne throughout summer. 'Aureus' has golden leaves.
Thymus doerfleri makes a 7.5cm (3in) tall carpet, up to 45cm (1½ft) wide, of grey-green hairy leaves. It bears lilac-pink flower clusters in early and mid summer.
Thymus x 'Doone Valley' is mat-forming, 7.5cm (3in) tall and 30cm (1ft) wide, with green and gold variegated leaves and round spikes of lavender flowers.
Thymus herba-barona makes a caraway-scented, dark green mat 5-10cm (2-4in) high and 40cm (16in) across, with lilac flowers in early summer.
Thymus praecox is the species formerly known as and still listed as *T. serpyllum*. It forms a mat up to 7.5cm (3in) high and 60cm (2ft) across. Blooming in the summer, it is usually represented by named varieties, such as 'Albus' (white); 'Annie Hall' (pink); 'Coccineus' (crimson); and 'Elfin' (bright green foliage, pink flowers).

Cultivation

Plant between autumn and early spring in well-drained soil in a sunny position. Shear the plants over after flowering to maintain dense, compact shapes.
Propagation Divide and replant in early spring or late summer. Alternatively, take heel cuttings in late spring and early summer and root in a cold frame.
Pests and diseases Trouble free.

TOADFLAX – see *Linaria*

Thymus x 'Doone Valley'

Thymus praecox 'Coccineus'

Townsendia
townsendia

Townsendia formosana

- ☐ Height 5-15cm (2-6in)
- ☐ Spread 10cm (4in)
- ☐ Flowers late spring and early summer
- ☐ Well-drained soil
- ☐ Sunny position
- ☐ Evergreen perennial

Townsendias are hardy but short-lived plants with aster-like flowers. They are excellent in troughs and rock garden pockets but dislike winter wet.

Popular species
Townsendia exscapa grows 5cm (2in) tall and 10cm (4in) wide. White or pink flowers, with prominent yellow centres, are borne on short stems above narrow grey leaves.
Townsendia formosa, often listed as *T. formosana*, is a tufted plant 10cm (4in) tall and wide. The flowers are violet-blue with orange discs.
Townsendia parryi, often biennial, is 15cm (6in) tall and 10cm (4in) wide. The daisy-like flowers of lavender-blue with yellow centres are carried above a rosette of spatula-shaped leaves.

Cultivation
Plant in spring in well-drained, but moisture-retentive soil in a sunny position.
Propagation Sow seed in autumn in a cold frame; plant out in mid spring.
Pests and diseases Generally trouble free.

Trifolium
clover

Trifolium 'Purpurascens Quadrifolium'

- ☐ Height 5-10cm (2-4in)
- ☐ Spread 45-60cm (1½-2ft)
- ☐ Foliage plant
- ☐ Any well-drained soil
- ☐ Sunny position
- ☐ Evergreen perennial

Several unusual alpine clovers are sometimes offered by specialist growers, but the only clover generally available is a decorative form of the common white clover, *Trifolium repens*. Despite its name, 'Purpurascens Quadrifolium', this clover may have three, five or six leaves as well as the 'lucky' four.

While the pea-like flowers are of little ornamental value – although they do attract bees – the foliage is attractively coloured dark purple with a green edge. Rooting at the leaf nodes as it spreads, the plant can be invasive and should be kept away from more delicate plants. It makes semi-evergreen ground cover, suitable for small bulbs.

Cultivation
Plant from mid autumn to mid spring in any well-drained soil in a large sunny rock garden or on a bank.
Propagation Divide and replant in mid spring. Rooted runners can be detached, potted up and grown on.
Pests and diseases Powdery mildew may disfigure the foliage.

Tropaeolum
nasturtium

Tropaeolum polyphyllum

- ☐ Height 15cm (6in)
- ☐ Spread 90cm (3ft)
- ☐ Flowers early and mid summer
- ☐ Fertile, well-drained soil
- ☐ Sunny position
- ☐ Perennial

Dwarf varieties of the half-hardy annual nasturtium can be planted in rock gardens, but the perennial *Tropaeolum polyphyllum* is a better choice. It is prostrate with trailing stems, 45cm (1½ft) or more long, set with grey-green, palmate leaves. In early and mid summer each stem is covered with trumpet-shaped yellow flowers, sometimes shaded orange. Each is about 12mm (½in) across and has a 2cm (¾in) long spur.

Because of its growth habit trailing nasturtium looks best where the stems can trail over a slope or wall. After flowering the stems die back and the plant overwinters as a resting tuber.

Cultivation
Plant the tubers in early or mid spring in fertile, well-drained soil, in sheltered sunny positions.
Propagation Divide and replant established clumps in early spring.
Pests and diseases Aphids may infest flowers and foliage.

Tsuga

dwarf eastern hemlock

Tsuga canadensis 'Cole'

☐ Height 15-90cm (6-36in)
☐ Spread 25-90cm (10-36in)
☐ Foliage plant
☐ Moist, well-drained soil
☐ Partially shaded position
☐ Evergreen conifer

The eastern hemlock, *Tsuga canadensis*, is a tall conifer which has sported several dwarf, slow-growing forms suitable as specimens in rock gardens. The sizes given below are reached after about ten years. The narrow foliage, arranged in two rows along the branches, has twin silver bands underneath.

Popular varieties

'Cole' ('Cole's Prostrate') is prostrate, 15cm (6in) high, with ground-hugging branches spreading to a carpet 90cm (3ft) wide.
'Minuta' forms a small-leaved bun, 25cm (10in) tall and wide.
'Nana Gracilis' grows as a flat-topped mound, 45cm (1½ft) tall and 90cm (3ft) wide, with graceful arching branches.
'Pendula' has weeping branches that make a dense mound 90cm (3ft) tall and 60cm (2ft) wide.
'Rugg's Washington Dwarf' is a dense, globular or mound-shaped variety, about 60cm (2ft) high and wide.

Cultivation

Plant from mid autumn to early spring in a partially shaded and sheltered site. Tsugas thrive in deep, well-drained but moisture-retentive soil and dislike shallow chalk.
Propagation Take heel cuttings of lateral shoots in early autumn and root in a cold frame.
Pests and diseases Trouble free.

Tsuga canadensis 'Pendula'

Tulipa

tulip

Tulipa kaufmanniana

☐ Height 10-38cm (4-15in)
☐ Spread 7.5-15cm (3-6in)
☐ Flowers early to late spring
☐ Well-drained soil
☐ Sunny position
☐ Bulb

The hardy dwarf species tulips may lack the flamboyance of the large hybrids used for bedding, but they have the grace and charm characteristic of most rock garden plants. The flowers are typically goblet-shaped, sometimes with slender-pointed petals, sometimes cup- or bowl-shaped. They all open wide in full sunshine and close up at night, and most are borne one per stem. The leaves are generally grey-green to rich green and lance-shaped.

Popular species

Tulipa aucheriana is 10cm (4in) tall with scented, starry, yellow-centred, rose-pink flowers in mid spring.
Tulipa batalinii has cream-yellow flowers on 15cm (6in) stems in mid to late spring.
Tulipa biflora has up to five starry flowers on each 15cm (6in) stem. White with yellow centres, shaded green and red outside, they open in early and mid spring.
Tulipa clusiana chrysantha (lady tulip) is 15-20cm (6-8in) high, with yellow flowers in mid spring. The petals are flushed red on the outside.
Tulipa eichleri, up to 30cm (12in) high, bears scarlet flowers with a

Tulipa batalinii

Tulipa linifolia

basal black blotch edged with yellow. They open to 10cm (4in) wide in early and mid spring.

Tulipa kaufmanniana (water lily tulip), the parent of many hybrids, is a variable species, 10-25cm (4-10in) high. In early spring it opens star-like, 7.5cm (3in) wide flowers of creamy white, centred yellow, and flushed red and yellow on the outside. The flowers of 'Heart's Delight' are carmine-red on the outside, pale rose inside; those of 'Shakespeare' are carmine-red edged salmon outside, and shaded scarlet and gold inside.

Tulipa linifolia, up to 20cm (8in) tall, has a rosette of narrow leaves. Scarlet flowers with black bases and pointed petals open in mid to late spring. *T. maximowiczii* is similar but flowers slightly earlier, and the petal bases are less distinctly marked bluish black.

Tulipa pulchella grows 10-15cm (4-6in) high, with small flowers opening flat, often three to a stem, in late winter or early spring. The flowers are crimson to purplish red with a white-edged bluish base. The narrow leaves are edged with red. 'Violacea' is deep purple-violet with a yellow base.

Tulipa sylvestris, 38cm (15in) tall, has yellow flowers with reflexed outer petals. They open during mid and late spring.

Tulipa tarda is 10cm (4in) tall and bears starry white flowers in early spring, heavily suffused with yellow in the centres. The flowers are carried in clusters of up to five. The leaves are slender and strap-shaped.

Tulipa turkestanica, 25cm (10in) tall, has up to nine starry flowers per stem. Creamy white with orange-yellow centres, they open in mid spring.

Tulipa urumiensis is also multi-flowered, growing 10cm (4in) tall. In mid spring it opens yellow, star-shaped flowers that are olive-green and red on the outside.

Cultivation

Plant the bulbs 7.5-10cm (3-4in) deep and 7.5cm (3in) apart (*T. kaufmanniana* 15cm/6in apart) during late autumn in good well-drained soil in rock garden sites where they can be baked by the sun; *T. sylvestris* accepts partial shade. Most dwarf tulips can be left to multiply where they grow, but they can also be lifted and stored after the foliage has died down.

Propagation Separate and replant offsets when plants are lifted; depending on size they will flower after a couple of years.

Pests and diseases Slugs feed on top-growth and bulbs; tulip fire (botrytis) may cause scorched areas on leaves and flowers. Mice dig up and eat the bulbs.

Tulipa aucheriana

Vaccinium

blueberry

Valeriana montana

Vaccinium vitis-idaea

☐ Height 10-30cm (4-12in)
☐ Spread 30-45cm (1-1½ft)
☐ Flowers mid spring to mid summer
☐ Moist acid soil
☐ Sunny or partially shaded position
☐ Evergreen shrub

Blueberries belong to the heather family and, like most of their relatives, must have lime-free soil. The genus *Vaccinium* includes several large decorative and fruiting shrubs, but the following are small enough for a rock garden or a peat bed. Those described are hardy evergreens. The bell- or urn-shaped flowers are followed by edible fruits.

Popular species

Vaccinium nummularia grows about 30cm (1ft) tall and wide. Moderately hardy and suitable for a shady, sheltered site in mild areas, it has compact arching branches with round, dark green, leathery leaves. In mid and late spring the tips of the shoots bear clusters of pink to rosy red flowers, followed by shining black fruits.

Vaccinium oxycoccos (cranberry), syn. *Oxycoccos palustris*, is a prostrate creeper growing 45cm (1½ft) wide and 7.5cm (3in) high with tiny oval leaves, glossy green above and silvery below. In late spring and mid summer it bears pink flowers with reflexed petals, followed by red fruits.

Vaccinium vitis-idaea (cowberry) forms a spreading mat 10-25cm (4-10in) high and 45cm (1½ft) wide, with dark green, box-like leaves on the arching stems. Fully hardy, it has clusters of white or pinkish urn-shaped flowers in late spring and early summer, followed by red fruits.

Cultivation

Plant dwarf blueberries between mid autumn and early spring in acid, moisture-retentive and rich soil. Choose a sunny or slightly shaded spot.

Propagation Layer any long shoots in early autumn. The rooted portions can be severed and replanted after one or two years. Alternatively, take half-ripe cuttings in mid summer and root them in a cold frame; set out the young plants in a nursery bed in mid autumn of the following year and grow on for two or three years before transferring to their final positions.

Pests and diseases Trouble free.

Valeriana

dwarf valerian

☐ Height 10-23cm (4-9in)
☐ Spread 23cm (9in)
☐ Flowers late spring to late summer
☐ Any well-drained soil
☐ Sunny position
☐ Perennial

Dwarf valerians are neater versions of their border cousins, with basal mats of glossy leaves, and flat heads of small white or pinkish tubular flowers on short stems. The seeds are feathery. Easily grown, they are good choices for rock gardens and paving cracks.

Popular species

Valeriana arizonica spreads to about 23cm (9in) and is at the most 15cm (6in) tall. It is a clump-forming, rhizomatous plant with fresh green leaves and heads of pale pink flowers during late spring.

Valeriana montana has a spread of about 15cm (6in) and usually grows 10cm (4in) high. It has somewhat woody rhizomes and, from mid to late summer, bears flat heads of lilac, pink or white flowers.

Valeriana saxatilis has much the same dimensions as *V. montana*, but the flowering stems generally lack leaves, and the heads of dainty white flowers appear in early summer.

Cultivation

Plant valerians between mid autumn and early spring in ordinary well-drained soil in a sunny spot. They will tolerate light shade, and thrive in limy soils.

Propagation Divide and replant in early autumn or spring.

Pests and diseases Generally trouble free.

Verbascum

dwarf mullein

Verbascum 'Letitia'

□ Height 25-30cm (10-12in)
□ Spread 25-30cm (10-12in)
□ Flowers early to late summer
□ Any sharply-drained soil
□ Sunny position
□ Evergreen sub-shrub

The tall border mulleins, many biennials among them, are noted for their large basal leaf rosettes and massive candelabras of flowers. Alpine species, however, are moderately hardy, sub-shrubby plants with greyish hairy leaves and yellow flowers carried in sprays or clusters.

Ideally, dwarf mulleins should be grown in sunny screes and similar situations with protection from winter wet, or in the shelter of an alpine house.

Popular species

Verbascum dumulosum makes a rounded shrub about 30cm (1ft) tall and wide. The ovate leaves are covered with soft grey hairs. Sulphur-yellow flowers are carried in

Verbascum dumulosum

rounded clusters for much of the summer.

Verbascum 'Letitia' is a hybrid between *V. dumulosum* and *V. spinosum*. It forms a compact shrub about 25cm (10in) tall and wide, with grey-green, toothed leaves. Loose spikes of clear yellow flowers with brown basal blotches are carried from early to late summer.

Verbascum spinosum, up to 30cm (1ft) tall and wide, is a shrublet of twiggy, congested growth with toothed and spiny, grey leaves. Profuse, clear yellow flowers are borne in the leaf axils during early and mid summer.

Cultivation

Plant in spring in very well-drained soil, such as a scree mixture. Rock crevices, dry walls, and raised beds against sunny walls are all suitable positions. Dead-head after flowering. The hairy leaves are easily damaged by winter wet, but the plants can be protected with raised panes of glass. Alternatively, grow them in an alpine house. Cut away any dead growth in spring.

Propagation Take 5cm (2in) heel cuttings during summer and root in a cold frame.

Pests and diseases Generally trouble free.

Veronica

dwarf speedwell

Veronica cinerea

□ Height 7.5-38cm (3-15in)
□ Spread 20-45cm (8-18in)
□ Flowers early spring and summer
□ Any well-drained soil
□ Sunny position
□ Evergreen perennial

Dwarf speedwells are hardy mat-forming plants for troughs, screes, paving cracks and walls. Their spikes of small saucer-shaped flowers in blue, pink and white provide a mass of colour throughout summer.

Popular species

Veronica armena, about 10cm (4in) tall and 20cm (8in) across, has prostrate branching stems clothed in finely cut, grey-green leaves. Bright blue flowers appear in late spring and early summer.

Veronica cinerea, 10cm (4in) high and 40cm (16in) wide, has toothed, narrow grey-green leaves, and pale blue flowers in early and mid summer.

Veronica fruticans, syn. *V. saxatilis*, is 15cm (6in) tall and 30cm (12in) wide. Sub-shrubby, it has oval leaves and deep blue flowers with a red eye in summer.

Veronica gentianoides makes mats 45cm (1½ft) across of glossy lance-shaped leaves. In early summer it bears 38cm (15in) tall spikes of palest blue flowers. 'Var-

Veronica gentianoides

Vinca minor

Vinca
lesser periwinkle

☐ Height 5-10cm (2-4in)
☐ Spread 90-120cm (3-4ft)
☐ Flowers early spring to mid summer
☐ Ordinary well-drained soil
☐ Partially shaded or sunny site
☐ Evergreen sub-shrub

iegata', with leaves boldly marked creamy white, is less vigorous, while 'Nana' has flower spikes only 23cm (9in) tall.

Veronica pectinata, which forms a mat, up to 38cm (15in) wide, of toothed grey-green leaves, is about 7.5cm (3in) tall. Short spikes of deep blue flowers appear in late spring and early summer. 'Rosea' has pink flowers.

Veronica prostrata, syn. *V. rupestris*, grows as a leafy mat 40cm (16in) across with 20cm (8in) tall spikes of deep blue flowers in summer. 'Trehane' bears violet-blue flower spikes.

Cultivation
Plant in well-drained soil in a sunny site between early autumn and early spring. Dead-head after flowering.

Propagation Divide and replant in spring; or take cuttings of lateral shoots in summer and root in a cold frame.

Pests and diseases Powdery mildew may affect the leaves.

The lesser periwinkle, *Vinca minor*, is a hardy sub-shrub with trailing and creeping stems set with glossy, elliptical leaves. Up to 10cm (4in) tall and 1.2m (4ft) wide, it makes good ground cover in light shade or sun. Five-petalled flowers, usually blue and 2.5cm (1in) across, appear from early spring to mid or late summer.

Numerous varieties are available and include: 'Alba' (white); 'La Grave' (large sky-blue); and 'Multiplex' (double, red-purple). Less vigorous forms with variegated leaves include: 'Argenteo-variegata' (cream-white, blue flowers); and 'Aureo-variegata' (golden-yellow leaf markings, blue flowers).

Cultivation
Plant in any well-drained soil in partial shade from early autumn to early spring. In early spring, trim the plants back to curb their spread if necessary.

Propagation Self-rooting at the leaf nodes, the trailing stems can be severed and replanted. Cuttings taken in early autumn or early spring will root in open ground.

Pests and diseases Trouble free.

Veronica prostrata

Viola

viola, violetta, violet

Viola tricolor

Viola cornuta

☐ Height 7.5-25cm (3-10in)
☐ Spread 15-40cm (6-16in)
☐ Flowers late winter to mid autumn
☐ Fertile, moist soil
☐ Sunny or partially shaded position
☐ Perennial

Violas are indispensable in rock gardens and scree beds. Sun and shade-loving species occur, with charming five-petalled flowers in a wide range of colours and a long-flowering season.

Popular species and varieties

Viola aetolica, syn. *V. saxatilis aetolica*, is a clump-forming species, about 5cm (2in) high and 15cm (6in) across. It bears mid green oval leaves, and clear yellow, flat-faced flowers in late spring and early summer.

Viola biflora is 7.5cm (3in) tall and spreads to 30cm (1ft). It has heart-shaped, bright green leaves and yellow flowers, generally in pairs, from early summer to early autumn. This species prefers partial shade.

Viola cornuta (horned violet) makes 30cm (1ft) wide mats of oval to lance-shaped leaves, above which violet-purple, spurred flowers on 25cm (10in) stems are carried from early summer to early autumn. Named forms include the neat 'Minor', particularly suitable for a rock garden. 'Boughton Blue' has clear blue flowers.

Viola gracilis is up to 15cm (6in) tall and 30cm (1ft) wide with oval leaves and deep violet, long-spurred flowers in summer.

Viola lutea is a mat-forming species, about 10cm (4in) high with a spread of 15cm (6in). Yellow flowers, veined with brown or purple, are carried above the oval to lance-shaped leaves in summer.

Viola odorata (sweet violet), up to 15cm (4in) high, spreads by runners, to 30cm (1ft) or more across. The fragrant violet-coloured flowers appear from late winter to mid spring above heart-shaped leaves. Thriving in partial shade, it has many named forms, including: 'Alba' (white); 'Coeur d'Alsace' (rose-pink); and 'Sulphurea' (cream-yellow).

Viola papilionacea, with broad heart-shaped leaves, is 20cm (8in) high and 30cm (1ft) across. Dark blue or purple flowers appear from mid spring to mid summer. Best in partial shade.

Viola pedata (bird's-foot violet) has deeply divided leaves and makes a tuft 12cm (5in) high and 7.5cm (3in) across. Violet-purple, yellow-eyed flowers are borne in mid and late spring. Best grown in the alpine house.

Viola tricolor (heartsease) is up to 15cm (6in) high and wide. The flowers vary from cream and yellow to dark blue and purple-black; there are also bi- and tricolours. It is a self-sowing annual or biennial, or a short-lived perennial, and blooms from mid spring to mid autumn – often longer. It tolerates partial shade. One parent of the garden pansies, heartsease is also involved in the violetta hybrids, whose 2.5cm (1in) wide flowers are in keeping with other rock garden plants. Among the many available violettas are: 'Iden Gem' (dark blue); 'Little David' (creamy white); and 'Martin' (deep mauve-purple).

Cultivation

Plant in early and mid autumn or

Violetta hybrid 'Martin'

early to mid spring in fertile, moist but well-drained soil in a sunny or shady site. Dead-head regularly to extend the flowering season.

Propagation Sow seeds in early or mid spring, outdoors in a moist, shady site, or in a cold frame. Grow on in nursery rows or prick out the seedlings into pots; plant out in early to mid autumn. Alternatively, take cuttings of basal shoots in mid summer.

Pests and diseases Slugs, rust and leaf spot may damage leaves and flowers.

Viola lutea

Waldsteinia

waldsteinia

Waldsteinia ternata

- ☐ Height 10cm (4in)
- ☐ Spread 45cm (1½ft)
- ☐ Flowers late spring and early summer
- ☐ Well-drained soil
- ☐ Sun or partial shade
- ☐ Evergreen perennial

Excellent for ground cover, the hardy *Waldsteinia ternata*, syn. *W. trifolia*, spreads from woody rhizomes to wide mats of toothed, dark green, lobed leaves. In autumn, the foliage takes on bronzy tints. Clusters of buttercup-yellow, saucer-shaped flowers are freely borne from late spring onwards.

Cultivation
Plant in autumn or spring in any well-drained soil in sun or partial shade.
Propagation Divide and replant in autumn or spring.
Pests and diseases Trouble free.

WALLFLOWER – see *Erysimum*
WHITLOW GRASS – see *Draba*
WILLOW (DWARF) – see *Salix*
WILLOW HERB – see *Epilobium*
WINTER ACONITE – see *Eranthis*
WINTERGREEN – see *Gaultheria*
WOOD SORREL – see *Oxalis*
WOODRUFF – see *Asperula*
YARROW – see *Achillea*

Zauschneria

Californian fuchsia

Zauschneria californica

- ☐ Height 30-45cm (1-1½ft)
- ☐ Spread 45cm (1½ft)
- ☐ Flowers late summer to mid autumn
- ☐ Well-drained soil
- ☐ Sheltered sunny position
- ☐ Shrubby perennial

The Californian fuchsia, *Zauschneria californica*, is a shrubby perennial, hardy in mild areas and, once established, long-lived. It is valued for its fuchsia-like flowers borne at the end of summer and well into autumn. It needs all the sun and warmth it can get and good drainage for the roots.

Clump-forming from a woody rootstock, the plant produces slender arching stems, set with lance-shaped, grey-green leaves, to a height and spread of 45cm (1½ft). The vivid scarlet, tubular flowers, with flared mouths like some fuchsia species, are carried in loose sprays throughout late summer. The sub-species *Z. californica microphylla* (or *Z. cana* as it is sometimes known) has smaller and narrower grey leaves, while *Z. californica latifolia* has broader leaves. The most reliable form is

'Glasnevin' ('Dublin Variety'), which has rich green leaves and flowers of a more intense scarlet.

Cultivation
Plant in autumn or spring in well-drained soil in a sunny sheltered position – at the back of a rock garden or trailing from retaining walls or raised beds. Except in frost-free areas, protect the base of the plants with a winter mulch or cloches. In spring, cut back any frosted stems to just above ground level.
Propagation Established clumps can be divided and replanted in mid spring though they do not split easily. It is easier to propagate from basal cuttings in late spring and root them in a propagator unit.
Pests and diseases Young growth may be attacked by aphids. In a severe infestation, leaves and stems can become distorted and may wilt and die.

Pool marginals Primulas and variegated water irises are dwarfed by a huge *Gunnera manicata*.

A-Z of water plants

Plants are an essential part of every garden pool. They add to its decorative appeal and also play an important role in creating a well-balanced environment for animal life.

Of the many plants that can be grown in or near water, water lilies are undoubtedly the best loved and most enchanting, with their exquisite cup-shaped blooms that open during the day and close at night. Many species, and even more hybrids, are available in every colour except blue. They grow in water depths ranging from 15cm (6in) to 90cm (3ft); other deep-water aquatics include water hawthorn (*Aponogeton*), pond lilies (*Nuphar*) and golden club (*Orontium*).

Other plants which also grow in deep water are known as floaters and oxygenators. Floaters, which include frogbit and water soldier, may be less spectacular than water lilies, but they are useful for covering the water surface and thus providing shade for fish. Oxygenators, which are submerged, include Canadian and curly pondweeds; though invisible, they are essential for controlling algae and maintaining a balanced ecosystem in the pool.

Another, larger, group of water plants are the marginals, which grow in shallow water at the pool edge. Water irises, sweet flag, marsh marigolds, rushes and arums are just a few examples. Away from the water, but in the boggy ground by streams and ponds, moisture-loving perennials, often known as bog plants, find their perfect habitat – hostas, primulas, water avens and hogweed, ferns, gunneras and purple loosestrife all grow more abundantly here than in dry garden borders.

A pool needs little attention once established. Water lilies and marginals should be lifted, divided and replanted every few years, and floating plants may need thinning at the start of the growing season. Few pests trouble water plants, apart from water lily aphids and water lily beetles. Do not use insecticides, which can be harmful to fish, but dislodge the pests with a forceful spray from a hose.

GROWING WATER PLANTS

Garden pools contain a mixture of plant and animal life, exotic lilies floating on the surface and fish darting among submerged oxygenators.

All garden pools should be sited in full light or the plants will not flower. The water should be clear, with about half its surface free from vegetation. In order to maintain fresh, healthy water it is essential that a balance between plant and animal life is achieved.

Murky green water is caused by a build-up of algae – microscopic plants that thrive on sunlight and feed on mineral salts in the water. Such salts are released through the decomposition of fallen leaves and other organic materials – peat and garden compost should never be used in a pool. Oxygenators – plants that live beneath the water surface – prevent the incidence of algae by feeding on any mineral salts and by shading the pool. They also take in the carbon dioxide exhaled by fish and other animals and in turn release oxygen, which is essential to fish and snails.

Planting water lilies

The size and depth of the pool determine the type and number of water lilies it can hold. Hundreds of named varieties are available, and they are generally divided into a number of categories. Miniature types require a water depth of 10-23cm (4-9in) and are ideal for tiny pools and water-filled tubs. They have a surface spread of 30-45cm (1-1½ft).

Small water lilies need slightly deeper water – about 15-30cm (6-12in) – and spread to 45-75cm (1½-2½ft) across. Medium types are suitable for large pools. They need a water depth of 15-45cm (6-18in) and will spread to 75-90cm (2½-3ft) across. Large water lilies should only be chosen for pools with a depth up to 90cm (3ft) and an expanse of water broad enough to accommodate their spread of up to 3m (10ft).

Water lilies and other true aquatics, such as water hawthorn and water fringe, are best planted in purpose-made plastic baskets obtainable from water garden nurseries. They restrict excessive growth and make it harder for fish to disturb the soil. Established plants, sold in containers, can be put in the pool at any time, but it is cheaper to buy young plants for setting out in late spring.

Prepare a planting mixture of good heavy loam (avoid humus of any kind) and add a couple of handfuls of sterilized bonemeal to each bucket, and sufficient water to make a pliable mixture.

Line the basket with a proprietary nylon or polythene liner or

▼ **Pool harmony** Surface-floating water lilies and submerged oxygenators create a balanced ecosystem in which fish and other animal life flourish.

▲ Pool depths A series of pools are set at different levels to hold aquatics of various types. The deepest pool is reserved for water lilies. The lush waterside planting includes rushes, ornamental grasses, luxuriant clumps of hostas and, on the right, the imposing purple-leaved *Ligularia dentata*.

▶ Water iris The blue-flowered *Iris laevigata* thrives in shallow water at pool margins. It colonizes readily and bears its deep royal blue flowers in early summer, well before the water lilies open their exquisite flower cups.

▲ **Duckweed** Charming as a contrast to large lily pads, duckweed should nevertheless be discouraged from ornamental pools. It spreads rapidly and soon obscures the entire water surface.

◄ **Bog plants** The shady moist soil by a woodland stream is ideal for perennials such as candelabra primulas, globe flowers (*Trollius*) and ferns.

▼ **Crimson beauty** The brilliantly coloured water lily 'James Brydon' and the creamy water hawthorn are centre-pieces in a pool in late summer. Vertical contrast is provided by the variegated leaves of sweet flag (*Acorus calamus*).

▲ **Poolside plants** Many garden perennials perform far better in the moist soil by the water's edge than in herbaceous borders. Notable examples include hostas and astilbes with their tall feathery plumes in shades of pink. The yellow-flowered mimulus will also grow in shallow water.

◀ **Icy pond** In deepest winter, water continues to fascinate, mirroring in its glassy surface the surrounding landscape rimmed with frost. Sombre and still conifers add touches of green.

145

hessian and fill it with the soil mixture to 2.5cm (1in) of the top. The rootstock of water lilies vary. Some are tuberous, with bulky anchorage roots and a ruff of fibrous roots just below the crown; they should be planted vertically in the soil. Others are rhizomatous, with long fleshy anchorage roots, and should be planted horizontally. Make sure that the growing points of the shoots on both types protrude just above the soil surface. This can be covered with a 2.5cm (1in) layer of fine shingle to prevent disturbance by fish.

Don't immerse newly planted water lilies to their final depth immediately. In an established pool, set the basket on a pile of bricks so the shoots are just above the surface. Remove a few bricks every few weeks as growth progresses until the basket is standing on the bottom.

Planting oxygenators
Oxygenating plants spend their lives underwater. They are usually

▶ **Formal pool** The straight lines of a formal concrete pool can appear severe, but here the eye is irresistibly drawn to the focal point in one corner. An ornate urn holding a tall spiky *Cordyline australis* perfectly complements a serene Victorian bust.

▼ **Streamside planting** The banks of natural streams are ideal, semi-wild habitats for moisture-loving plants, such as tall candelabra primulas, ferns and self-sown Welsh poppies.

sold as bundles of unrooted cuttings and can be anchored to a pool bottom with a heavy zinc strap. For preformed pools, use perforated plastic pots filled with the same soil mixture as for water lilies.

Planting floating plants
Floating water plants, such as frogbit, water hyacinth and water soldier, don't need planting at all. Simply place them on the surface of the water; their trailing roots absorb nutrients from the water.

Planting marginals
Marginal plants, which grow around the edge of the pool or in wet mud, prefer no more than 5-7.5cm (2-3in) of water above their roots. Most preformed pools are designed with a shelf around the edge to accommodate them. They can be planted in aquatic baskets like water lilies.

▲ **Arum lilies** The exotic marginal *Zantedeschia aethiopica* raises its glistening white spathes above hosta clumps.

◀ **Kingcups** The golden buttercup heads of *Caltha palustris* are familiar sights by the marshy edges of streams and ponds. Less common are the golden spathes of the great bog arum (*Lysichiton americanus*), whose leaves can reach dramatic heights and are unsuitable for small garden pools.

▼ **Candelabra primulas** The bright tiered whorls of *Primula pulverulenta* appear in early summer on stems which are 30cm (1ft) tall.

Acorus

sweet flag

Acorus calamus 'Variegatus'

☐ Height 30-90cm (1-3ft)
☐ Water depth 7.5-12cm (3-5in)
☐ Foliage plant
☐ Sunny site
☐ Hardy marginal aquatic

The common name of *Acorus* – sweet flag – describes the plant well. Its foliage and form are reminiscent of yellow flag iris, and when the leaves are crushed they release a sweet cinnamon-like aroma, making this one of the most fragrant, as well as striking, waterside plants.

Sweet flag is grown for its upright sword-shaped leaves which form a dramatic edge to a pool. It does have flowers – resembling upright catkins – in summer, but they pale into insignificance among the handsome leaves.

Popular species

Acorus calamus has dark green sword-shaped leaves reaching 60-90cm (2-3ft) high. It should be planted at a water depth of 7.5-12cm (3-5in). 'Variegatus' has rich green leaves striped with white.
Acorus gramineus, Japanese sweet flag, grows only 30cm (1ft) high and has narrow evergreen grass-like leaves. The flowers rarely appear.

Cultivation

Plant in early to mid spring in shallow water or moist loamy soil by the pool edge, and preferably in full sun.
Propagation Divide and replant clumps in spring.
Pests and diseases Trouble free.

Alisma

water plantain

Alisma plantago-aquatica

☐ Height 45-60cm (1½-2ft)
☐ Water depth 5-10cm (2-4in)
☐ Flowers in summer
☐ Sunny site
☐ Hardy marginal aquatic

Water plantain (*Alisma plantago-aquatica*) is often found in the wild in Britain, growing in muddy ground around pools, slow rivers and canals. In water gardens it is a useful marginal aquatic, its loose spikes of small pale pink or cream-white flowers adding a delicate touch to any planting scheme.

The flowers open in summer. They are borne 45-60cm (1½-2ft) above the lance-shaped to oval-shaped, bright green leaves which are arranged in a rosette at the base of the plant.

Cultivation

Plant in early to mid spring along the water's edge at a water depth of 5-10cm (2-4in). The soil should be loamy, and the site in full sun. Alternatively, plant in a basket or crate and sink this into the water.

Dead-head after flowering before the ripening seeds disperse.
Propagation Divide and replant overcrowded clumps in spring.
Pests and diseases Trouble free.

Aponogeton

Cape pondweed, water hawthorn

Aponogeton distachyos

☐ Spread 45cm (1½ft)
☐ Water depth 23-60cm (9-24in)
☐ Flowers early summer to early winter
☐ Sunny or shaded site
☐ Near-hardy deep water aquatic

Cape pondweed or water hawthorn (*Aponogeton distachyos*) is something of a curiosity in British gardens. It was one of the first Southern Hemisphere aquatics to be used here as an outdoor plant, being introduced as long ago as 1788. It is also one of the few water plants which tolerate shade. Unlike most other deep water aquatics which need to be kept in check, it is not invasive.

In spring Cape pondweed puts up oval, green floating leaves. Soon after, the flowers appear in a display that may continue from mid spring until early winter. When first open they are pure white with black anthers, but after four or five days they become cream-coloured or green-white and subsequently turn com-pletely green as they fade. The flowers, which have a waxy texture, measure up to 10cm (4in) across. They are arranged in a V-shaped cluster held above the surface of the water. They have a delicate hawthorn-like scent, hence one of the plant's common names. As cut flowers, they will last several days.

Cultivation

Grow Cape pondweed in still or slow-moving water, in neutral or slightly acid soil. It will tolerate partial shade, though the flowers are more profuse in full sun.

Set each tuber in a basket or crate of rich soil, covered with fine washed shingle. Place in the bottom of a pool, at a depth of at least 23cm (9in), to ensure the tubers survive the winter.

Alternatively, push the tubers into the mud on the bottom of the pool, or wrap each tuber in a small piece of turf, weighing it down with a stone and dropping it into

Aponogeton distachyos, flowers

place. In large pools, set the tubers at least 15cm (6in) apart.
Propagation Divide old tubers with several crowns in late spring and replant.
Pests and diseases Trouble free.

ARUM LILY – see *Zantedeschia*

149

Arundo

giant reed

Arundo donax

- ☐ Height 3-6m (10-20ft)
- ☐ Spread 1m (3ft)
- ☐ Foliage plant
- ☐ Moist soil
- ☐ Sunny, sheltered site
- ☐ Half-hardy perennial

The elegant giant reed (*Arundo donax*) originates from southern Europe, and in Britain is hardy only in mild localities, where it can reach a height of 6m (20ft) in a season. Although it will adapt to growing in well-drained herbaceous borders, it thrives in rich moist soil by the water's edge and needs a position in full sun, sheltered from cold winds.

The thick stems bear broad, floppy blue-green leaves, particularly ornamental in the form 'Variegata', which is broadly striped with creamy-white. In good summers, these grasses produce dense sprays of yellow-green spikelets in early autumn.

Cultivation

Plant in mid spring in rich, deep and moist soil, and in sun and shelter. Cut the stems back to ground level in mid autumn and cover the crowns with a deep winter mulch of leaf-mould or leaves.
Propagation Divide and replant the roots in late spring.
Pests and diseases Generally trouble free.

Asclepias

milkweed

Asclepias incarnata

- ☐ Height 1.2m (4ft)
- ☐ Spread 60cm (2ft)
- ☐ Flowers mid summer to early autumn
- ☐ Moist acid soil
- ☐ Sunny site
- ☐ Hardy perennial

Most species of milkweed are vigorous and spreading plants best suited to wild gardens, but one, *Asclepias incarnata*, also known as swamp milkweed, thrives in the boggy ground by a pool or stream. It is easy to grow and, like other milkweeds, exudes a milky sap when cut. The stout erect stems bear lance-shaped, rich green leaves and are topped in mid and late summer with showy clusters of horned, reflexed, rosy-pink flowers; they are followed by large hairy seed pods.

Cultivation

Plant in mid autumn or mid spring, in rich moist soil, preferably acid, and in full sun. Cut the stems back to ground level in late autumn.
Propagation Divide and replant in autumn or spring. Or sow seeds in spring.
Pests and diseases Generally trouble free.

Astilbe

astilbe

Astilbe x *arendsii* 'Cattleya'

- ☐ Height 60-90cm (2-3ft)
- ☐ Spread 30-60cm (1-2ft)
- ☐ Flowers early to late summer
- ☐ Rich, moist soil
- ☐ Sunny or lightly shaded site
- ☐ Hardy perennial

The elegant astilbes are popular plants for herbaceous borders, but they flourish most luxuriantly in moist and boggy ground in close proximity to water. In such conditions, their deeply cut, rich green foliage, bronze-coloured in spring, becomes particularly lush, and the tall fluffy flower spikes grow especially dense and long-lasting. They often fade to attractive russet colours and can be used dried for winter decoration.

Astilbe x *arendsii* is a hybrid race of strong-growing plants in a range of pastel and strong colours; they include 'Bressingham Beauty' (rich pink); 'Cattleya' (pale pink); 'Irrlicht' (creamy white); and 'Ostrich Plume' (deep coral pink).

Cultivation

Plant astilbes between mid autumn and early spring. They need rich, permanently moist soil and thrive in sun or light shade. Cut the plants down to ground level in mid autumn.
Propagation Divide and replant in early to mid spring, shading the new divisions until they are growing strongly and making sure they do not dry out.
Pests and diseases Trouble free.

Azolla
fairy moss

Azolla caroliniana

☐ Surface floating
☐ Any water depth
☐ Foliage plant
☐ Sunny site
☐ Hardy floating aquatic

An introduction from North America, *Azolla caroliniana*, is becoming increasingly common in the wild in Britain. Each plant is only 1-2cm (½-1in) across, but the species colonizes rapidly, particularly during a long hot summer when it can take over an entire garden pool.

The minute fronds – for this is a true fern – float on the surface of still water, forming a dense pale green carpet. In late summer and early autumn they may assume a very attractive pinkish-red tint. During the winter the plant is submerged.

Cultivation
Scatter the plants over the water surface in late spring or early summer.

Control by scooping up unwanted plants with a net.
Propagation Buy new stock from a nurseryman or transfer from one pool to another with a net.
Pests and diseases Trouble free.

BOG ARUM – see *Calla palustris*
BOG BEAN – see *Menyanthes*

Buphthalmum
buphthalmum

Buphthalmum speciosum

☐ Height 1.2-1.5m (4-5ft)
☐ Spread 1-1.2m (3-4ft)
☐ Flowers late summer
☐ Moist poor soil
☐ Sunny site
☐ Hardy perennial

A member of the daisy family, *Buphthalmum speciosum*, syn. *Telekia speciosa*, is a strong-growing robust plant suited to boggy ground by woodland streams where it can be allowed to spread by its invasive underground runners. Given plenty of room, this is a magnificent, fully hardy perennial with mid green, coarsely toothed leaves that are heart-shaped at the basal rosettes and oval on the branching stems.

In late summer, the stems are topped with large, rich yellow daisy flowers with darker centres.

Cultivation
Plant in mid autumn or early spring, in a sunny position and in moist to boggy soil by the edge of water. Avoid rich soils which encourage the plants' natural tendency to spread.
Propagation Even if new plants are not wanted, it is a good idea to lift and divide buphthalmums every few years, in autumn or spring, in order to keep them within bounds.
Pests and diseases Trouble free.

Butomus
flowering rush

Butomus umbellatus

☐ Height 90cm (3ft)
☐ Water depth up to 15cm (6in)
☐ Flowers early to mid summer
☐ Sunny site
☐ Hardy marginal aquatic

The flowering rush (*Butomus umbellatus*) is one of the most beautiful of waterside plants. In spring it pushes up spears of green sword-shaped and rush-like leaves. These have sharp edges and may be tinged purple. They give the plant an average height of 90cm (3ft).

In early to mid summer, the tall flower spikes begin to overtop the leaves. The effect is rather like that of a large-flowered allium – slender stems carrying open heads of rose-pink, cup-shaped flowers. Each flower head may be composed of up to 30 flowers measuring 10-15cm (4-6in) across.

This elegant plant is best grown in the mud alongside a stream or pool. Though it is a hardy plant native to Britain, take care to prevent more exuberant neighbours from swamping it.

Cultivation
Plant in early to mid spring at the margins of pools or the muddy banks of slow-moving streams. Plant directly in the ground or use an aquatic basket or container and sink this into the water. The plants will tolerate a water depth of up to 15cm (6in) and thrive in a sunny site.
Propagation Increase by dividing and replanting the rootstock of mature plants in spring.
Pests and diseases Trouble free.

Calla

calla lily, bog arum

Calla palustris

- ☐ Height 25cm (10in)
- ☐ Water depth 5-10cm (2-4in)
- ☐ Flowers late spring to early summer
- ☐ Sunny site
- ☐ Hardy marginal aquatic

Where the water merges imperceptibly with the land, at the edge of a shallow pool, the lovely calla lily (*Calla palustris*) can add much to the scene. Here its creeping stems will grow through the marshy soil and shallow water to send up thick, glossy, heart-shaped leaves which stand 25cm (10in) high.

The summer display of small white arum flowers is full of charm. Flowering starts in late spring and continues through early summer, with each bloom lasting for a couple of weeks. They are followed by bright red or orange seed heads. Sometimes there may be a second show of flowers in late summer.

Cultivation

Plant in late spring in fertile soil at the edge of a pool up to a water depth of 5-10cm (2-4in). A sunny or partially shaded site is suitable.
Propagation Increase by dividing and replanting mature or crowded clumps in mid spring.
Pests and diseases Trouble free.

Caltha

kingcup, marsh marigold

Caltha palustris 'Flore Pleno'

- ☐ Height 30-60cm (1-2ft)
- ☐ Water depth up to 15cm (6in)
- ☐ Flowers mid spring to early summer
- ☐ Sunny or lightly shaded site
- ☐ Hardy marginal aquatic

In late winter few sights are more encouraging by the poolside than the new emerging heart-shaped leaves of kingcups. The great golden buttercup-like flower heads follow in spring on thick, fleshy stems.

Popular species

Caltha palustris grows into a 30-45cm (1-1½ft) high clump of dark green, heart-shaped leaves. It bears a profusion of single golden-yellow flowers. Varieties developed from it include 'Alba' (white flowers) and 'Flore Pleno' (double golden-yellow flowers).
Caltha polypetala, giant kingcup, reaches 60cm (2ft) high and has a sprawling habit. The leaves and golden-yellow flowers are larger than those of *C. palustris*.

Cultivation

Plant between early spring and early autumn in sun or light shade. If planted above the water

Caltha palustris 'Alba'

level, the soil must be continuously moist. Kingcups tolerate a water depth of up to 15cm (6in).
Propagation Divide and replant the roots between late spring and early summer.
Pests and diseases Rust may develop on the foliage.

CANADIAN PONDWEED – see *Elodea*
CAPE PONDWEED – see *Aponogeton*

Cardamine
cuckoo flower

Cardamine pratensis 'Flore Pleno'

- ☐ Height 30-45cm (12-18in)
- ☐ Spread 30cm (12in)
- ☐ Flowers late spring and early summer
- ☐ Moist soil
- ☐ Shady site
- ☐ Hardy perennial

Cuckoo flower or lady's smock (*Cardamine pratensis*) is a native wild flower commonly found on wet meadowland. In gardens, it is represented by the form 'Flore Pleno', a clump-forming perennial with basal rosettes of mid green leaves divided into numerous leaflets. From late spring onwards, slender and wiry, leafy stems bear loose spikes of delicate, lilac-pink flowers, like miniature stock.

Cardamines are valued for their early flowering; they thrive in moist, even wet, ground, on streamside banks and in bog gardens.

Cultivation
Plant between early autumn and late winter, in any type of soil that is wet or permanently moist. Flowering is most profuse in partial shade.
Propagation Divide and replant established clumps after flowering or in late winter just as the plants start to grow.
Pests and diseases Generally trouble free.

CINQUEFOIL, MARSH – see
Potentilla

Claytonia
spring beauty

Claytonia virginica

- ☐ Height 5-15cm (2-6in)
- ☐ Spread 20cm (8in) or more
- ☐ Flowers in early spring
- ☐ Fertile, moist soil
- ☐ Partial shade
- ☐ Evergreen perennial

The hardy little spring beauty from North America (*Claytonia virginica*) is aptly named, for it unfolds its cup-shaped flowers at the first touch of spring sun. They are white or pale pink, with deep pink stripes, and are borne on branching stems clothed with narrowly spoon-shaped, near-succulent leaves. The evergreen foliage is bronzy-red when young, but later turns bright glossy green.

Spring beauty is a creeping, spreading plant, ideal for ground cover in moist shady woodlands, wild gardens and boggy areas.

Cultivation
Plant in mid autumn in good moist soil and in a shady site. Claytonia is a tuberous-rooted plant and is sometimes slow to become established, but thereafter spreads rapidly.
Propagation Offsets are formed on mature clumps. Lift them in early to mid autumn, separate the offsets and replant them immediately.
Pests and diseases Slugs and snails are the chief enemies.

COMMON ARROWHEAD – see
Sagittaria
CORKSCREW RUSH – see
Juncus
COTTON GRASS – see
Eriophorum

Cyperus
sweet galingale

Cyperus longus

- ☐ Height 45-60cm (1½-2ft)
- ☐ Water depth up to 45cm (1½ft)
- ☐ Flowers late summer to early autumn
- ☐ Sunny or partially shaded site
- ☐ Hardy marginal

Sweet galingale (*Cyperus longus*) is a rush-like plant which needs moisture around its roots. It is popularly planted as marginal shelter at the edge of lakes and large pools.

A hardy, rather invasive perennial with a tough creeping rootstock, sweet galingale can be grown in a small garden pool provided that the roots are restricted in a container.

The wide, ribbed, dark olive green leaves are a feature in themselves, and an added attraction are the heads of red-brown flower plumes which appear in late summer and early autumn.

Cultivation
Plant between mid spring and early summer along the margin of a pool or in an aquatic basket filled with rich soil and lowered into the water up to a depth of 45cm (1½ft). The site can be sunny or partially shaded.

Remove all flower heads before the seeds ripen. Clean up and cut down old foliage in autumn.
Propagation Lift established plants in mid to late spring, cut off young rooted growths and replant, discarding the old woody centres.
Pests and diseases Trouble free.

Cypripedium
lady's slipper orchid

Cypripedium calceolus

Cypripedium reginae

- ☐ Height 30-60cm (1-2ft)
- ☐ Spread 30cm (1ft)
- ☐ Flowers late spring to mid summer
- ☐ Moist, acid soil
- ☐ Partial shade
- ☐ Hardy perennial

The true lady's slipper orchid (*Cypripedium calceolus*) is a native plant of Britain and grows wild in a few secretive places. It is a protected species, but rhizomes of this and other cypripediums can be obtained from specialist orchid growers. They are fully hardy perennials – though often temperamental in their growth pattern – and among the most beautiful plants for a bog garden.

Typically, these orchids bear lance-shaped, mid green leaves that wrap like sheaths around the stems and are pleated or prominently ribbed. The flowers have a conspicuous pouch or slipper-like lip beneath the spreading, fused petals and sepals.

Popular species
Cypripedium calceolus (yellow lady's slipper) is a lime-tolerant species; it grows 30-45cm (1-1½ft) high, with long sheath-like leaves. Each erect stem bears up to three flowers in late spring. They are up to 12.5cm (5in) across, with twisted maroon-purple sepals and petals and a large pale yellow lip. The variety *pubescens* has hairy leaves and stems, with purple-flushed brown lips and yellowish petals.

Cypripedium japonicum is about 45cm (1½ft) high. In early summer it bears solitary flowers that are silvery white spotted with red; the lip is white and crimson. The variety *formosanum* is creamy white, the large lip marked with purple-red.

Cypripedium reginae, syn. *C. spectabile*, is a showy species, with stems up to 60cm (2ft) high enfolded by broad, densely hairy pleated leaves, usually in pairs. The flowers are borne one to three to a stem; they are fragrant and pure white, the large lip heavily streaked and mottled with rose-purple.

Cultivation
Plant the rhizomes in early or mid spring, setting them 5cm (2in) deep, those of *C. reginae* at half that depth. All need good, moist to boggy, acid soil and partial to full shade. Mulch annually with well-rotted garden compost or a peat substitute.

Propagation As the clumps become established, they spread and form new rhizomes which can be divided and replanted in spring.

Pests and diseases Aphids and scale insects may infest the leaves. Discoloration and leaf spot are usually caused by unsuitable growing conditions.

Cypripedium japonicum var. formosanum

Eichhornia
water hyacinth

Eichhornia crassipes

- ☐ Height 15-23cm (6-9in)
- ☐ Water depth 15-45cm (6-18in)
- ☐ Flowers in summer
- ☐ Sunny site
- ☐ Tender floating aquatic

Water hyacinth (*Eichhornia crassipes*, syn. *E. speciosa*) is the only species in this genus of tropical evergreen floating plants which is widely grown in Britain. Being tender, it should be overwintered in a heated greenhouse, but the trouble is worth it for the charming lavender-blue hyacinth-like flowers borne in summer. The glossy dark green leaves are roughly heart-shaped. The stems are inflated and act as floats, keeping the plants buoyant.

Though normally found as a floating plant, water hyacinth will grow in mud where the water depth is insufficient for it to float.

Cultivation
Place the plants on the surface of the pool in early summer. The soil at the bottom of the pool should be rich and at least 5cm (2in) deep. Full sun is essential. Bring the plants into a greenhouse in early autumn and overwinter in wet soil at a temperature of 13-16°C (55-61°F).
Propagation New plants are produced on runners in summer. When a young plant is showing several well-formed leaves it is ready to be detached.
Pests and diseases Trouble free.

Elodea
Canadian pondweed

Elodea canadensis

- ☐ Any water depth
- ☐ Foliage plant
- ☐ Sun or partial shade
- ☐ Hardy submerged aquatic

Canadian pondweed (*Elodea canadensis*, syn. *Anacharis canadensis*) belongs to the group of aquatic plants known as oxygenators. They are essential in any still-water pool as they supplement the oxygen and consume some of the carbon dioxide exhaled by fish and plants. They discourage the growth of algae and promote the existence of beneficial microscopic animals while providing shade and shelter for fish.

Canadian pondweed is a vigorous, submerged perennial whose fleshy stems and dark green, lance-shaped leaves are rarely seen on the pool surface. Minute white, purple-tinged flowers are borne throughout summer.

Cultivation
Plant in mid spring, inserting small bundles of unrooted cuttings, popularly known as slips, into the mud at the bottom of the pool or in aquatic baskets of loamy compost lowered into place. The plants grow prolifically and need thinning out in late autumn – use a rake to pull out surplus growth.
Propagation If necessary, take cuttings in mid spring and treat as slips (see above).
Pests and diseases Trouble free.

Eriophorum
cotton grass

Eriophorum angustifolium

- ☐ Height 30-45cm (1-1½ft)
- ☐ Planting depth up to 15cm (6in)
- ☐ Flowers mid to late spring
- ☐ Sunny site
- ☐ Hardy marginal aquatic

This attractive low-growing perennial is a good choice for growing in moist soil around the edge of a pool; it will also grow in water up to a depth of 15cm (6in). In Britain it grows naturally on damp moorland and is useful for ground cover on exposed ground where few other marginals would thrive.

Eriophorum angustifolium has dense tufts of rush-like foliage, but the main attraction is its tassels of cotton-wool-like flower heads. They appear in mid to late spring 30-45cm (1-1½ft) above the ground.

Cultivation
Plant in moist soil along the water's edge in spring. Ideally the site should be sunny.
Propagation Increase in autumn or spring by lifting, dividing and replanting mature plants.
Pests and diseases Trouble free.

FAIRY MOSS – see *Azolla*
FLOWERING RUSH – see *Butomus*
FORGET-ME-NOT – see *Myosotis*
FROGBIT – see *Hydrocharis*

Geum

water avens

Geum rivale

- ☐ Height 30cm (12in)
- ☐ Spread up to 45cm (18in)
- ☐ Flowers late spring to late autumn
- ☐ Moist soil
- ☐ Sunny site
- ☐ Hardy perennial

Flowering almost continuously from late spring and well into autumn, water avens (*Geum rivale*) is invaluable for providing colour in boggy ground or the margins of a pool. It is undemanding and easy to grow, 30cm (12in) or more high and clump-forming with mid green, strawberry-like leaves. The nodding, bell-shaped flowers have purple-red calyces and pink to yellow petals veined with purple.

'Leonard's Variety' is rose-pink flushed with golden-yellow; 'Album', a white-flowered form, is sometimes available.

Cultivation
Plant between early autumn and early spring in any fertile, moisture-retentive soil and preferably in full sun. In late autumn, or when flowering has finished, cut the stems back to ground level.
Propagation Divide and replant established clumps every three or four years in early or mid spring.
Pests and diseases Generally trouble free.

GIANT KINGCUP – see *Caltha*
GIANT REED – see *Arundo*

Glyceria

manna grass, reed sweetgrass

Glyceria maxima 'Variegata'

- ☐ Height 60-90cm (2-3ft)
- ☐ Water depth up to 15cm (6in)
- ☐ Flowers in summer
- ☐ Sunny position
- ☐ Hardy marginal aquatic

The bright green 1.2-1.8m (4-6ft) *Glyceria maxima*, a plant of wet meadows and watersides, is too invasive for the average garden scene. The form 'Variegata', however, is shorter and more decorative. It will grow in a dry site, though the leaves tend to lose their colour as the summer progresses. The waterside, or shallow water up to a depth of 15cm (6in), is the best site.

In spring, young leaf shoots of green striped with pink-flushed-white emerge. As the long narrow leaves open out, the pink fades and grassy inflorescences of cream flowers wave in the breeze.

Cultivation
Plant in early autumn or spring in a sunny position by the water's edge, or in pots in up to 15cm (6in) of water. If planted above the water level, the soil should be moisture-retentive.
Propagation Lift, divide and replant in spring.
Pests and diseases Trouble free.

GOLDEN CLUB – see *Orontium*
GREAT BOG ARUM – see *Lysichiton*
GREATER SPEARWORT – see *Ranunculus*
HOGWEED – see *Heracleum*

Heracleum

giant hogweed

Heracleum mantegazzianum

- ☐ Height 3-3.5m (10-12ft)
- ☐ Spread 1.2-1.8m (4-6ft)
- ☐ Flowers mid and late summer
- ☐ Deep moist soil
- ☐ Sun or partial shade
- ☐ Hardy perennial

Giant hogweed (*Heracleum mantegazzianum*) is truly gigantic, often growing to a height of 5m (16ft) in a season. Too massive for a small pool, it is impressive by a large pond or lake in semi-wild settings. Its stout fluted stems, often purple-spotted, shoot upwards and are clothed with enormous deeply lobed mid green leaves. Massive round heads, up to 45cm (18in) across, of white, starry flowers are borne in mid and late summer.

Giant hogweed is a short-lived perennial, often of biennial growth, but it seeds itself freely and can become a nuisance unless it is dead-headed before the seeds ripen in early autumn.

Cultivation
Plant between mid autumn and early spring, in any deep moist soil, and in full sun or light shade. Cut the tall stems back to ground level after flowering.
Propagation Seeds can be sown in an outdoor nursery bed in spring and the seedlings transplanted to their growing positions in autumn.
Pests and diseases Generally trouble free.

Hosta

hosta, plantain lily

Hosta ventricosa 'Aureo-marginata'

Hosta plantaginea

☐ Height 45-90cm (1½-3ft)
☐ Spread 45-60cm (1½-2ft)
☐ Flowers mid summer to autumn
☐ Moist rich soil
☐ Partial shade or sunny site
☐ Hardy perennial

Hostas are primarily grown for their striking foliage, which comes in an array of colours, shapes and textures. The large leaves are heart or lance-shaped, smooth, crinkled or prominently veined and vary in colour from the palest green to blue, edged or overlaid with white, gold or silver.

They do flower, with tall slender stems bearing loose clusters or spikes of bell- or funnel-shaped flowers that are white or in shades of pink, purple and mauve.

Hostas grow well in herbaceous borders, but are particularly vigorous and luxuriant in moist soil at the margins of pools and streams. In such situations they form increasing clumps of foliage; they retain their leaf colourings best in dappled shade.

Popular species

Hosta plantaginea is a distinctive, all-green species growing 45-60cm (1½-2ft) high. It bears long-stemmed, glossy bright green, heart-shaped leaves from which rise, in late summer, flowering stems topped with pure white flowers. It is one of the few hostas that performs best in full sun.

Hosta sieboldii, syn. *H. albo-marginata*, grows about 45cm (1½ft) high, with narrow lance-shaped, glossy green leaves with a thin but distinctive white margin. It bears funnel-shaped flowers, lilac striped with violet, from mid to late summer. 'Louisa' is a white-flowered variety.

Hosta ventricosa, syn. *H. coerulea*, is a vigorous species up to 90cm (3ft) high. It bears heart-shaped,

blue-green leaves, and mauve to violet flower spikes in late summer. In the variety 'Aureo-marginata', the leaves are prominently splashed with yellow.

Cultivation

Plant in mid autumn or early spring, spacing the plants 45cm (1½ft) apart – 60cm (2ft) for *H. ventricosa* – and setting the crowns flush with the soil surface. All hostas need rich and moist though not waterlogged soil, and generally a site in dappled shade – in sun make sure that the roots never dry out. Dead-head after flowering and in autumn clear away dead and rotting leaves.

Propagation Division in early spring, just as growth starts, is the usual method. Ideally, hostas should be left undisturbed; they are long-lived and in time develop tough woody crowns which are difficult to split. For propagation purposes, divide and replant hostas while they are still young.

Pests and diseases Slugs and snails can reduce entire leaves to skeletons.

Hosta sieboldii 'Louisa'

Houttuynia

houttuynia

Houttuynia cordata 'Variegata'

- ☐ Height 30-45cm (1-1½ft)
- ☐ Water depth 2.5-5cm (1-2in)
- ☐ Flowers in summer
- ☐ Dappled shade
- ☐ Hardy marginal aquatic

Houttuynia cordata is a hardy herbaceous perennial which thrives in boggy ground or shallow water. Unlike most aquatics, it needs a site in dappled shade.

It spreads rapidly by means of underground stems, and can be invasive under ideal conditions.

The upright bright red stems bear pointed heart-shaped leaves which have a blue-green and rather metallic appearance sometimes suffused with red. In summer small spikes of white flowers with white bracts appear. 'Flore Pleno' is a variety with large white bracts, and 'Variegata' (syn. 'Chamaelon') has leaves variegated with cream and red.

Cultivation

Plant in spring or autumn in soft moist soil or shallow water to a depth of 5cm (2in). Dappled shade is essential. Plant dormant runners horizontally, 7.5cm (3in) deep. Container-grown plants should be planted at pot depth.

Propagation Divide in spring or autumn. Pot pieces of underground stem, each with a growing point or developed shoot, in potting compost and grow on until well rooted. Transplant to the growing position.

Pests and diseases Trouble free.

Houttuynia cordata

Hydrocharis

frogbit

Hydrocharis morsus-ranae

- ☐ Surface-floating aquatic
- ☐ Any water depth
- ☐ Flowers in late summer
- ☐ Sunny site
- ☐ Hardy perennial

The small bronze-green kidney-shaped leaves and tiny simple white flowers, composed of three petals and a yellow centre, make frogbit (*Hydrocharis morsus-ranae*) a graceful floating aquatic.

As a perennial, it dies down in winter, and the only evidence of its presence is the submerged dormant buds at the bottom of the pool. It is extremely hardy and will grow almost anywhere. Given its small size, it is a particularly good subject for a small pool or wooden water barrel.

Cultivation

Place the plants on the water in spring in full sun. Frogbit will thrive in pools above acid or neutral soil, but it is not suitable for unlined ponds with lime-rich soil. Any water depth is suitable.

Control the spread by pulling out unwanted plants with a rake.

Propagation Increase by breaking up colonies with a net in spring and summer.

Pests and diseases Generally trouble free though certain species of snails can devastate the foliage.

Iris

iris

Iris laevigata

Iris pseudacorus 'Variegata'

Iris pseudacorus

- ☐ Height 45cm-1.2m (1½-4ft)
- ☐ Water depth 5-45cm (2-18in)
- ☐ Flowers late spring to early summer
- ☐ Sunny site or dappled shade
- ☐ Hardy marginal aquatic

There are irises for every possible garden situation, from miniatures for rockeries and sink gardens to stately border irises and imposing aquatic types. *Iris laevigata* and the varieties developed from it flourish in shallow water and at the margins of pools and streams, while *Iris pseudacorus* thrives in deep water. Both have dramatic, upright sword-shaped leaves and typical iris flowers from late spring to early summer.

Popular species

Iris laevigata grows best in water up to 15cm (6in) deep. It has smooth pale green leaves 45-60cm (1½-2ft) long. In early summer, two to four royal blue flowers open at the tip of each branching stem. Popular varieties include: 'Albo-purpurea' (white with purple-blue markings); 'Regal' (cyclamen-red); 'Rose Queen' (rose-pink); 'Snowdrift' (white and yellow, double flowers); and 'Variegata' (soft blue flowers and white and green-striped leaves).

Iris pseudacorus, yellow flag or flag iris, thrives in a water depth of up to 45cm (1½ft). Reaching 90cm-1.2m (3-4ft) or more high, it has blue-green distinctly ridged leaves. The branching, shiny stems carry five or more yellow flowers, usually marked with brown veins, in late spring and early summer. Varieties include: 'Golden Queen' (golden flowers) and 'Variegata' (golden and green variegated leaves).

Cultivation

Plant the rhizomes along the margins of pools or streams in good deep, moist soil in early to mid spring. Or plant directly in muddy soil beneath shallow water or in aquatic baskets lowered to the bottom in deeper pools. The site can be in full sun or light shade.

Propagation Divide the rhizomes after flowering every three years. Replant immediately.

Pests and diseases Iris sawflies feed on the foliage.

Iris laevigata 'Albo-purpurea'

Juncus
corkscrew rush

Iuncus effusus 'Spiralis'

- ☐ Height 38-45cm (15-18in)
- ☐ Water depth up to 7.5cm (3in)
- ☐ Foliage plant
- ☐ Sunny or partially shaded site
- ☐ Hardy marginal aquatic

Most species of the large *Juncus* genus are too coarse and rampant for the water garden, but the corkscrew rush (*Juncus effusus* 'Spiralis') is sufficiently ornamental to merit a position around a garden pool. It has a sprawling, rather untidy habit, but the virtually leafless stems are interesting – dark green and with a permanent wave that varies from tight curls to perfect corkscrews and spirals. The brown flower clusters, borne in early to mid summer, are insignificant. The plants grow 38-45cm (15-18in) high.

Cultivation
Plant around the margins of a pool in mid to late spring. The site can be sunny or partially shaded. Any soil, even the poorest, is suitable and the plants will thrive in a water depth of 7.5cm (3in).

Remove congested stems from time to time and cut out any that fail to develop the spiralling shape.
Propagation Increase by dividing and replanting clumps in mid to late spring. Use a sharp knife to sever the tough rootstocks.
Pests and diseases Trouble free.

KINGCUP – see *Caltha*
LADY'S SLIPPER – see *Cypripedium*
LADY'S SMOCK – see *Cardamine*

Lobelia
cardinal flower

Lobelia siphilitica

- ☐ Height 30-90cm (1-3ft)
- ☐ Spread 30-38cm (12-15in)
- ☐ Flowers mid summer to early autumn
- ☐ Rich, moist soil
- ☐ Light shade and shelter
- ☐ Hardy perennial

The hardy lobelias are quite distinct from the ubiquitous bedding types, being tall branching perennials with magnificent spikes of two-lipped tubular flowers. They grow naturally in boggy ground.

Popular species
Lobelia cardinalis grows 75cm (2½ft) high. It is a short-lived and clump-forming species with bright green or coppery, lance-shaped foliage. Spikes of brilliant red flowers are borne from mid to late summer.
Lobelia fulgens resembles *L. cardinalis* but bears bronze-purple leaves and more showy flower spikes on thick branching stems up to 90cm (3ft) high.
Lobelia siphilitica, 60-90cm (2-3ft) high, is fully hardy. It has narrowly oval, pale green leaves and, from mid summer until autumn, huge spikes of clear blue flowers.

Cultivation
Plant in mid spring in rich, moist to wet soil, in dappled shade or sun, and in shelter. It is advisable to lift *L. cardinalis* in autumn and overwinter it in a cold frame.
Propagation Divide and replant established clumps in spring. *L. cardinalis* can also be increased from stem cuttings in summer.
Pests and diseases Trouble free.

Lobelia fulgens

Lysichiton

skunk cabbage, great bog arum

Lysichiton americanus

☐ Height 60cm-1.2m (2-4ft)
☐ Crown level with the water surface or moist soil
☐ Flowers early to late spring
☐ Sunny or partially shaded site
☐ Hardy marginal aquatic

Abundance of water often promotes growth, resulting in many water plants being of massive proportions. Skunk cabbage, or great bog arum, is one example. Its huge waxy arum-like flower spathes, which appear in early to late spring, are often 30cm (1ft) high. The leaves, which unfurl later, may grow to 1.2m (4ft) long.

These are dramatic and long-lived plants for growing in wet ground around pools and streams where the soil is deep, rich and moist. Specialist growers supply two- to three-year-old specimens which take a couple of years to settle down and begin flowering.

Popular species

Lysichiton americanus is the largest species, reaching 60cm-1.2m (2-4ft) high. It has grass-green leaves and deep golden-yellow spathes. In mid to late summer the ripening seed heads are another attraction.
Lysichiton camtschatcensis is similar to *L. americanus*, but smaller. It grows 60-90cm (2-3ft) high and has

Lysichiton camtschatcensis

pure white flowers which do not seed. The leaves are blue-green.

Cultivation

Plant container-grown specimens between mid spring and early summer, taking care not to damage the fleshy roots. They need a soil depth of at least 30cm (12in) and rich moist loam. The site can be sunny or partially shaded.
Propagation Division is the easiest method though divided plants may take two or three years to establish themselves. Remove the young plants which form around the rhizomes and pot them up in loamy compost. Plant out in spring.
Pests and diseases Trouble free.

Lysimachia

creeping Jenny, moneywort

Lysimachia nummularia 'Aurea'

☐ Height 2.5-5cm (1-2in)
☐ Spread 45cm (1½ft) or more
☐ Flowers early and mid summer
☐ Any moist soil
☐ Sunny site
☐ Evergreen perennial

Creeping Jenny (*Lysimachia nummularia*) is a fully hardy prostrate plant much used for ground cover in rock gardens, on banks and in borders, although it is a true evergreen waterside perennial, thriving in moist soil or shallow water. The prostrate stems spread and trail indefinitely, rooting where they touch the soil or spilling over the water's edge. They are clothed with tiny rounded, mid green leaves and studded in summer with bright yellow, cup-shaped flowers.

The variety 'Aurea' has soft yellow-green foliage.

Cultivation

Plant between mid autumn and mid spring in shallow moist soil at pool margins or close to the rim where the shoots can trail over the water. Creeping Jenny does equally well in full sun or dappled shade, but the yellow-leaved 'Aurea' tends to lose its bright colour in a shady site.
Propagation Stem sections, 7.5-10cm (3-4in) long, taken in mid spring or early autumn and inserted directly in the growing site, root readily.
Pests and diseases Generally trouble free.

Lythrum

purple loosestrife

Lythrum salicaria 'Firecandle'

- ☐ Height 60cm-1.5m (2-5ft)
- ☐ Spread 45cm (1½ft)
- ☐ Flowers summer and autumn
- ☐ Moist soil
- ☐ Partially shaded site
- ☐ Hardy perennial

The magnificent tall red-purple flower spikes of purple loosestrife (*Lythrum salicaria*) can be found growing by watersides all over the British countryside. Several varieties have been developed from the species and thrive in moist soil around ornamental garden pools and streams. They are also ideal in woodland settings. The flower spikes appear from early summer to early autumn, some 60cm-1.5m (2-5ft) high, among mid green lance-shaped leaves.

Popular varieties

'**Firecandle**' has rich purple-pink flowers.
'**Lady Sackville**' has bright rose-pink flowers.
'**Robert**' has vivid rose-red flowers.
'**Rose Queen**' has paler pink flowers than most other varieties.

Cultivation

Plant in autumn or spring in wet soil by the water's edge. The site can be sunny or partially shaded. Cut back in autumn.
Propagation Divide and replant in autumn or spring.
Pests and diseases Trouble free.

MANNA GRASS – see *Glyceria*
MARSH MARIGOLD – see *Caltha*

Mentha

water mint

Mentha aquatica

- ☐ Height 30cm (1ft)
- ☐ Water depth 5-12cm (2-5in)
- ☐ Flowers in early summer
- ☐ Sunny site
- ☐ Hardy marginal aquatic

Water mint (*Mentha aquatica*) is a versatile plant, thriving in wet mud or on the surface of shallow pools. It grows in sun or shade – in shade the hairy oval leaves are bright green, while in full sun they turn purple.

The small mauve-lilac flowers, arranged in tight rounded clusters, appear in late summer. A distinctive characteristic of the plant is its strong minty smell.

Cultivation

Water mint is an invasive plant, so it is advisable to plant it in an aquatic basket and sink this in wet mud or shallow water along the margins of a pool or stream. Plant in spring or autumn. The site can be shaded or in full sun.
Propagation Increase by removing rooted suckers and replanting in late spring to early summer.
Pests and diseases Trouble free.

Menyanthes

bog bean

Menyanthes trifoliata

- ☐ Height 25cm (10in)
- ☐ Water depth up to 10cm (4in)
- ☐ Flowers in early summer
- ☐ Sunny site
- ☐ Hardy marginal aquatic

The bog bean (*Menyanthes trifoliata*) grows wild in Britain, most commonly in the north. It is useful for covering the margins of garden pools with its scrambling stems. Mud just covered with water provides the best growing conditions for these plants.

Thick green trailing stems carry three-lobed, clover-like leaves. Bare flower stalks appear in early summer, carrying spikes of pure white, heavily fringed flowers from pinkish tinged buds. They have a charming effect when massed.

Bog bean spreads, but is rarely invasive.

Cultivation

Plant the rhizomes in spring, setting them 30cm (1ft) apart in wet soil at the pool's edge, so that their roots can grow into the water. The site should be sunny. Bog bean will also grow in a water depth of up to 10cm (4in).
Propagation Divide the rhizomes into sections, each with a healthy growing tip, and replant immediately.
Pests and diseases Trouble free.

MILKWEED – see *Asclepias*

Mimulus

monkey-musk, monkey flower

Mimulus luteus

☐ Height 30cm (12in)
☐ Water depth up to 7.5cm (3in)
☐ Flowers late spring to late summer
☐ Sunny or lightly shaded site
☐ Hardy marginal aquatic

Monkey-musk (*Mimulus luteus*) is ideal for providing colour throughout summer. It belongs to a genus of mainly hardy annuals and perennials, all of which require moist soil. Monkey-musk is a true aquatic and will grow in water up to a depth of 7.5cm (3in).

It has mid green oval leaves and snapdragon-like golden yellow flowers sometimes marked with maroon or crimson-brown spots.

Cultivation

Plant in spring in moist soil along the margins of a pool or stream. Monkey-musk will thrive in water up to a depth of 7.5cm (3in). It does equally well in sun or light shade.

Cut down faded flower stems in late autumn.

Propagation Divide and replant in spring. Alternatively, sow seeds under glass in late winter, prick out seedlings into boxes and then pot on. Harden off in a cold frame before planting out in late spring or early summer.

Pests and diseases Trouble free.

Miscanthus

silver grass

Miscanthus sinensis 'Gracillimus'

☐ Height 1.2-3m (4-10ft)
☐ Spread 90cm (3ft)
☐ Foliage plant
☐ Rich moist soil
☐ Sunny site
☐ Hardy perennial

These tough and robust grasses make admirable shelter plants by the waterside, and create handsome focal points where space allows. They grow rapidly, up to 3m (10ft) each season, if given deep rich and moist soil.

Popular species

Miscanthus sacchariflorus (Amur silver grass) is an ultra-hardy species, growing 2-3m (7-10ft) high from a rhizomatous, slowly spreading rootstock. The stout stems bear narrow, arching leaves, mid green with paler midribs; they persist well into autumn, turning russet-brown before dying.

Miscanthus sinensis, syn. *Eulalia japonica*, grows to 1.5m (5ft) and forms wide-spreading clumps. It bears arching, blue-green grassy leaves with white midribs. The species and its varieties sometimes produce feathery flower panicles in early and mid autumn. 'Gracillimus', 1.2m (4ft) high, has exceptionally narrow leaves, and sometimes white inflorescenses in autumn; 'Silver Feather' is free-flowering with tall silky flower plumes that fade to bronzy-red in autumn; 'Variegatus' is outstanding for its green leaves striped with bright primrose yellow.

Cultivation

Plant in early to mid spring, in deep rich and moist soil and in a sunny site; these grasses look particularly dramatic where their graceful outlines are reflected in water. In late autumn, or in early spring, cut all stems and dead foliage back to ground level.

Propagation Divide and replant during early and mid spring.

Pests and diseases Powdery mildew shows first as white or brown patches which later become a grey-white coating on the foliage.

MONEYWORT – see *Lysimachia*
MONKEY-MUSK – see *Mimulus*

Miscanthus sacchariflorus

Myosotis

water forget-me-not

Myosotis palustris

☐ Height 23cm (9in)
☐ Water depth up to 7.5cm (3in)
☐ Flowers mid spring to mid summer
☐ Sunny or partially shaded position
☐ Hardy marginal aquatic

The well-known forget-me-not group includes one moisture-loving species – *Myosotis palustris* (syn. *M. scorpioides*). A hardy evergreen, it thrives in moist soil found along the margins of a pool or stream and will also grow in shallow water up to a depth of 7.5cm (3in).

Numerous pale blue flowers with pale yellow eyes are carried in sprays at the tips of long stems between mid spring and mid summer. They are set off perfectly by a foil of green spoon-shaped leaves covered with rough hairs. The plants reach 23cm (9in) high. 'Mermaid' is a popular variety; it bears deep blue flowers with a deep yellow eye, and dark green, narrow leaves.

Cultivation

Plant in mid to late spring or early to mid autumn in deep fertile soil at water level, or covered by up to 7.5cm (3in) of water. It thrives in full sun or partial shade.

Trim off flower heads as they fade, to prolong the flowering season.

Propagation Water forget-me-not can be increased by seed or by cuttings. Sow the seeds in mid to late spring in a cold frame. Prick the seedlings out into an outdoor nursery bed and grow them on; transplant to the flowering sites in early autumn.

Alternatively, take basal cuttings in early spring or late summer to early autumn. Root them in a cold frame, making sure the compost is kept moist. When well rooted, plant out in the permanent positions.

Pests and diseases Grey mould can rot the flowers and mildew may show as a white powdery coating on the stems and leaves.

Nuphar

pond lily

Nuphar lutea

☐ Surface floater
☐ Water depth to 1.2m (4ft) or more
☐ Flowers in summer
☐ Hardy aquatic

Pond lilies resemble true water lilies (*Nymphaea*) but are coarser plants and inferior in bloom. Like water lilies they have thick and leathery leaves, as much as 40cm (16in) across, that float on the water surface, as well as fern-like and translucent, submerged foliage. The flowers, usually yellow or orange, are much smaller and more rounded, with fewer petals; they have an unpleasant smell and self-seed readily.

These characteristics notwithstanding, nuphars have their strong points: they thrive where water lilies would not succeed, in running water, deep ponds and in shady situations. The most commonly grown species is the yellow pond lily (*Nuphar lutea*), which spreads to at least 1.5m (5ft) and should only be introduced to large pools and natural ponds and streams. The miniature *Nuphar pumila* is suitable for rock pools with cold, flowing or still water.

Cultivation

Plant the rhizomes in spring, siting them in the muddy soil at the bottom of a large pool or lowering them in aquatic baskets. Nuphars will grow in sun or shade, most vigorously in full sun. Remove the flowers as they fade.

Propagation Divide congested clumps periodically in spring.

Pests and diseases Trouble free.

Nymphaea
water lily

Nymphaea 'Amabilis'

- ☐ Surface floater
- ☐ Water depth 15cm-1.2m (6in-4ft)
- ☐ Flowers in summer
- ☐ Sunny site
- ☐ Hardy shallow and deep water aquatics

Water lilies are the marvels of the ornamental water garden, with their elegant blooms which appear over a long period in the summer. An enormous range of varieties is available, offering the gardener a choice of sizes and flower colours. They are planted in the mud at the bottom of a pool or in perforated aquatic baskets, but flowers and leaves float on the water surface. They are easy to grow, long-lived and demand little attention, though the larger types can be invasive.

The flowers are cup-shaped with several rows of petals, the outer ones lying almost flat as the inner ones open. The shape of the petals varies from variety to variety with some having pointed petals which give them a starry appearance. The central boss of stamens is usually orange or yellow. A few are almost completely double.

In spring, the rounded or heart-shaped leaves unfurl and float on the water, except where overcrowd-ing forces them above the surface. The colour of the glossy, leathery leaves is pale to mid green, some-times splashed or flushed with maroon. Leaf size is determined by the vigour of the plant.

Popular species and hybrids
Water lilies are usually divided into categories according to size and required water depth. Minia-ture, small and medium types are suitable for the average-sized garden pool.

MINIATURE TYPES have a surface spread of 30-45cm (1-1½ft). The leaves are 5-7.5cm (2-3in) across and need a water depth of 15-23cm (6-9in). Popular varie-ties include: *N. pygmaea* 'Alba' (scented and pure white flowers); *N. pygmaea* 'Helvola' (sulphur-yellow, star-shaped flowers and maroon-spotted leaves); and 'Paul Hariot' (orange flowers and leaves spotted maroon).

SMALL TYPES have a spread of 45-75cm (1½-2½ft) and require a water depth of 30-45cm (1-1½ft). The leaves are 10-18cm (4-7in) across. The most commonly grown species is *N. candida* (white flowers). Hybrids include: 'Albatross' (pure white flowers with prominent golden centres);

Nymphaea x marliacea 'Albida'

'Fire Crest' (rich pink flowers with orange stamens); 'Froebelii' (rich red flowers); *N. x laydekeri* 'Lilacea' (soft rose-pink flowers); *N. x laydekeri* 'Purpurata' (wine-red flowers); *N. x marliacea* 'Chromatella' (large primrose-yel-low flowers); 'Rose Arey' (scented, cerise-pink flowers); and 'Sioux' (yellow flowers suffused with red).

MEDIUM TYPES have a spread of 75cm-1.05m (2½-3½ft). They need water 45-60cm (1½-2ft) deep, and the leaves are 18-25cm

Nymphaea 'Attraction'

Nymphaea 'General Pershing'

Nymphaea 'Gladstoniana'

(7-10in) across. Varieties include: 'Amabilis' (starry pink flowers); 'Atropurpurea' (dark crimson flowers, young reddish foliage); 'Attraction' (white tipped, deep red flowers); 'Conqueror' (large deep red blooms flecked white); 'Escarboucle' (deep crimson-red flowers); 'General Pershing' (wine red flowers); 'Gladstoniana' (large pure white flowers); 'Gloire de Temple sur Lot' (double cream-white flowers); 'James Brydon' (pinkish-red flowers and purple young leaves); *N.* x *marliacea* 'Albida' (white flowers); *N.* x *marliacea* 'Carnea' (pale pink flowers); 'Moorei' (yellow flowers, spotted brown leaves); 'Sunrise' (golden-yellow, fragrant flowers, leaves flecked brown); and 'William Falconer' (dark ruby-red flowers with golden anthers).

Cultivation

Choose a sunny position for water lilies. Either plant directly in the mud at the bottom of a pool or in perforated aquatic baskets which are then sunk into position. Whichever method is used the soil should be fertile and loamy. Mix light or clay soil with rotted cow manure or coarse bonemeal.

Miniature water lilies need a soil depth of 7.5-10cm (3-4in), small types 10-15cm (4-6in) and medium types 15-20cm (6-8in).

Plant the tubers or rhizomes between mid spring and early summer. In baskets, set them so that the soil is level with the growing point of the rootstock. When planting directly in the mud, reach down and push the rootstocks into the soft mud.

Water lilies require little attention after planting. Remove excessively large leaves if necessary, and thin plants in small pools. Mid to late spring is the best time to do this. Either drain off the water or lift out the basket. Examine the rootstocks and, using a sharp knife, sever strong-growing tubers and rhizomes, 15-20cm (6-8in) from the growing point; trim off the true roots beneath. Use the severed pieces for propagation.

Propagation After thinning in spring, replant the severed sections or remove offsets from the main rootstock with a sharp knife. Insert the offsets in small pots of loamy compost and stand them in a bowl or tank with water just covering the pot rim. Keep in full sun, and plant out when fully rooted.

Pests and diseases Water lily aphids infest leaves and flowers, and water lily beetles eat strips out of the leaves. Leaf spot and stem rot are the chief diseases.

Nymphaea x *marliacea* 'Carnea'

Nymphoides

water fringe

Nymphoides peltata

☐ Surface floater
☐ Water depth 15-45cm (6-18in)
☐ Flowers in summer
☐ Sunny site
☐ Hardy aquatic

This water lily look-alike is useful for new pools as it spreads quickly, providing interest while other plants are still establishing themselves.

In summer *Nymphoides peltata* bears dainty yellow cup-shaped flowers with fringed petals; they are held well above the water surface. The floating rounded leaves are similar to those of a water lily but smaller – they reach only 5cm (2in) across – they are light green mottled with maroon and brown and have wavy margins.

Cultivation
Plant directly in the mud at the bottom of a pool, or in loam-filled baskets which can then be sunk into position. A water depth of 15-45cm (6-18in) is ideal. The best time to plant water fringe is in mid spring and early summer.

Control the spread by thinning in late spring.
Propagation Water fringe is best increased by removing offsets from the main rootstock with a sharp knife in late spring. Insert in pots of loamy compost and stand them in a bowl with water just covering the rim. Plant out when fully rooted.
Pests and diseases Water lily aphids may infest the leaves and flowers. Leaf spot and stem rot can also be a problem.

Orontium

golden club

Orontium aquaticum

☐ Surface floater
☐ Water depth up to 45cm (1½ft)
☐ Flowers late spring to early summer
☐ Sunny site
☐ Hardy aquatic

Golden club (*Orontium aquaticum*) was brought to Britain from the United States in the 1770s. It has been endearing itself to British gardeners ever since, and is considered one of the loveliest aquatic plants.

It is fully hardy and adaptable to different growing conditions. When grown in shallow water or at pool margins, it bears a profusion of large sturdy, oval to round leaves coated with a bluish-green, water-repellent wax. The leaves are borne on tough stalks up to 45cm (1½ft) tall.

In deep water, however, the leaves float on the surface in near circular clumps; they are then strap-shaped rather than oval and retain their attractive appearance well into autumn.

The flowers, which appear from late spring and into early summer, betray the golden club's relationship with the Arum family, although it lacks the usual white spathe wrapping. The flowers are bright golden, slightly knobbly spikes borne on white-tipped pencil-thick stalks which rise gracefully from the leaf bases before arching outwards.

Cultivation
Plant the tubers between early spring and early summer, ideally in good loamy soil at the pool bottom, with a water depth up to 45cm (1½ft). Alternatively, plant in boggy ground at the pool edge; the roots penetrate deeply and need plenty of soil depth.

Remove the faded spikes after flowering and rake out the yellowing foliage in autumn before it can foul the water.
Propagation As established clumps become overgrown, they should be lifted and divided, in early spring, after flowering or in early autumn. Use a sharp knife to cut through the tough rootstock; discard the old wooden

Orontium aquaticum

centres and replant outer, younger sections at once.

Alternatively, sow fresh seed in early summer. Sow in shallow boxes of loamy seed compost and keep the pans submerged until seedlings appear. Transplant them individually to small pots kept in water up to their rims and grow on until the young plants are sturdy enough to be planted out in the pool.

Pests and diseases Generally trouble free though water lily aphids and water lily beetles can sometimes be troublesome.

PICKEREL WEED – see *Pontederia*
POND LILY – see *Nuphar*

Pontederia
pickerel weed

Pontederia cordata

☐ Height 60-75cm (2-2½ft)
☐ Water depth 7.5-23cm (3-9in)
☐ Flowers mid summer to early autumn
☐ Sunny site
☐ Hardy aquatic

Pickerel weed (*Pontederia cordata*) is one of the few true blue aquatic plants, and for this reason alone it is well worth growing. It will grow in boggy ground by the pool's edge but thrives better in shallow water. In such a position the blue of the flowers is patterned with light reflected from the ripples below.

The plants root in mud, from which their smooth fleshy stems grow strongly to a height of about 60-75cm (2-2½ft), carrying upward-pointing heart-shaped leaves. Flower spikes push through the membranes at the leaf bases and come into full colour in mid summer, often continuing until autumn. They consist of small purple-blue flowers, surrounded by soft hairs.

Cultivation
Plant between mid spring and early summer in a 10-15cm (4-6in) layer of loam and cover with 7.5-23cm (3-9in) of water. Position in full sun at the margins of a pool or slow-flowing stream.

Propagation Lift the plants in spring and cut off side branches with a sharp knife. Replant, pushing the rootstock 5cm (2in) into the loam. Do not cover with more than 7.5cm (3in) of water until the plants are well established.

Pests and diseases Trouble free.

PURPLE LOOSESTRIFE – see *Lythrum*
PURPLE MARSHLOCKS – see *Potentilla*

Potamogeton

curled pondweed

Potamogeton natans

☐ Any water depth
☐ Foliage plant
☐ Sunny or shaded site
☐ Hardy submerged aquatic

None of the two dozen or so native pondweeds can be called beautiful, but in small pools in particular they are valuable oxygenators – they take in carbon dioxide from the water and release oxygen, thus preventing the growth of algae. The leaves also provide much-needed shelter for fish.

One of the most decorative, and most commonly grown in garden pools, is *Potamogeton crispus* – curled pondweed. A completely submerged species, it has branched stems ranging from 30-90cm (1-3ft) long and narrow wavy-edged leaves that resemble seaweed; they are a beautiful bright translucent green and may turn bronze with age.

It is a vigorous plant, especially in the year or two immediately after planting, but it slows down later and is easily reduced with a rake.

Potamogeton natans is a similar species, but has flatter, floating leaves; it can be highly invasive.

Cultivation

Plant in spring, in mud at the bottom of a pool. Thin by pulling out plants by hand or with a rake.
Propagation If necessary, take cuttings in spring and insert bunches of them in the mud at the bottom of the pool.
Pests and diseases Trouble free.

Potentilla

marsh cinquefoil, purple marshlocks

Potentilla palustris

☐ Height 30cm (12in)
☐ Spread 30cm (12in) or more
☐ Flowers late spring to mid summer
☐ Moist or wet, acid soil
☐ Sunny site
☐ Hardy perennial

The little marsh cinquefoil (*Potentilla palustris*) is a British native plant inhabiting wet places. It is unassuming and easy to grow, in shallow water at pool margins or in permanently boggy ground by ponds and streams. It bears strawberry-like, divided leaves, hairless and mid to dark green.

From late spring onwards, slender stems carry loose clusters of buttercup-like flowers that open out to stars; they are deep purple surrounded by maroon sepals. The plants self-seed and also spread by underground stolons.

Cultivation

Plant in mid to late autumn or in early and mid spring, in shallow water or in constantly wet ground. Marsh cinquefoils will not tolerate lime in the soil and they often fail if grown in hard water. Choose a site in full sun.

Cut the faded stems back to ground level after flowering.
Propagation Detach rooted stolons from established plants in early spring and replant at once.
Pests and diseases Generally trouble free.

Primula

primula, primrose

Primula helodoxa

☐ Height 15cm-1.2m (6in-4ft)
☐ Spread 12-38cm (5-15in)
☐ Flowers early to late spring and early to mid summer
☐ Fertile, moist or boggy soil
☐ Light shade
☐ Hardy perennial

All primulas thrive in moist soil, but certain species are particularly associated with boggy conditions and are invaluable for colonizing by water and streamsides. From early spring and into high summer, they provide swathes of colour with their graceful spikes.

While primulas do not appreciate waterlogged soil, bog plants are at their best in permanently moist ground, preferably in light shade. They are fully hardy plants, with basal rosettes of oval, coarsely textured leaves that range in colour from pale to mid and dark green.

Popular species

Primula beesiana is one of the finest species for moist soil. It is a candelabra type producing its 60cm (2ft) high, loose spikes of yellow-eyed, rose-carmine and fragrant flowers in early and mid summer. The pale green, slightly mealy leaf rosettes spread to 30cm (1ft).

Primula bulleyana, another candelabra primula, has dark green leaves with red midribs. Clump-forming to 30cm (12in) across, it carries 75cm (2½ft) high stems set with tiers of golden-yellow flowers from reddish buds in early summer.

Primula beesiana

Primula denticulata

Primula denticulata, the drumstick primula, grows 30cm (12in) tall and 23cm (9in) wide. It flowers from early to late spring, with ball-shaped flower clusters on sturdy stems; they are pale lilac to deep purple. White, blue and red varieties are available.

Primula florindae, giant cowslip, is one of the tallest species, with stems up to 1.2m (4ft) high. It forms wide clumps of large mid green, heart-shaped leaves from which rise, in mid summer, tall stems that terminate in loose clusters of nodding, bell-shaped flowers, soft yellow in colour and scented. This species will grow in shallow water at the pool edge.

Primula helodoxa, a candelabra-type species, grows 60-90cm (2-3ft) high with a spread of 25cm (10in). It often retains its pale green, glossy leaves throughout winter. Tall-stemmed tiers of golden yellow flowers are borne in summer.

Primula japonica is outstanding among moisture-loving primulas. It grows 75cm (2½ft) high and 30cm (1ft) across, with tier upon tier of yellow-centred, crimson-purple flowers from late spring on. Pink, red, blue and white seed selections are available.

Primula pulverulenta resembles *P. japonica*, but has mealy flower stems with dark-eyed, wine-red to crimson flower clusters. The pink-flowered 'Bartley' strain is particularly fine.

Primula rosea is a small-growing species, rarely more than 15cm (6in) high and wide, but ideal for carpeting boggy ground by the waterside. It bears clusters of deep rose-pink flowers in early and mid spring.

Primula sikkimensis, Himalayan cowslip, is an outstanding species up to 45cm (1½ft) high and 30cm (12in) across. The long and narrow, pale green leaves are finely toothed. It flowers from early to late summer, with slender spikes of fragrant, pale yellow bell flowers.

Cultivation

Plant primulas between mid autumn and early spring, in rich boggy but not waterlogged soil by the edge of pools and streams. A lightly shaded site is ideal, though *P. japonica* will tolerate sun.

Dead-head after flowering. Primulas often seed themselves and hybridize with other species to produce flowers in colours different from their parents.

Propagation Bog primulas spread rapidly and should be regularly divided and replanted every three or four years, after flowering.

New plants are easily raised from seed sown as soon as ripe, in early autumn. Sow in boxes and overwinter in a cold frame. Prick the seedlings out into small pots, plunge them outdoors and keep them thoroughly moist until planting out in autumn or the following spring.

Pests and diseases Aphids distort flowering stems, and caterpillars, slugs and snails feed on the foliage. Crown, foot and root rot affect underground tissues and lead to the collapse of plants. Various virus diseases, for which there is no cure, cause stunting of growth and distortion of flowers. Destroy affected plants.

RAGWORT – see *Senecio*

Primula pulverulenta

Ranunculus

greater spearwort

Ranunculus lingua 'Grandiflora'

☐ Height 1.2-1.5m (4-5ft)
☐ Water depth 10-15cm (4-6in)
☐ Flowers late spring to early autumn
☐ Sunny or partially shaded site
☐ Hardy marginal aquatic

The greater spearwort (*Ranunculus lingua*) is one of Britain's native plants, increasingly rare but still to be found in marshes and fens. It is a tall, stately perennial, spreading widely from underground runners. In cultivation, it is represented by the improved form 'Grandiflora'.

Growing in shallow water, the greater spearwort puts up stout stems 1.2-1.5m (4-5ft) high, carrying narrow, blue-green leaves often as much as 30cm (1ft) long on pinkish-green stems. The flowers, borne in elegant sprays from late spring until early autumn, are glossy, large golden buttercups. 'Grandiflora' grows up to 90cm (3ft) high.

Cultivation
Plant between early autumn and mid spring in soil that is continually wet or in water up to a depth of 15cm (6in).

Greater spearwort spreads quickly and can become invasive. In small pools it should be thinned annually, in autumn or early spring.
Propagation Lift and divide the rhizomes in spring. Replant immediately.
Pests and diseases Trouble free.

REED SWEETGRASS – see *Glyceria*
REEDMACE – see *Typha*
RUSH, ZEBRA – see *Scirpus*

Sagittaria

common arrowhead, water-archer

Sagittaria sagittifolia

☐ Height 60cm (2ft)
☐ Water depth up to 45cm (1½ft)
☐ Flowers mid to late summer
☐ Sunny site
☐ Hardy aquatic

The main attraction of *Sagittaria sagittifolia* is its elegant arrow-shaped foliage. In spring it emerges as long grass-like almost translucent leaves below the water surface, and as the season progresses typical triangular arrow-like leaves rise above the water on stout stems up to 60cm (2ft) in height. The foliage is pale green sometimes spotted with brown.

Loose clusters of white, three-petalled flowers with yellow-brown centres are borne in mid to late summer.

The plants spread rapidly and should not be introduced to small pools.

Cultivation
Plant in early to mid spring along the margins of slow-moving streams and ponds. A water depth of up to 45cm (1½ft) is suitable, above fertile soil at least 15cm (6in) deep. Push the tubers 5-7.5cm (2-3in) deep into soft mud, taking care not to damage the growing shoots.

Thin out in the growing season by uprooting unwanted specimens.
Propagation In early to mid summer remove and replant the smallest of young offsets.
Pests and diseases Aphids, particularly water lily aphids, may infest leaves and flowers.

Scirpus

zebra rush

Scirpus tabernaemontani 'Zebrinus'

- ☐ Height 90cm (3ft)
- ☐ Water depth up to 15cm (6in)
- ☐ Foliage plant
- ☐ Sunny site
- ☐ Hardy marginal aquatic

In this large genus of bulrushes, one species – *Scirpus tabernaemontani* – is particularly outstanding in the ornamental pool. 'Zebrinus', commonly called zebra rush, is a decorative plant distinguished by cream and white horizontal markings along its stems. The inflorescences are insignificant. The plant looks particularly striking growing along the water's edge, where its forms increasing clumps.

Cultivation
Plant in good loamy soil around the margins of a pool or the edge of a stream in mid to late spring. Sun is essential if the variegations are to be strong. Zebra rush thrives in water up to a depth of 15cm (6in) and needs a sheltered site. It is not recommended for cold and exposed gardens.

Cut out any plain green stems as soon as they appear.
Propagation Increase by lifting and dividing mature clumps in mid to late spring, using a sharp knife to cut the tough rootstock. Replant the divided pieces immediately.
Pests and diseases Trouble free.

Senecio

marsh ragwort

Senecio aquaticus

- ☐ Height 60cm (2ft)
- ☐ Spread 45-60cm (1½-2ft)
- ☐ Flowers early summer to late autumn
- ☐ Wet soil
- ☐ Light shade
- ☐ Hardy perennial

The native marsh ragwort (*Senecio aquaticus*) belongs to the large ragwort and groundsel family. It is essentially a plant of the wild garden, colonizing readily in wet meadows and along streams. It is a vigorous plant, with deeply cut, lyre-shaped, mid green leaves clothing the branching stems.

From early summer until well into autumn, marsh ragwort is rarely out of flower, the stems topped with large rounded clusters of pale yellow, daisy-like flowers.

Cultivation
Plant between mid autumn and mid spring in any permanently boggy soil. A partially shaded site is suitable. Cut the stems down to the ground in late autumn.
Propagation Marsh ragwort can be rampant. Divide and replant established clumps in spring.
Pests and diseases Trouble free.

SILVER GRASS – see
Miscanthus
SKUNK CABBAGE – see
Lysichiton
SPRING BEAUTY – see
Claytonia

Stratiotes

water soldier

Stratiotes aloides

- ☐ Height 10-20cm (4-8in)
- ☐ Water depth up to 60cm (2ft)
- ☐ Flowers in summer
- ☐ Sunny site
- ☐ Hardy floating aquatic

Water soldier (*Stratiotes aloides*) is a curious plant to introduce to a garden pool. It resembles the top of a pineapple – a clump of 30cm (1ft) long sword-like leaves sitting on the bottom of the pool. In summer it releases oxygen and rises to the surface, producing small white, three-petalled flowers. After pollination the whole plant sinks again into the depths.

In view of its largely submerged existence, water soldier cannot claim to make much of a show. It is, however, an interesting plant and provides a home for small pond creatures.

Cultivation
Place on the mud at the bottom of a pool in water up to a depth of 60cm (2ft).

Water soldier reproduces rapidly by means of offsets – keep under control by thinning out.
Propagation In mid autumn separate offsets from the parent and replant.
Pests and diseases Pond snails can be a nuisance.

SWEET FLAG – see *Acorus*
SWEET GALINGALE – see
Cyperus

Typha
reedmace

Typha minima

☐ Height 30cm-1.8m (1-6ft)
☐ Water depth up to 15cm (6in)
☐ Flowers in summer
☐ Sunny site
☐ Hardy marginal aquatic

Reedmace – often incorrectly called bulrush – is a familiar waterside plant with its brown poker-like flower heads. It is suitable only for large pools.

Popular species
Typha latifolia grows about 1.8m (6ft) high and forms large clumps of blue-green foliage.
Typha minima, at 45-75cm (1½-2½ft) high, is suitable for garden pools. It bears green grass-like leaves and slender flower heads.

Cultivation
Plant in mid to late spring in rich deep soil along the water's edge or up to a water depth of 15cm (6in).
Propagation Cut the rhizomes into 2-7.5cm (1-3in) pieces in spring and replant.
Pests and diseases Trouble free.

WATER-ARCHER – see *Sagittaria*
WATER AVENS – see *Geum*
WATER FRINGE – see *Nymphoides*
WATER HAWTHORN – see *Aponogeton*
WATER HYACINTH – see *Eichhornia*
WATER LILY – see *Nymphaea*
WATER MINT – see *Mentha*
WATER PLANTAIN – see *Alisma*
WATER SOLDIER – see *Stratiotes*

Zantedeschia
arum lily

Zantedeschia aethiopica 'Lime Lady'

☐ Height 60-90cm (2-3ft)
☐ Spread 30-60cm (1-2ft)
☐ Water depth 15-30cm (6-12in)
☐ Flowers early and mid summer
☐ Sunny site
☐ Hardy and half-hardy marginal

The stately arum lily (*Zantedeschia aethiopica*) is a magnificent and exotic perennial that thrives by the pool edge or, in mild districts, in shallow water. It is handsome in leaf – large arrow-shaped, dark glossy green leaves in dense rosettes. From early summer onwards, tall flower stems rise above the foliage, each topped with a dazzling white spathe (modified leaf) surrounding a golden spadix.

Named forms are generally hardier than the species itself and will grow in drier conditions. They include 'Crowborough' and 'Lime Lady.'

Cultivation
Plant in spring in good but not over-rich moist soil or in shallow water in mild areas. Protect the fleshy crowns with a strawy winter mulch or lift them and store, in pots, in a frost-free greenhouse.
Propagation Divide and replant the rhizomes in spring.
Pests and diseases Corm rot may occur on heavy cold soils. Various virus diseases cause mottling of the foliage, with distorted flowers.

Zantedeschia aethiopica

ACKNOWLEDGEMENTS

Photographer's Credits
A-Z Botanical 107(tr), 153(c); Agence Bamboo 17(l), 57(r), 60(tl), 98(b), 103(r), 106(l), 110(tl), 112(tl), 114(tr), 149(l), 151(r), 155(tl), 175(tl); Gillian Beckett 34(r), 37(l), 38(l), 39(r), 40(br), 43(br), 45(l), 46(c), 49(tl), 52(tl), 54(tr), 58(b), 59(l), 65(tl,br), 67(tr), 68(tl), 73(tr), 74(bl), 78(tl), 84(br), 87(tl), 99(bl,r), 111(br), 120(l), 127(l), 128(tl); Biofotos (Heather Angel) 89(c), 148(r), 149(r), 158(tr), 163(c), 169(l), 171(l,c), 173(r), 174(c,r); Bruce Coleman Picture Library 155(c); Eric Crichton front cover (bc), 14(tl), 15(t), 17(r), 18(tl), 19(tl,br), 23(b), 24(tr), 25(tr), 26(tc), 29(r), 33(tr), 36(tl), 40(tr), 41(tl), 48(r), 49(tr), 53, 54(tl,br), 57(l), 58(tr), 60(tr), 64(t), 66(t), 68(bl), 70(br), 71, 72(tl,br), 73(br), 74(t), 75(l), 76(tr), 78(tr), 79(tr), 81(l), 82(tl), 83(r), 85(tl), 87(tr), 88(t), 89(l,r), 90(t), 93(r), 95(tr), 96(tr), 97, 100(c), 101(tl), 103(l), 105(l), 107(c), 108(tl), 109(tr), 110(tr), 112(tr), 115(l), 118(l), 119(bl,tr), 121(bl), 122(tl,br), 126(tl), 128(tr), 129(r), 130(t), 132(bc,tr), 133(tr), 136(bl,tr), 137, 138(b), 151(l,c), 152(b), 158(tl,b), 159(br), 164(l), 168(br), 173(l), 174(l); Philippe Ferret 148(l), 152(tc), 155(r), 162(b), 166(l), 167, 168(tl), 170(r); Andrew Gagg (Photoflora) 26(tr); Garden Picture Library (J. Ainsworth 110(br), 117(tr), (Brian Carter) 13(b), 18(c), 20(tl), 21(r), 24(bl), 31(l), 32(l), 42(r), 43(tl), 47(tr), 51(cr), 56(tr), 86(tr), 91(r), 102(bl,tr), 108(bl), 109(tl), 131(c), 162(tr), 168(tr), 169(r), (John Elliot) 82(bl), 85(bl), 86(b), 99(tl), 129(l), 135(tl), (Chris Fairweather) 171(r), (John Glover) front cover (c), 47(br), (Marijke Heuff) 120(r), (Roger Hyam) 154(b), (Clive Nichols) back cover, (Joanne Pavia) 8, 124(bl), (J.S.Sira) 90(br), (David Russell) 157(tr), 164(br), (Ron Sutherland) 172(br), (Brigitte Thomas) 2-3, (Steven Wooster) 160; ; John Glover front cover (bl), 11(l), 12(bl), 33(c), 145, 147(bl), 175(b); Derek Gould 15(b), 18(br), 23(tr), 26(tl); Patrick Johns 28(r), 52(bl), 55(tr), 69(tl,b), 84(tl); Michèle Lamontagne 22(l), 25(br), 33(l), 44(c), 51(tr), 63(l,r), 66(c), 67(br), 70(t), 73(tl), 96(tl), 100(r), 104(tl), 122(tr), 135(bl), 136(tl); Andrew Lawson 105(c), 109(br), 133(tl), 139(r); Tania Midgley front cover (cr), 10, 14(b), 44(r), 45(r), 57(bl), 58(tl), 64(br), 80(r), 84(tr), 114(tl), 124(tl), 140, 147(t), 152(tl), 156(l), 163(r); Natural Image 24(tl), 25(cr), 31(r), 36(bl), 41(tr), 76(c), 85(br), 92(br), 93(l), 94(tl), 96(br), 108(tr), 112(b), 114(b), 118(tr), 123(tr), 124(tr), 125(tl), 126(c,r), 128(br); Clive Nichols front cover (br), 1, 4-7, 11(r), 143; Photos Horticultural front cover (t), 12(tl), 14(tr), 16(t), 20(tr), 21(tl), 23(tl), 27, 28(tl), 29(tl), 30, 35(l), 36(tr), 37(tr), 39(tl), 40(tl), 41(br), 43(tr), 45(c), 46(tr), 48(l), 49(br), 50(tl), 51(tl), 52(tr), 56(l), 59(r), 60(bl), 61(r), 62, 63(c), 65(tr), 67(tl), 68(tr), 75(tr), 77, 78(br), 79(tl,br), 80(l), 82(tr), 83(l), 86(tl), 91(tl), 92(tr), 94(bl), 95(br), 98(tl), 101(bl), 102(tl), 104(bl), 105(r), 106(r), 107(tl), 116(t), 121(t), 125(tr), 127(r), 130(b), 131(l), 132(tl), 134, 135(tr), 138(t), 139(tl), 147(br), 150, 153(tl), 154(t), 156(c,r), 157(tl,br), 159(t), 161(tr), 162(tl), 165, 166(br), 172(t), 175(tr); Harry Smith Collection front cover (cl), 12(r), 16(br), 17(c), 18(tr), 19(tr), 20(bl), 22(r), 25(tl), 26(bc), 32(r), 34(l), 35(r), 38(r), 42(l), 44(l), 46(tl), 47(tl), 50(r), 55(l), 61(l), 69(tr), 72(tr), 73(bl), 76(l), 81(r), 87(br), 88(br), 92(tl), 93(c), 95(tl), 98(tr), 100(l), 101(tr), 104(tr), 113, 115(r), 116(b), 117(l), 119(tl), 123(tl), 125(bl), 131(r), 133(br), 146, 153(r), 161(tl,br), 164(tr), 170(l).

Illustrators
Gill Tomblin – Reader's Digest 144.

Printing & Binding PRINTER INDUSTRIA, GRÁFICA S.A. BARCELONA
Separations COLOURSCAN OVERSEAS CO PTE LTD, SINGAPORE; Paper PERIGORD-CONDAT, FRANCE
53-017-1